PRAISE FOR

SELDOM DISAPPOINTED

"A warmly old-fashioned reminiscence from the dean of the American regional mystery."
—*Kirkus Reviews*

"Hillerman reveals the real author. . . . A great yarn."
—Glenn Griffin, *Denver Post*

"A splendid and disarming remembrance of things past."
—*New York Times Book Review*

"[Tony Hillerman] commits his own world—and his optimist's attitude—to the page."
—*New York Daily News*

"Beloved, imitated, admired and, above all, avidly read, Hillerman has, at age seventy-five, undertaken a memoir. Read it for insight into a master writer's background and technique. Read it to be acquainted with a quiet man from small-town Oklahoma who knows how to tell a good story."
—*Sunday Oklahoman*

"Man of mysteries seldom disappoints."
—*Chicago Tribune*

"What shines through this memoir is Hillerman's love of the written word."
—*Bergen Record* (New Jersey)

"*Seldom Disappointed* is no disappointment. . . . An amazing reporter's eye at work."
—John Sandford, *Fort Worth Star-Telegram*

About the Author

TONY HILLERMAN is the former president of the Mystery Writers of America and has received their Edgar and Grand Master awards. His other honors include the Center for the American Indian's Ambassador Award, the Silver Spur Award for the best novel set in the West, the Navaho Tribe's Special Friend Award, the National Media Award from the American Anthropological Association, the Public Service Award from the U.S. Department of the Interior, the Nero Wolfe Award, the Lifetime Achievement Award from the Oklahoma Center for the Book, an honorary lifetime membership in the Western Literature Association, and the Grand Prix de Littérature Policière. In addition to his election to Phi Beta Kappa, Tony Hillerman has been named Doctor of Humane Letters at Arizona State University and at Oregon's Portland State University. He lives with his wife, Marie, in Albuquerque, New Mexico.

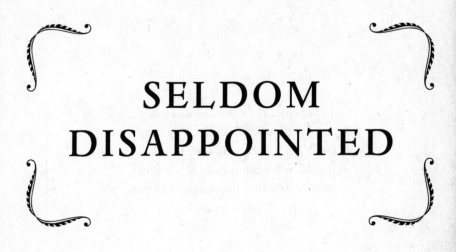

SELDOM DISAPPOINTED

A Memoir

TONY HILLERMAN

Perennial

An Imprint of HarperCollins*Publishers*

*To Marie, who wanted me to do this,
and to all you other writers, wannabes,
shouldbes, willbes, and hadbeens included,
I dedicate this effort. You're the ones who
know it ain't easy. May you get as lucky as
I have been.*

All the photographs in the insert courtesy of the author except where noted.

A hardcover edition of this book was published in 2001 by HarperCollins Publishers.

HarperCollins books may be purchased for educational, business, or sales promotional use. For information please write: Special Markets Department, HarperCollins Publishers Inc., 10 East 53rd Street, New York, NY 10022.

First Perennial edition published 2002.

Designed by Elliott Beard

The Library of Congress has catalogued the hardcover edition as follows:

Hillerman, Tony.
  Seldom disappointed : a memoir / by Tony Hillerman.—1st ed.
    p. cm.
  ISBN 0-06-019445-6
    1. Hillerman, Tony.   2. Novelists, American—20th century—
    Biography.   I. Title.
  PS3558.I45 Z474 2001
  813'.54—dc21   2001024160

ISBN 0-06-050586-9 (pbk.)

11 ❖/RRD 15 14 13 12 11 10 09

Contents

Illustrations follow pages 88 and 280.

SELDOM
DISAPPOINTED

1
Papa's Melon—
and What
Happened Next

Outside on this New Mexico morning the dandelions add festive color to our yard while I sit inside casting back in my memory for autobiographically useful material. I intend this to be a recitation of good luck and happy outcomes but my mind turns up only fiascos and misfortunes.

The first memory popping up is of sitting on our front porch in Sacred Heart on a torrid Oklahoma Sunday watching Papa trudging up the section line carrying a huge Black Diamond watermelon. The Black Diamond is the most delicious fruit known to humanity and this was more than a normal Black Diamond. Papa had been nurturing it all summer on the Old Hillerman Place, picking off competitive melons and, when it wilted, helping it along with a couple of lard buckets of water in one of his agronomy experiments. The previous Thursday he had declared it ripe and rigged up a little arbor of sticks and leaves to give it cooling shade. He announced that after Mass Sunday he would carry it home, put it in a washtub of well water to chill it, and when the cool of twilight came we five Hillermans would eat it, inviting anyone who happened to pass on our dusty street to come in and have a slice.

Alas, it was not to be. During the long walk in the humid heat Papa's perspiration had made the melon slippery. As he reached for our gate latch it slid from his grasp, crashed to earth, and shattered. I recount this incident, trivial though it sounds, because seventy something years later I still recall my reaction was as much confirmation as sorrow. At some level in my psyche even then I had sensed that this Black Diamond was too good to be true. I must have mentioned this to Mama when she was comforting us kids, because it's the first time I recall hearing her favorite aphorism.

"Blessed are those who expect little," Mama would say. "They are seldom disappointed."

I was about five then and probably didn't appreciate the doubled-edged irony in that beatitude. Looking back at life, I find I have often received more than I ever expected and suffered less than my share of disappointments.

The absolute earliest memory I finally managed to retrieve also involved a fiasco and, like so many to come, it produced a positive effect. I was sitting on one of those little hills red ants form of the tiny bits excavated from their tunnels. We were living on the Old Hillerman Place then, which means I was a toddler. I was scooping up sand and pouring it into the ants' exit hole. Why? Perhaps to block this passage and keep occupants from swarming out to attack me. Alas, those already out were crawling all over me, biting away. Before Mama heard my howls and rescued me, I had accumulated enough bites to make this incident a sort of family legend.

The next affair that pops from the memory bank is the dismal afternoon at Oklahoma A&M when I fell so soundly asleep in College Algebra that I toppled from my chair into the aisle and the professor sent me off to get a drop card. Turning away from that, I dredge up the terminal night of my career as an infantryman when I had gone along on a dinky little raid intended to capture two German prisoners. My role was to tote the stretcher on which we would carry a captive in case we wounded him. Instead I rode back on it myself. Part of the way, that is. The fellow carrying the front end stepped on an antipersonnel mine, which killed him and broke the stretcher. I'm a little hazy about the rest of that trip, recalling the final lap was made with me the passenger in a "fireman's carry" formed by a couple of friends, recalling being dropped into a frigid February creek, reviving while being strapped onto a stretcher on a Jeep, and being aware I was going somewhere to get some sleep.

Next to come to mind was my original literary agent delivering her verdict on my first novel. Don't want to show it to anyone, she said. Why not? It's a bad book. Have to think of your reputation as well as mine. Why bad? It falls between the stools, halfway betwixt mainstream and mystery. No way to promote it. And where does the bookseller shelve it? Stick to nonfiction, said my agent. I can sell that for you. How about me rewriting it? Well, if you do, get rid of the Indian stuff.

Unpleasant as those affairs sound, every one was lucky in a way. The sleepy tumble into the classroom aisle resulted in an Algebra grade of W (for withdrawal) instead of the otherwise inevitable F with its negative effect on one's grade point average. The fiasco at the Alsatian village of Niefern provided the "Million-Dollar Wound" for which all sane members of World War II infantry rifle companies yearned and which got me home at just the right time. My agent's advice caused me to seek a second opinion, which sent me to Joan Kahn, the Einstein of mystery editors, who saw possibilities in the Navajo cultural material and subsequently forced me to be a better plotter than I had intended.

Even the lost contest with the ants had a good outcome. It established me as a kid from whom not much should be expected. It remains a vivid memory because through my boyhood I heard it described at countless family gatherings. It provoked grins and chuckles from uncles, fond head pats from aunts, and helped establish my reputation among cousins. They used it to illustrate my tendency to be impulsive ("Antnee didn't worry about those ants already out. He just tried to put the stopper in."), stubborn ("Antnee wasn't going to quit a loser."), and a slow learner ("Antnee had nine ants biting on him before he started yelling for help.").

I should explain I was called Antnee until the draft board sent me off to the induction center because no child can pronounce all three syllables of Anthony (Ann-tho-knee) and Papa didn't want me called Tony. Later, grown-ups began calling me "Little Gus" (Papa, August Alfred Hillerman, was Gus) and I became "Puss Guts" to my male peers.

The Gus and Lucy Hillermans of Sacred Heart included three kids—big sister Margaret Mary, big brother Barney, and me. I will begin with Papa, because he was the first to go, and the one I knew the least. Since Papa never talked about himself, that knowledge came mostly from overheard conversations. He was born in Missouri to a German immigrant farm couple. Except for part of a year in a college, he was mostly self-educated. He drifted into West Texas when very young, taught ranch kids in a one-room rural school, where (as I heard him tell an uncle on the front porch one summer night) the teacher's first job was proving he could whip the bigger boys by doing it. (Papa had replaced a fellow who had failed the test.) He leased land, planted wheat, and made a great crop the first year. The second year it didn't rain and Papa "harvested the whole crop in my hat." He worked as a cowboy, established some sort of endurance legend by riding a horse from the Oklahoma Panhandle about two hundred miles to somewhere else in an amazingly short time. He became a farrier and shoed mules in a coal mine. He and a brother moved into Indian Territory and established a store at Violet, a violent little river-crossing settlement that sprouted up on the margin of Cherokee Strip to provide hospitality for those who needed to cross the border fast when they heard the U.S. marshals coming from one direction or the Indian police posse from the other. When law and order reached Oklahoma Territory and erased Violet, Papa moved to Sacred Heart.

Here I am left with a host of unanswered questions, which went unasked because Papa worked himself to death before I grew mature enough to be interested. Somewhere in this period Papa had married—a union which left him a widower with two daughters to raise. I'd guess Sacred Heart, with the only Roman Catholic church in the territory and its school, drew him as a more civilized place to raise motherless girls. It certainly offered no economic lures.

Sacred Heart had come to exist late in 1876 because a railroad coveted land near Shawnee Mission, Kansas, to which the Army had moved the Potawatomi Tribe to get them off land white folks coveted farther east. One group of Potawatomis had won the "citizens" before their tribal name by helping General Andrew Jackson's ragtag army defeat the British in the Battle of New Orleans in the War of 1812. When Jackson became President he rewarded their heroism by giving them U.S. citizenship. They were then rounded up and hauled off to the Kansas prairie. Benedictine missionaries joined them there, built a school, hospital, and so forth. This grew into a substantial settlement, which came to be called Shawnee Mission, which attracted immigrant farm families, which made the land valuable, which inflamed the greed of railroad moguls. The Potts were forced to move again.

The government didn't repeat the mistake of giving the Potts fertile land. In Oklahoma it allotted them an expanse of brushy scrub oak and eroded clay hills so devoid of fertility, timber, known mineral deposits, or anything else of value it was considered safe from the avarice of white folks. The Benedictine priests and monks tagged along, built another school, infirmary, etc., and registered the place with the U.S. Post Office as Sacred Heart.

Meanwhile, the Great White Father in Washington had decided

the dozens of Indian tribes resettled in Oklahoma didn't need all that territory and in 1889 Oklahoma was opened to home-steaders and here came a flood of whites. The overwhelming majority of these were refugees from the ruined Confederate States of America, solidly Protestants. A few were immigrants from Northern states, mostly with family origins in mainland Europe, and mostly Roman Catholics. Sacred Heart drew these faithful as a magnet draws iron filings.

Poor land or not, it attracted Papa. It also attracted another Catholic widower, an Englishman named Christopher C. Grove, who came south from Nebraska with two sons and two daughters in his wagon. The youngest was Lucy, fated to become my mother. She was born in Nebraska in 1885 and was three when Oklahoma Territory was opened to white settlement.

Small as was Sacred Heart the romance that produced me didn't move fast. They married in 1920, when Mama was thirty-five and Papa forty-seven. Thus they were forty and fifty-two respec-tively by the time I was born—old enough one would think to be running short of patience for the foolishness of kids. But that was not to be.

Readers who expect exciting accounts of child abuse, which showbiz celebrities have made popular, will be disappointed. Instead of the flogging we probably deserved, discipline went like this: For a mild disobedience, broken rule, or out-of-line unruli-ness, Mama would stand us at attention and scold us, individually and in total privacy. (I never actually saw or heard her scolding my siblings but I presume they received the same treatment I did. Surely I wasn't the only malefactor.) For more grave or repeated offenses, Mama would tell me (Barney and Margaret Mary, too?) that she would tell Papa when he got home from work.

That sounds mild, but it produced awful hours of waiting for sundown, for the sight of Papa trudging homeward down the dirt path along the section line, for sitting on the porch trying to overhear Mama's infraction report, and finally for the summons into the kitchen for the hearing, the judgment, and the sentence.

Papa sat in a kitchen chair (he'd been on his feet all day) and you stood. He would describe your offense as he had heard it and ask if that was accurate. It was. He'd ask your explanation and you would provide whatever justification you'd been able to come up with. To illustrate I will use a triple offense I recall from the autumn of 1934. The rules violated were playing in the cotton yard while cotton bales were stored there, shooting a BB gun at another kid, and playing with matches. My justification: lured into the cotton yard to talk to Billy Delonie (not to play). Billy was shooting kitchen matches in his BB gun (we almost never had real BBs) and had let me use it to take my turn. The match had hit a rock, ignited, and started the fire, which we had stomped out.

Had I been shooting the match at Billy? Well, yes, because he didn't think I could hit him and dared me to do it. Had Mama previously warned me thrice not to play around the cotton bales? I thought it was only twice. Papa then explained about family rules and considered my responses. The now popular "everybody else is doing it," excuse was not allowed because we had learned we operated by family rules. About now Papa would repeat this injunction, remind me never to judge the behavior of others because they had their own set of rules, and then he would decide that I had better go out and get a switch. I return with a switch (neither painfully large nor ridiculously small) from a backyard peach tree. I hand this to Papa. He examines it and me. Did I think I could remember family rules without a switching? I do indeed think so. All right, he says. Remember, now, and go see if your mother needs some help.

Since neither Mama nor Papa ever actually laid a hostile hand on me, my best claim to child abuse involves clothing. The summer before it was time to join Margaret Mary and Barney in the long walk up Church Hill and down the other side to St. Mary's Academy. Mama ordered a set of blue coveralls from Sears, Roebuck—to be my principal costume for the first grade. Mama said I looked cute in them. Alas, so did the grade school boys, clad in the bib overalls uniform of farm kids. Thus I became the swan among the ducklings, an object of scorn and derision. But a little bit of serious sobbing into Mama's apron solved that problem and got me back into my own overalls.

As a matter of fact, I can dredge up nothing much to complain about in my formative period. We children spent those years of the Great American Depression/Great Oklahoma Dust Bowl living miles below the current poverty level but happily protected by love and the invincible ignorance of the young. Life in Sacred Heart then (and now, for that matter) was not complicated by any possibility of getting rich. Everybody was poor and when you're a kid you don't know you're deprived unless you see someone who isn't. That didn't happen around Sacred Heart.

As I remember our village in the 1930s it first had two filling-station/general stores (quickly reduced to one) and thirteen residences, including the brick two-story Zoeller house of the folks who owned the cotton gin. I estimate the population at fifty but when I tried this number on Margaret Mary in 1999 she called it inflated. Her count was thirty-four, and she named them for me. However, Margaret Mary didn't include some folks on the outskirts, Mrs. Bondeau and her alcoholic son, for example, who lived almost invisibly north of the section line and across the creek, or Mrs. Brown, who lived with her sons in a house on Mission property and was often away at Norman, having what we called "nervous breakdowns" treated at the Oklahoma Mental Hospital there. Nor did my sister's census grant citizenship to the various Benedictines looking after the almost empty monastery on the other side of Church Hill, or the Sisters of Mercy who taught at St. Mary's Academy, or the come-and-go oil field workers who sometimes lived a month or two in the house in the Zoeller pear orchard.

Whichever count you adopt, Sacred Heart was small enough so we were considered country kids, as opposed to town kids who lived in Konawa, and large enough so that Barney and I didn't quite make it as "farm boys" since in our prepuberty years we did "chores" instead of fieldwork. The human species always divides itself into us and them.

Our urban center was the place where the north-south section line joined the east-west section line—both roads being rarely graded dirt, dusty when dry in those Dust Bowl years and only marginally passable when it rained. Papa and Uncle Frank (Uncle Frank being the husband of one of Papa's sisters) operated a filling station and general store on the east side of this junction just across the road from the Zoeller store. Behind the Zoeller Store was The Gin, our only industry, which operated a couple of autumn months when the wagons rolled in with the cotton harvest.

Atop Church Hill, looking down on all this, was the new church—built of poured concrete after a 1901 fire destroyed the old church (much finer in my mother's memory) at the monastery in the valley behind the hill.

In my boyhood, the monastery was still managing to maintain itself as a little spot of French culture in the wilderness. The abbot had long since faced reality and moved the school to Shawnee. Not only was Shawnee (oh, blessed town!) the home of Marie Unzner, who was to be my wife, partner, and best friend from 1948 until today, but it was the seat of government of Pottawatomie County, the site of the Potawatomie Indian Agency, and surrounded by flat, rich river-bottom farmlands, which offered folks hope of making a living.

At Sacred Heart during my boyhood, the old monastery buildings stood mostly empty but they retained their formal red-brick dignity. The monastery-seminary itself was a great U-shaped structure with basement, two stories, and attic dormers. Around it stood a stone bakery, a convent where the nuns had lived, barns, stables, a grain silo, and so forth. A row of great trees lined the entrance road but the formal gardens were being overgrown and the swans my mother remembered fondly in the garden pond were no longer in residence. Margaret Mary believed they had been transported to Shawnee to adorn the campus of St. Gregory's College, which the Benedictines founded there. Barney and I were pretty sure they had been eaten by Seminole Indian boys. (The Potawatomi and Hillerman tribes were uneasy about the Seminoles, who had oil money and more of what TV sportscasters now call "athleticism.")

Years later my infantry company liberated a villa in Alsace that looked enough like the old monastery to provoke an awful flood of nostalgic homesickness. The owner had fled, leaving on his walls pictures of horses and autographed photographs of himself with Heinrich Himmler and other important Nazis. One of my companions opened the wall safe with a grenade and we left with pockets full of worthless Vichy French francs and a bundle of good cashable deutsche marks. We were caught and made no profit from the burglary but even that affair proved lucky. Being arrested caused us to be hauled back to the villa, where we had to count out the money under the eyes of a clean, well-fed, well-paid major wearing a West Point ring. That caused us to miss a nasty little fight to clear Grube, a Lower Vosge village held by an SS armored unit. (Better to be embarrassed than shot at.)

But back to Sacred Heart. Adjoining the monastery grounds and at the very edge of the area that I include in our village, stood St. Mary's Academy. The Sisters of Mercy decided that Potawatomi Indian girls had as much right to an education as boys the Benedictines enrolled. They built a great wood frame building, two stories with basement and lined all around with porches. While the boarding students were mostly Indian girls, the sisters also admitted day students, including boys.

Oklahoma in those days required an eighth-grade education. Sacred Heart offered either St. Mary's or Georgetown School.

Why was the public grade school at Sacred Heart, a village in which no one could remember a George ever living, named Georgetown? My guess is that since Sacred Heart was a very

Roman Catholic, Popish, Mackerel Snapper–sounding name and the board of education was 100 percent Protestant, the board considered Georgetown a better choice. But why did my brother and I, white males, go to a boarding school for Indian girls? Mostly, I guess, because of the religious instruction it offered. Partly because even though Georgetown School had two rooms it hired only one teacher, a young man who instructed grades one through four in one room and handled five through eight in the other. That arrangement wouldn't have bothered Papa, who had been the only teacher in just such a school in Texas. What might have bothered him was the notion that the teacher was a right-wing Ku Klux Klan Republican. The books in Papa's little bookcase dealt with law and political philosophy and the ones I remember best were the complete works of a rabid left-wing writer who published *The Iconoclast*, a firebrand pro-workingman, pro-union, anticapitalist newspaper. Had Papa been born in Munich instead of Missouri, he'd never have survived the Nazis.

I have not mentioned any youth recreational facilities in the foregoing. A swing set sat under the only tree at Georgetown School but it was rarely used because it was downwind from the two outhouses. St. Mary's Academy had a swing set, merry-go-round, and slide in its playground, but boys were kept on the other side of the fence. (The sisters forgave us for not being Potawatomies, but not for being male.) There were usually only about nine or ten boys enrolled, not enough for regular baseball or football (basketball had not yet found its way to rural Oklahoma), so we played One-Eyed Cat, dodge ball, and similar stuff in the pig pasture behind the barn.

Our favorite pastime was Ape, which involved scratching two lines in the dirt about fifty feet apart and then drawing lots to determine who would be Ape. Ape would post himself between the lines, and we would run from line A to line B with Ape trying to catch us. When the Ape caught one he became another Ape, helping in the catching process, until finally the single runner left was the winner. Usually this was my cousin Robert, a contemporary of my brother Barney. He was fleet, agile, taciturn, and strong; he did everything well and was my boyhood hero.

Then along came the Eisheid Brothers, Jimmy and Billy, and the game changed. The Eisheids were visitors from another planet, city boys. Every rural kid knew city boys were sissies, but the Eisheids hadn't got the word. Instead of submitting when caught as we played Ape, the Eisheids would struggle. This idea seemed manly. It spread. Soon making a capture involved pinning the runner to the ground. Thus we'd return to the classroom after recess marked with grass stains and gravel scratches. Then the Eisheids took it another step. They had to admit they were captured. Jimmy usually would submit after a couple of fingers were bent backward to their limits, but not Billy. He had to be choked. The technique was to cut off his air supply, ask him if he was caught, release the pressure long enough to register his "No," and then choke him again. This continued until Billy said yes. The first time Billy passed out, producing the panicky screaming that brought one of the sisters rushing out to investigate, we persuaded her that Billy had merely fainted. The second time it happened she was skeptical. The third time she pretended she would take Billy to Konawa to see Dr. Giesen (the only medico in our end of the county). That forced the truth out of Billy. And that put an end to Ape.

The kids at Georgetown School had only one game. It was baseball. It went on year-long and it provided material for the only thing I ever published about my hometown—the introduction to a scholarly book about one- and two-room schools in the Great Plains States. The Georgetown team entered the Oklahoma American Legion grade-school baseball tournament. They won their way to the finals and went up to Oklahoma City to do battle with a huge urban grade school in Capitol Hill.

If I expect you to believe this could happen I must explain that rural education in the 1930s was much different (at least in Pottawatomie County) than it is today. The law requiring completion of the eighth grade didn't say when. Farm kids missed a lot of days in spring plowing and planting time, and even more during the wheat harvest and cotton-picking months. The larger boys would also skip when roughneck or roustabout jobs were available at well-drilling sites in the oil patch. Therefore, while city grade schools were fielding teams of thirteen- and fourteen-year-old eighth graders, the age level at Georgetown with just a few kids to pick from, ranged from ten-year-old third graders up to Nag Nonie, who was completing his eighth grade at twenty-one. Three of my cousins were on the team. Nibs, who was about nineteen, Goober, who was seventeen, and thirteen-year-old Larry—all sons of Uncle Chris Grove, who loved literature but loved baseball even more. Georgetown took ten players to the big city. One got drunk the night before the big game and was sent home. (Oklahoma retained alcohol prohibition until after World War II, which made it easy for kids to get whiskey just as the current "war on drugs" now makes it easy for them to get whatever we are prohibiting.) That left nine. The Capitol Hill coach objected to the 210-pound twenty-one-year-old third baseman, arguing that if there wasn't an age limit for grade-school baseball there damn sure should be. Nag was declared ineligible. That left an eight-man nine, but Georgetown was winning anyway because the Capitol Hill kids couldn't hit our nineteen-year-old pitcher's fast ball. Alas, it was then decided the rules required a full team and Georgetown had to forfeit the game.

After grade eight, we boys had to catch the school bus to Konawa High for the second lap on our road to enlightenment. That came at about the time our family was leaving Sacred Heart, moving a mile and a half down the section line to a little farm my mother owned. But there's a bit more to be told about life in the village pertinent to the point of this memoir. It concerns the development of Barney and me as War Lovers.

2
Preparing
for War

Perhaps obsession with war games is normal for young males. Or perhaps in the 1930s it was the product of the international saber-rattling, which was dominating newspapers, magazines, and radio. Mussolini was trying to re-create the Roman Empire by conquering Ethiopia, the Japanese were doing their invasion of Manchuria, and the German General Staff was testing its new tanks and fighters against Stalin's equipment in the Spanish Civil War. The newscasts delivered by our radio (when the battery was charged) were alive with accounts of bombing raids and battles. So was the Sunday *Kansas City Star*, to which Papa subscribed, and the back issues of *Life*, which our family dentist saved for us. *Life* editors were as fond of war as were we boys.

Our war games included one with marbles. Each player placed

his army on the battlefield, took turns getting one shot with each marble at the enemy marbles. Marbles hit were dead. The last kid with marbles left won. It didn't stay simple. Soon we were digging networks of marble-depth trenches, molding marble-sized tanks of clay with matchstick cannon barrels, etc. Barney wrote our version of the Geneva Convention war rules. Each marble could be moved three inches after each turn, each tank could be moved a foot, etc. We played increasing complicated versions of this well into our high school years.

As grade schoolers, we were also playing Cavalry and Comanches, riding imaginary horses through the woods, creeks, and cow pastures, carrying wooden sabers, horseweed stalks as lances, and using clay balls (carried in old socks hung from the side buttons of our overalls) as ammunition. The rules required one hit by a missile to fall and cheating was rare. Sacred Heart offered a limited recruiting pool for our wars, and the genuine farm boys away from the village were kept busy chopping cotton, plowing, and so forth. Usually we had only Barney and me, Cousin Cecil from down the section line, the three Delonie boys, and, when circumstances brought them in from the city, the Eisheids. Sometimes Cecil's big brother Robert would join us, but Robert matured earlier than we did and usually was involved with more serious affairs.

The Delonie boys, being Indians, were assigned Comanche roles. But every Saturday evening the Rex Theater in Konawa would be opened and a movie would be shown. These movies in the 1930s tended to be westerns and the Delonie boys saw one of these. This made them aware that in Cavalry vs. Indian battles the Indians lose. Henceforth, even though as Potawatomis they had no aversion to shooting Comanches, we Hillerman boys had to alternate in the roles.

For our trench warfare, fought in the mountainous slag heap of cotton hulls left beside the gin, we chose up sides. Now cotton hulls are ground, bagged, and sold as mulch. Then they were dumped, year after year, forming towering piles. Dig away the newly dumped and you reached levels where pressure and decay had compressed them into layers about the texture of sponge cake. In these great hills of rotted hulls we created networks of trenches and tunnels in which to reenact the awful slaughter of World War I.

Nature had improved this ideal site with a row of bois d' arc (Osage orange) bushes rimming the dump. The "oranges" they produced resembled grapefruit in shape and color but were harder and heavier—ideal cannonballs. Hits with hard-thrown clay balls and rubber-gun bands stung a little and they remained our small arms. But before we discovered the Osage orange cannonball the only elements of danger adding spice to the game were the occasional cave-ins of trenches or collapse of tunnels, which left one buried and scared for a bit. Being hit with an Osage orange really hurt, producing bruises, cut lips, loose teeth, bloody noses, and so forth. That added nervous tension to the game. It also finally ended it.

One of the Delonie boys (Tommy, probably too little to be playing this anyway) stuck his head out of a trench to snap off a rubber-gun shot just in time to be hit right between the eyes by an Osage orange. We revived him with water from the gin pond, but Tommy ran home screaming. A moment later his dad came roaring out the back door of his house, also screaming. We abandoned our trenches and fled, never to resume the game.

We didn't abandon the cotton yard, however, nor other war games. On summer evenings we rolled tires. The little skinny tires off Model A or B Fords were fighter planes. Truck tires were bombers. The idea was to maneuver your tire into position to side-swipe an enemy tire and send it wobbling into a crash.

The inner tubes that came out of these worn-out tires were cut into bands—ammunition for rubber guns. Barney had made an arsenal of eleven of these for us. Eight were single-shot pistols, fired by squeezing the clothespin on the handle. Three were automatic rifles, an invention of his. They were loaded by stretching the bands from the end of the barrel and pressing them over a string into a sequence of notches. These were fired, single shot or in a murderous burst, by pulling the string. The pain when shot at close range was such that we finally had to ban them from our indoor version of the game.

When winter and early darkness made the cotton yard inhospitable we moved our war into the kitchen. To explain that I must pause and explain our home. That requires explaining "Shotgun Houses." They were American ingenuity's answer to the need of oil field workers, who would spend a few months drilling a well then move to wherever they could find a job drilling another one. The house that met their needs had a light wood frame and was narrow enough to be hauled on a flatbed truck. On our lot east of the cotton yard Papa had arranged two of these in a T-shape. The house fronting the street was a heavier three-room version. The room on the east end doubled as the parlor, den, and parental bedroom.There Mama and Papa entertained guests and there the radio was kept. When working it brought us "Little Orphan Annie," "Jack Armstrong," "Amos and Andy," Frank Buck capturing his wild rhinos, the news and reconstituted rebroadcasts of St. Louis Cardinal games. And it was there the five Hillermans knelt each evening to thank the Lord for another day completed. I can still remember the feel of the linoleum under my knees, and the print of a Cruxifixion scene with Christ looking down at us from the cross. The prayers Papa led were mostly thanks for blessing our family with such happiness, but we never forgot to include an appeal for rain.

The room in the center became the entrance foyer, storage area, and hallway. The west-end room was the kitchen, dining room, and laundry. Here we took our baths in a round galvanized tub filled with water pulled from the backyard well and heated in buckets on the cookstove.

The exit door of this west room opened into the backyard. There stood the rain barrel, which caught runoff from the roof to augment bath and laundry water, the woodpile which fueled the cookstove, the well from which hung the pulley and well rope by which we hoisted drinking and cooking water to the surface, and the root cellar. The cellar was equipped with rows of shelves holding the year's supply of Irish potatoes, sweet potatoes, onions, etc., and row upon row of Mason jars containing beets, peas, green beans, corn, pickles, peaches, pears, applesauce, blackberries, and assorted jams and jellies—mostly grown in Mama's garden or on our trees, and all peeled, prepared, cooked, and preserved in the torrid heat of the Oklahoma summer prior to the invention of air conditioning.

Behind this root cellar was the "chicken fence," which separated our yard from the territory occupied by the chicken house, the chickens, the barn, and Bossy, our milk cow. The family outhouse stood demurely out of sight beyond the chicken house.

The rest of home was formed by a smaller two-room shotgun house tacked on to the front one to form a stem of the T. This provided the bedroom shared by Margaret Mary, Barney, and me and a storeroom at the end, occupied by boxes of apples, clothing waiting for the season to change, and so forth.

More important to me, the storeroom held a huge (by boyhood standards) and sinister black trunk. The parental cover story was that it held family keepsakes, heirlooms, photo albums, documents, and other such valuable and irreplaceable stuff and it was therefore off-limits for kids. But in the awful reality that comes to boys in their dreams I understood it was actually the den of a gorilla. On windy nights I would hear him scratching and the lid creaking as he tried to push it open. Barney finally tired of being awakened with my elbow in his ribs and my whispered demands for an explanation of the noises. He got me out of bed, took me back there, opened the trunk, and showed me it was so crowded with photo albums, old correspondence, documents, what must have been a wedding dress, and so forth, that no gorilla was plausible.

That helped, but the gorilla reappeared years later when I was doing my sleeping in the Army's Third General Hospital at Aix-en-Provence. My most popular nightmare there had me trudging through a rainy woods, carrying my mortar, hearing the whistle of artillery rounds and the sharp sound of tree bursts, passing Sergeant Arras, who was lying face up in the ditch looking at me and saying something I couldn't understand. But the gorilla also showed up often, and now I would hear the storeroom door creaking open and I'd know that if the light were a little better I'd see him looking out at me.

Aside from the sinister storeroom, I have nothing but good memories of that house. Papa had built a porch across the front of it and screened in part of that for sleeping on those nights when the heat was intolerable. The entire structure was mounted on pedestals of concrete blocks, which made it relatively level. The roof never leaked, and air circulated through it in such a way that on torrid summer days the wet towels Mama hung on the screens provided a nice touch of evaporative cooling. Even the odd way the floors warped in our kids' room wasn't all bad. The boards bowed up in the middle, which meant lost marbles could always be quickly found in the corners.

The downside of the warping was caused by dogs sleeping in the dust under the house. Country dogs collect fleas, even our own beloved German shepherds, Lad and Wags. Fleas have survived down through untold eons by developing fantastic jumping skill plus a radar system for detecting warm-blooded food supplies passing by. Thus we three warm-blooded Hillerman kids learned not to linger over the cracks between the warped boards of our bedroom floor during the summer. When hot weather made fleas active we countered with a run-and-jump method of getting to bed.

The winds of winter also leaked through the cracks. On bad days, the linoleum on the kitchen floor rose and fell with the gusts. I remember a happy house, but not a cozy one. Even when the wood fire was raging in Mama's cooking stove and the heating stove was going full blast, the kitchen could be warm above the knees but chilly at ankle level.

Not long before we left the place to move to Mama's farm, Sacred Heart was blessed by the arrival of a natural gas line and Franklin Roosevelt's New Deal paid off with a Rural Electrification Administration power line. Now we had electric lighting and it was practical to move our war game indoors during winter nights. The new battleground became the kitchen. Here's how it worked.

Barney, as keeper of the arsenal, would hand out rubber guns to those who had not come armed. We would stand on opposite sides of the kitchen table, the light switch would be flicked off by the Starter, each participant would find a hiding place while silently counting to fifty ("one thousand one, one thousand two," etc.). Then in the tense, silent darkness the battle would begin.

You'd listen, breath held. You'd hear the sound of bumping. Should you snap off a shot? Was it a trick to cause you to give away your position? Finally there would be an uproar—shooting, falling chairs, yelling, and banging. The Starter would switch on the light, expended rubber-gun bands would be retrieved and the game would be resumed. (As I write this it occurs to me that Mama and Papa, trying to read a few feet away in the living/bedroom, were long-suffering parents.) Eight winters later when my slumbers in the Army Hospital weren't being disturbed by walking past the wounded sergeant in the ditch or the storeroom gorilla my subconscious would put me on my stomach under the kitchen table in Sacred Heart, hidden by total darkness and the hanging edges of the tablecloth, the feel of the cold linoleum against my stomach, the total silence broken only by the muttering of wood burning in the kitchen stove. And over all that the dread awareness that the muzzle of Billy Delonie's rubber gun was probably about an inch from my eyeball. That nightmare was just as unnerving as the others.

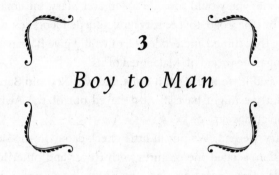

3
Boy to Man

If I make it to heaven, I'll ask my parents why they moved the family from our house in Sacred Heart two miles down the road to Mama's forty acres. I think I know the answer.

Papa must have become aware he was dying. Perhaps the store was failing—the victim of the Depression, of better roads on which customers drove into town to do their buying, and of Papa's policy of granting credit to anyone with a hungry family or a hard luck story. Whatever the reason, we built a house on Mama's place, and Papa added to the forty by buying a twenty across the section line and a worn-out eighty-acre farm a half mile down the road. He paid $1,100 for the eighty, which says a lot about the condition of the farm and the price of land in the 1930s. It took a conversation

with Barney, about thirty years later, before I came to really understand why he bought it.

I had guessed Papa thought we could grow enough cattle and
fodder on it to actually make a living. Barney thought it went
deeper than that.

Papa knew he would soon die. Margaret Mary, the smartest of
us, was on the road to security and independence as a nurse.
Restoring that ruined and eroded farm would give Barney and me
something to be proud of. Make men of us.

Well, said I, we didn't get it done, did we? No, said Barney, we
didn't. But we might have if we'd stayed out of the Army. And
aren't you glad we tried?

And try we had. We put in little check-dams on the slopes to
stop erosion, seeded the pastures with clover and other legumes
to provide some decent grazing, and kept our two horses busy all
summer pulling a breaking plow through the one good segment of
bottomland to kill the Johnson grass that engulfed it. Most ambi-
tious of all, we began a project to straighten a creek that snaked
through that bottom, wasting much of our potentially good alfalfa
acres. Barney thought we could scoop out a direct route through
the goosenecks for the stream and then dam the old route to force
the creek to use the new one. We made good progress that first
summer but the war came and got us before we finished it. Four
years later the Axis had lost its war but the creek had won this one.

My most vivid memories of those last months before Papa died
were of the dismal November. The rains we'd prayed for in the
summer heat had come, making it the coldest, wettest autumn
the old-timers could remember. For Barney and me it was fence-
building season, digging post holes, stringing roll after roll of
barbed wire, and keeping a little fire going for an occasional hand-
warming session. It was an ideal situation for two brothers pulled a
bit apart by adolescence to get reacquainted.

For example. A bitter Monday afternoon. After Mass on Sunday
I had seen a shiny new Nash roadster parked at the store in Sacred

Heart and had been captivated by it. I'll have one of those one day, I assured Barney. I would find a way to make a huge amount of money. Barney put on his older-brother hat and asked me why I wanted a huge amount of money. I said I'd buy a Nash. Maybe even a Packard. Barney was not impressed. If you have food to eat and a warm, dry home, there's just one thing money is really useful for, Barney told me. You can use it to buy your life back. Then you don't have to waste it doing things you don't like to do just to make money. I didn't understood this theory, so he explained it. Don't look for a way to make money; find a way to make a living doing what you like to do anyway. Otherwise you're just raising funds to buy yourself out of slavery.

That sounded foolish at the time. In 1993 I went back to the house we'd left behind fifty years earlier and made a side trip to see how the fence had fared. It was still doing its duty and seeing it recalled Barney's philosophy. Foolish or not, it turned out to be pretty much the rule we'd both followed.

4

The Second House

Our second house had also survived well. It was built on a concrete foundation with two bedrooms upstairs and a living room, bedroom, kitchen, and (praise God!) bathroom with indoor plumbing downstairs. That indoor bathroom—a first for our family and a rarity in the south end of Pott County—was luxury indeed.

This house was made possible because years earlier Papa and Uncle Frank had provided desperately needed money and years of "on credit" food to a starving-out farm family. The family had eventually given up and joined Steinbeck's Joads in the Dust Bowl migration to California. The bank at Konawa had foreclosed on the abandoned farm but Papa had found himself holding "mineral rights" to the tract. Such rights are generally worthless (I know, having been stuck with some down through the years) but this site proved a rare exception. It eventually attracted the interest of an oil company. Papa was paid about five thousand dollars for a drilling lease. The wildcat well was the usual dry hole, but the lease money paid to build our house. The indoor bathroom was possible because a Rural Electrification Administration power line went down the section road past Mama's forty, providing electricity for the house and the pump which put water into the bathroom and kitchen.

We moved into it in 1938, the grim bottom of the Depression. The price of cotton was so low it was being left unpicked in the fields and the Zoeller gin was closing. The beautiful Chester White boar on which Barney had lavished untold months of loving care and tons of table scraps won a blue ribbon at the county fair but brought him a check for only $7.23 when he sold it. The only jobs in our end of the county were with the WPA (when the Works Progress Administration had a project going) or day labor "rough-necking" at an oil well rig when someone had money to gamble on drilling. The only work I could find when our own crops were laid by was with hay baling crews. At fifteen, I could drive a buck rake as well as anyone else, or feed the baler, or even push the bailing wire through the slots. The pay was $1.25 for a ten-hour day and bring your own lunch. That 12.5-cents-per-hour scale made the 35-cents-an-hour wage I'd be making as an Oklahoma A&M college freshman seem generous.

I was no more aware of this economic crisis in American history than I was that Papa's heart was wearing out and the only help Dr. Giesen could offer him was an estimation of how many more months it would pump. Our menus, typical of the pre-refrigerator times, were seasonal but we ate well. There was a year-round supply of fresh eggs, fresh milk, fresh-churned butter (I'd guess that not 10 percent of today's Americans have ever experienced the delight of any of those three in their truly fresh, pre-refrigeration state), plus poultry, salt pork, and cottontail rabbits. Summer brought the whole array of things Mama produced in her garden, and Papa planted just about every sort of fruit tree, vine, or bush that would grow at our latitude—including three species of berries, four types of grapes, and apples, pears, plums, and peaches. Except for poultry and game, hot weather limited us to cured meat. The ice truck rolled out from Konawa and those who subscribed were provided little signs to stick in the screen door declaring whether they wanted twenty-five- or fifty-pound blocks to put in their iceboxes. But even fifty pounds lasted only about three days. Thus, eating fresh pork and beef was limited to winter with the season stretched a bit by the custom of neighbors sharing meat when they butchered. While the story was far different in the cities, I doubt if many farm families went hungry during the Depression.

The trouble wasn't food. It was lack of money to pay property taxes and to buy things you couldn't grow in Pott County—such as sugar, salt, flour, the other kitchen staples, barbed wire for fences, medicine, parts to keep the old auto running, etc. Gasoline that year sold at eight gallons for a dollar in Shawnee but like most folks on the fringe of the oil patch we didn't buy all of our gasoline. We kept a fifty-five-gallon oil drum on a rack into which we collected "drip"—the condensation that collects in natural gas pipelines where they sag at creek crossings. Taking this gasoline is illegal now and probably was then. But the oil companies didn't mind. If we didn't steal it they had to hire someone to tour the lines and drain them. But, alas, even that had its downside. Drip gasoline was rich with sulfur and cars that burned it trailed behind them that awful rotten-egg aroma, sure evidence of what we were up to and a cause of some loss of social status.

Whatever the parental motivation for leaving Sacred Heart the move was the big excitement of my boyhood. I quit being a village kid and became a farm boy. Moving two miles may not imply a dramatic change in life style but as village kids Barney and I did only "chores"—cleaning the chicken house, weeding Mama's garden, milking Bossy, feeding the hogs, chopping cookstove kindling, pulling water out of the backyard well to meet the needs of the kitchen, wash day, and Saturday baths and helping Mama with her efforts to make the yard pretty, etc. Now we were farmers.

Workwise, the really big improvement was for Margaret Mary, who had always carried the heavier load. Being big sister, the role of overseeing two younger brothers fell to her. So did the job of being assistant cook, clothes washer, ironer, house cleaner, bread baker, canner of food, etc. As Mama said: "A man may work from sun to sun, but woman's work is never done." In a house without electricity or indoor plumbing that work was hot, heavy, and endless. The change for Barney and me was mostly psychological. The chores remained but we were also doing dignified man's work behind a team of horses.

For me this gain in prestige was balanced by a loss. We were no longer in easy walking distance of the Sacred Heart church. Even though neither I, nor anyone else, ever considered me a pious kid, that graceful old place was important to me in ways I had to grow old before I began to understand. Now they may be beyond my powers to explain. But I'll try.

Our church was built at the summit of Church Hill, the highest in our part of Oklahoma. Therefore when I sat in the shade of its trees to think boyhood thoughts I could (by Pottawatomie County standards) see forever. To the east beyond the cemetery and over the Zoeller pear orchard, stretched the rolling expanse of the Mission Pasture. There, beyond the farthest hill, was the pond full of huge bullfrogs for those of us reckless enough to invade this forbidden territory and astute enough to bag them. To the west, over the roofs of the monastery buildings and St. Mary's Academy, an endless clutter of wooded hills fell away, waiting to be explored. And in every direction stretched the great blue dry-weather sky of Dust Bowl drought, and the towering clouds that waited for winter before delivering rain.

The hilltop was first to enjoy a breeze and the church interior was usually cool and dim. It breathed the perfume of Sunday's incense, old wood, candle smoke, and a sense of God's presence. Sometimes the church was locked because of rumors that the Ku Klux Klan was planning arson. But I had become our self-appointed librarian and that gave me not only access but a reason to be whiling away my idle time atop Church Hill.

The library, of which I was both founder and sole patron, occupied a storeroom adjoining the sanctuary. Its books were the odds and ends left behind when the Benedictines moved their school to Shawnee to become St. Gregory's College. Some were in Latin, German, or French and undecipherable for me. Some were devoted to the metaphysics of theology and beyond my understanding. But others—worn, torn, and hard-used castoffs though they were—were treasures to a kid who loved to read and had never been inside a real library.

I had found them collecting dust in stacks of boxes one Sunday, nosing around after doing my turn as altar boy at Mass. I told the young pastor we had at the time I'd sort them out and make a list for him. I suspect this bookishness and my habit of hanging around the church may have caused Father Bernard to consider me a potential recruit for the Order of St. Benedict.

Making the list took many a month since I needed to sample the contents before penciling in title, author, subject, and publication date into my Big Chief notebook. I started with the Lord North translation of Plutarch's *The Lives of Famous and Illustrious Men of Greece and Rome*, a sort of gossipy account of the machinations and misdeeds of the movers and shakers of the Classic Age and pretty racy stuff for a sixth grader. Then followed Prescott's *Conquest of Peru* and *Conquest of Mexico*, Darwin's *Evolution of the Species*, Washington Irving's *Conquest of Granada*, and so forth. I dipped into *The Lives of the Saints* now and then for a change of pace. I wasn't seeking a pious escape here from the bloody battles of the conquests. I picked those who attained sainthood not by praying but by dying—their martyrdom inspiring vivid descriptions of tongue extractions, beheadings, boilings in oil, burnings at stake, flayings, and impalements.

Such reading provided an endless source of questions for Father Bernard to answer and answer he did. Darwin's theories, said he, didn't conflict with our biblical Genesis stories because we understood that in these God taught in poetic metaphor. The biblical "days" of creation represented eons of time. Humanity separated us from the other primates when God touched the first of us with self-knowledge of Him and of life, death, good, and evil. The evolution theory was simply a briliant scientist's attempt to help us understand the dazzling complexity of God's creation—from the amazing strength of a grasshopper's legs to the way our brains translated the signals delivered by our optic nerves. He made the Gospels equally simple. Christ tried to teach us that happiness lay in helping others, selfishness was the road to damnation. His bottom line always boiled down to God loves us. He gave us free will, permission to go to hell if we wanted, rules to follow if we preferred both a happy life and heaven, and a conscience to advise us along the way.

About the time I finished my indexing Father Bernard was whisked away to a more important assignment, and my next source of books did not come with a philosophical spiritual adviser attached. It was the State Library of Oklahoma, which would respond to requests by mailing a catalog of volumes available. Patrons then noted books desired and sent stamps to cover the mailing costs. After about three nail-biting weeks a package would arrive, causing intense excitement among the Hillerman kids. On top of the books would always be a mimeographed form letter:

"Dear Library Patrons: We are sorry to inform you that not all of the books you requested are available at this time. Therefore substitutes were selected that we trust will meet your needs."

We would have requested something like *Little Women* and *Anne of Green Gables* for Margaret Mary, and stuff like *Captain Blood*, *Death on Horseback*, *Tom Swift and His Electric Runabout*, and *Red*

Badge of Courage for Barney and me. The package would contain such volumes as *History of the Masonic Order in Oklahoma*, *The Bobbsey Twins on Blueberry Island*, *The Decline and Fall of the Roman Empire*, *Tom Brown's School Days*, *Post-Bellum Cotton Economy on the Mississippi Delta*, and *Pollyana and Her Puppy*. They'd all be read before the time came to return them—even though our new life in our new location left less time for sitting around with a book.

For the first year or thereabout, Papa would drive our old Dodge into Sacred Heart and put in his regular ten- or eleven-hour day at the store. Margaret Mary would ride with him to complete the year at St. Mary's Academy and Barney and I would walk down to the intersection where the school bus stopped and ride into Konawa High School to be educated. On Saturdays and when school was out the marble version of our war games survived briefly under the trees in the backyard. Junior Johnson, Jr., the kid in the rented house across the section line, joined us, and his father, Junior Johnson, Sr., came over to see what his boy was doing and got interested. He accumulated his own bag of marbles and when unemployed would join the combat. But it didn't last long. The real war was coming.

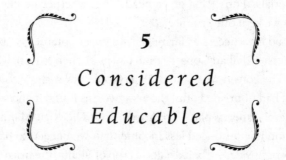

5

Considered
Educable

The autumn before I became a soldier, Mama called a fateful family meeting at the kitchen table and that discussion needs its historical context. The Japanese had bombed Pearl Harbor the previous December 7. Papa, who had been keeping himself alive mostly on willpower, died on the front room sofa the following Christmas morning. Barney turned eighteen in January and was running the farm while he waited for his draft call. Margaret Mary was completing her nurses' training in Oklahoma City. I graduated from Konawa High in May and turned seventeen a week later. When I did, Mama suggested that at least one of us boys should go to college.

Barney and I had spent that day with a cousin, setting up a headstone at Papa's grave—a solemn occasion that perhaps provoked

Mama's planning. A few days before he died, Papa had told us he wanted the cheapest possible funeral and extracted our promise we'd waste no money buying a headstone. We hadn't, but a monk at the monastery told us we could make a handsome white cross of cement, lime, and sand. He helped us make the form and provided the materials. Thus Papa got a headstone, whether he liked it or not, and we kept our promise.

We had less success as farmers. The sweet potatoes we planted to supply the Civilian Conservation Corps kitchen at Konawa went unsold. The cotton we planted (Papa would never allow cotton on his land) had flourished until the armyworms found it and wiped it out. The blackberry patch we leased from Old Man Mann down the section line produced less income than we needed to pay him. On the bright side, we baled a good crop of alfalfa, the price of beef had inched up, increasing the value of the thirty-five head of Angus and Herefords Papa had accumulated, and we'd made a little money peddling strawberries, grapes, apples, and watermelons in town. Add it together the net was probably enough to pay property taxes.

But all was in flux. Barney had lined up a common labor job at the Swift Packing Plant in Oklahoma City to add money to the family treasury during the lax autumn farming time but he'd soon be drafted. What did the future hold for us? Barney, replacing Papa as the family optimist, thought we could make a living farming. I was skeptical. Mama looked beyond that. One of us should go to college. It was a revolutionary idea those days when colleges were for the children of the affluent but we decided to try it. Since I had the better grades and lacked Barney's enthusiasm for agronomy I would be the family scholar. (Actually, Margaret Mary always had the best grades but she was away at nursing school and not involved in this conversation.) The decision was reached. Barney will run the farm until the draft calls him. I will enroll at Oklahoma Agricultural and Mechanical College. What next? In our family, the rule was trust in a loving God, fear nothing, and don't cross bridges until you get to them. The plan went like this. Family funds would pay my tuition for the fall semester, purchase my books, and cover room rent for the first month. By then I would have found work and would cover my own rent and expenses and accumulate enough cash to pay for the spring semester.

Before the social-economic revolution caused by the G.I. Bill of Rights sent literally millions of young men to college, student loans, student aid funds, and government scholarships had not yet been invented. The only people I knew who had been to college were Dr. Geisen, who served the sick of Konawa and the surrounding territory, and some (but not all) of my high school teachers. College was a place where upper-class folks, and a few in the middle class, sent their heirs. Thus Mama's notion that I should be sent off into the lofty realms of the ruling elite seemed downright amazing. But then, Mama was a downright amazing woman.

Decision made, there was no time to lose. Autumn was upon us and classes would be starting soon. I packed my Sunday clothes. Mama made a lunch for us. We got into our old sedan and headed for Stillwater.

In fact, classes were already in their second week. While Mama and Barney dealt with finding me a place to live and a job, I was sent to an academic adviser. Wanted to be an engineer, did I? Well, how had I done in math? I told him I'd made nothing but A's. Alas, he didn't know the only math offered at Konawa High then was one semester of Introduction to Algebra and a semester of plane geometry. Both were taught by the coach of the Konawa Tigers football team. Since the coach didn't understand either subject very well, and since no one seemed to sign up for them except members of the team, we'd spend a lot of our time going over single wing football plays, pass patterns, and so forth. Blissful in his ignorance, the adviser signed me up for College Algebra and Trigonometry, freshman English, Biology, Chemistry, and Chemistry Lab.

While the adviser and I were compiling this blueprint for disaster, Mama and Barney paid the $15 rental for the first month of my living quarters. For that I shared one half of a double bed in a tiny second-floor room of Mrs. Pulliam's old house on Stillwater's Twelfth Street. They had also gone to the college job placement office and collected a list of prospects. By late afternoon when Mama and Barney headed for home (people with cows to milk don't spend nights away from home) I had a six-day-a-week job as bus boy and dishwasher at Mrs. Wallen's boardinghouse, a weekend job as maid for a Stillwater dentist, and a "when needed" promise of work as cleaner of irrigation ditches for the College Department of Agriculture. The pay for dishwashing was three meals a day, except Sunday. The pay for the other jobs was 35 cents an hour.

Years later, after reading *Catcher in the Rye*, memories of that day came flooding back to me and I tried to pull them together into the raw material for a short story—working in the good-bye hug from Mama, shaking hands with Barney, standing on the mostly dead bermuda grass of Mrs. Pulliam's yard watching our sedan disappear down the street, the mixed feelings of fear, exultation, loneliness, and excitement. Suddenly I was a formally recognized adult. Free at last from boyhood, a career at which I had not felt myself successful. I was skinny, clumsy, slow of foot, the survivor of two tough pre-antibiotic bouts of pneumonia, and a struggle with malaria that kept me home from sixth grade classes for months. I had the sort of ears that made Ross Perot a favorite of cartoonists, a large and bony nose, and a tendency to do dumb things to minimize the risk of being considered a sissy by my peers. (For example, jumping out of a barn loft to show pals how paratroopers did it and, as paratroopers often did, tearing up ankle tendons.) Now I had a new start. I was simultaneously scared and jubilant, an emotional mix that was (and still is) beyond my ability to handle in fiction.

Imagine if you can the exact opposite of the movie-TV stereotype of college students and you have my six fellow occupants of Mrs. Pulliam's upstairs rooms. They tended to be grim, dead serious, tired, and on the razor edge of flunking out, going broke, or both. The exception was Sam Singletery Elliot, the offspring of an old and important Georgia family, and why he was reduced to living among us will be explained in a moment. The fellow with whom I would share a mattress for the semester was James Bean, the son of an Army captain. He had played linebacker at one of the huge Oklahoma City high schools. He was big, burly, short-tempered, and not happy to give up his privacy nor even the wall-side of his bed to a late-arriving country bumpkin.

Bean based his claim to the outside of the mattress neither on getting there first nor on his obvious physical superiority. He noted that his job (assistant cook and janitor in a sorority) required him to be in the kitchen at 5 A.M. Since the sorority was a two-mile walk away he had to hit the floor about 4 A.M. and I wouldn't want a 200-pound linebacker climbing over me at that hour seven mornings a week. He was a good, generous lad, once loaning me fifty cents to finance a plan to ask a girl in my Chem Lab out for a cup of coffee. She said no thanks but Bean and I became friends.

Bean was already eighteen. He had volunteered and was awaiting his call to arms. It came at semester end. I heard years later that he was killed in Italy, one of the thousands of young men General Mark Clark sacrificed in his egomanic race to get to Rome before the British.

Like Elliot, Bean was an exception in our group but only because he was from Oklahoma City, and therefore urbane. The rest of us were either farm kids or came from little crossroads villages. In those innocent days before female liberation, a high percentage of young ladies in college were there looking for eligible husbands. Mrs. Pulliam's roomers, supporting ourselves with a variety of 35-cent-an-hour jobs, were clearly not suitable nor competitive with the fraternity boys. Not one of us had a date that semester.

Our social involvement took place downstairs in Mrs. Pulliam's parlor, where she was attempting to teach us auction bridge. Sam

Singletery Elliot had the eligible look but was almost always in the game because he neither held a job nor did homework. Sam had fallen in love and Sam is worth a paragraph because he was part of the education I received at Oklahoma A&M.

From Sam I learned about a social class system that I had no idea existed outside the Victorian-era novels I'd read. I learned there are poor people and rich people and we were among the former. Sam was one of the latter group—a refugee among us at the moment because his family was out of sorts with him and had cut off his allowance. As I remember Sam's story he'd gone to some private school in Savannah, where his family was involved in shipping and banking. He had pledged the family's fraternity at Georgia Tech, did the party scene, and flunked out. An aunt in Tulsa had then taken charge and got Sam enrolled at A&M. Sam was tall, handsome, courteous, amiable, and big-hearted. I was fascinated by him, and so was another of Mrs. Pulliam's inmates, a wheat farmer's son named Darrell. By the middle of the semester we were Sam's friends and confidants.

But Sam needed something more than mere buddies.

He needed someone to really care for him and he had spotted this person. She was a Stillwater High School girl who walked past our place to and from class. Sam had the best room in the house all to himself, with a row of windows looking down on this fateful sidewalk. He had stopped going to classes because Monday through Friday, morning and afternoon, he had to be at these windows awaiting her passage. Meanwhile word of Sam's conduct seemed to have reached his family and even his tolerant Tulsa aunt lost patience. His cash flow stopped. Sam began selling off his extensive and expensive wardrobe.

I observed this with detached interest but Darrell lost patience. He demanded that Sam get this girl's name and telephone number and call her. Sam refused to risk rejection. Finally one icy afternoon just before Christmas vacation, Darrell rushed out to the sidewalk, stopped the girl, introduced himself, and told her about Sam. He invited her in, introduced her to Mrs. Pulliam, and ran upstairs to get Sam. I was away dishwashing when this happened so I report only by hearsay, but Darrell told me that Sam was furious, embarrassed, humiliated, and he had a hell of a time getting him to come down to Mrs. Pulliam's parlor. There he introduced Sam and girl and bowed out. A few minutes later the girl departed, waving good-bye to Sam. What came of that, I don't know. I went home for Christmas. When I got back Sam was gone.

The only reminder I had of him was a beautiful cashmere sports coat he sold me. (My outerwear had been a Konawa High School letterman's jacket awarded for my heroics as second-string right guard—but the A&M lettermen organization banned the wearing of such on campus and that had left me in shirtsleeves and sweater.) I think I paid Sam about four dollars for the coat. Years later after the war when I was trying to attract the attention of my future bride I was still wearing it.

Unfortunately, Sam had feet to match his size. While he had lots of shoes none fit me and shoes had become a serious problem.

Oklahoma A&M was a "land grant" college and thus required all able male students to enroll in Reserve Officers Training Corps programs. Just my cup of tea, I thought, until I learned that even pseudo-soldiers were required to wear brown shoes. I owned two pairs of shoes at the time—a pair of standard high-top work shoes, which I had left behind because they were worn out and too tight, and a pair of two-tone dress shoes. I had used my blackberry-picking money to order these from a catalog. They were Roblees, light tan with the top of the foot covered by very thin, very soft white calfskin perforated with a multitude of square holes—at the cutting edge of Pottawatomie County fashion as I saw it. I wore them with pride, but this attitude was not shared by our drill instructor when he finally noticed them.

"You can't wear those things," he said. "This ain't no party. Wear brown shoes."

I told him I didn't have brown shoes. He said get some by Wednesday, which was our next drill session.

I have no idea what a cheap pair of brown shoes would have cost in Stillwater in 1942. Whatever it was I didn't have it. My plan was to stall and it worked for a couple of weeks until he noticed me again and the conversation went something like this:

"Didn't I warn you about those damn party shoes?"

"Yes, Sergeant. I'm looking."

"Brown next week or your skinny butt is out of here."

The polish I borrowed made that lovely perforated calfskin less obvious—sort of like shoes look when one has been walking through a muddy cattle-holding pen—and it persuaded the sergeant I had tried. Try again, he said. I did. My plan now was to repolish until he gave up and delivered another ultimatum and deal with that if and when it happened. As usual with me, fortune smiled. The sergeant disappeared (off to the Aleutian Islands, I hoped) and was replaced by a corporal with less interest in footwear.

I have retained only a few memories of that first attempt to improve my education—an experience like Alice following Rabbit into Wonderland. At seventeen I had only an abstract notion of social structure and at the campus the ignorance that had been my shield was swept away. Margaret Mary still rejects the idea of our poverty and maybe she's right. We dressed in the costume of the community, we ate well, and when Papa and Mama worried about finances they didn't let us know it. But Stillwater was the world. Stillwater wasn't Bennington, Hanover, Beverly Hills, or New Haven, but social caste is relative. Its sororities, frats, even its dorms, were full of kids with CASH, with allowances, with some-body else paying their tuition, room rent, and expenses. Many of these students even had cars. I was seeing a world I had only read about. Trudging home one evening after getting the supper dishes washed at the boardinghouse, I passed the Sigma Alpha Epsilon frat where party festivities were beginning. Rows of convertibles, pretty coeds in party dresses, and dudes in tuxedos, and my first close look at the unequal distribution of wealth—what Bryan the Iconoclast was complaining about in his socialist editorials. An English professor would call what I was experiencing an epiphany.

I recall no sense of the resentment we have-nots are supposed to suffer when we first see the haves. It was more a sense of surprise. But since this is supposed to be an honest memoir, I'll also admit a touch of envy.

Maybe the dour mood I had brought to the sidewalk where I stood observing SAE festivities can be blamed on Albert Harjo, who was chief dishwasher of our boardinghouse, my supervisor, and a daily diminisher of happy moods. Albert was a big, burly Choctaw Indian, a junior studying electrical engineering, whose expression never fluctuated from glum, and who sang "I'll Never Smile Again," while we cleared eighteen tables and did the dishes. These sessions with dirty dishes and soapy water took place three times daily, six days a week, and lasted about 150 minutes. Albert's baritone voice never faltered. He knew every word of every verse of that mournful love song, and so did I after about the middle of the second week and so do I still a lifetime later. At semester end, Harjo went away to Marine boot camp and onward eventually to Iwo Jima, where the Japanese defenders made his song prophetic. As for me, when the semester ended I went home to the farm.

By then it was clear that college was not for me. Barney had received his draft notice and would be reporting for induction. I had saved most of what I'd earned as the dentist's janitor, ditch cleaner for the Aggie department, and equipment stacker for the ROTC unit, but it was short of second semester tuition. I had managed an A in English Composition, a D in Introduction to Chemistry, a W in Intermediate Algebra (saved from an F by being kicked out of class for sleeping), and a miraculous C in Trigonometry, spared another inevitable F by a genial young instructor.

The conversation as I remember it went something like this:

"What happened to you, kid? All A's on the first half of the semester and now all F's."

I explained I could memorize all the sine, cosine formulas, the various rules, etc., but now we were using algebra and I was lost. He asked what grade I had made in Intermediate Algebra. I told him I had to drop it. Didn't I know that I couldn't take Trig until I had passed Intermediate Algebra? No, I didn't. Well, what sort of grade had I made in Introductory Algebra. I told him I hadn't taken it either. Moment of silence. Did I know that I couldn't even enroll in Intermediate Algebra until I had passed Introductory? No, I didn't. Did I know I had two semesters of learning algebra ahead of me before I'd be eligible for his class. Now I do, I said. Another silence while he did some calculations. We have two more tests scheduled, he said. You'll make two more F's. Then I add your 4-point A's and your 0-point F's and divide and it comes out a 2-point C. Why bother coming to class. So I didn't and a C is what that fine young man awarded me.

A few years ago I went back to Oklahoma A&M (now Oklahoma State University) to make a speech and took the opportunity to find out what had replaced Mrs. Pulliam's old house when the wrecking crew carried out the city's condemnation order. There it stood, still awaiting demolition and looking better than I remembered it under a fresh coat of paint.

The narrow little window that lit our narrow little room (only eleven inches wider than the length of our bed) had a screen on it now and the squirrels had made a comeback, reoccupying the trees from which Darrell had harvested them. Darrell had sensed that Mrs. Pulliam's prohibition against cooking in our rooms was meant to be merely advisory—a gesture to placate the Stillwater fire marshal. His discreetly made squirrel stew came in handy on Sundays when those of us with dishwashing jobs had to find our food somewhere else. It has occurred to me that social economists could learn something about measuring hard times by counting the ducks and geese surviving on state university ponds and the squirrel population in campus trees.

But no more squirrel stew for me. Barney's "Greetings" notice came. He drove Mama and me to Maud and waved his farewell as the draft board's bus pulled away. I drove Mama home—conscious of the significance of that change behind the steering wheel and wise enough to understand that Mama's matter-of-fact cheerfulness was for my benefit. The road home from Maud took us through Sacred Heart and Mama suggested we stop a moment at the church. "Let's say a prayer he comes home safe," she suggested. We knelt for a while in the back pew and I think it was then that I first realized the reality of war. That Barney might never come back. I prayed as fervently as I ever have. Had I known he would get himself into the airborne infantry's glider-flying business, I would have known I was praying for something close to a miracle.

Along with obtaining custody of the car keys, I had more or less, at least in my own mind, became farm manager—for which I had no more competence than I had for trigonometry. Mama must have been aware of that and that I was dying to follow my big brother into uniform. We talked about it that evening at a supper dominated by Barney's vacant chair and came to a decision. If I wanted to go, I could go. We would shut down the farm, sell off the livestock, and close the house. She would move to Oklahoma City. She would find a job. What then? I can't remember that the question ever occurred to me. My only justification for that sort of selfishness is that teenagers tend to think of their mother as Superwoman.

I don't remember her attending the auction we held out at the barn of our farming equipment. The Depression and the drought had made such auctions rural America's Ceremony of Failure. She must have known she would never return to her home here. Having seen what war does to mothers' sons in her nursing of

World War I wounded, she could have had no illusions about that either. I suspect the auction of our wagon, worn plows, cultivators, hay rakes, and harness was a scene she was happy to miss. My only recollection is of Blackie and Dan, our mismatched and trouble-prone plow horses, being bought by my cousin, Joe Grove. I knew even then that Joe didn't need them and bid as an act of kindness. Many years later I asked him if he'd ever worked them. No, he said, he wanted to keep them for Barney and me.

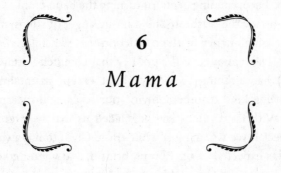

6

Mama

Before we get to the real war, you must get acquainted with Mama, the hero of this book. Without her understanding I would never have had a chance to wear the combat infantry badge, which we former grunts consider America's highest military decoration, nor would I have become a writer. Mama's own life had taught her that youth must have its adventures, whatever the risk. She passed that wisdom along, and also somehow taught me that daydreaming has its values. Her most important lesson was not to be afraid of anything—a variation on Father Bernard's theme. Since God loves us, there is no rational justification for fear. If we do our part by using the good sense He gave us, He's not going to let anything happen that isn't somehow or other for our own good. Slam a door on your hand? While she was dealing with the injury, she would be telling us, first, to offer the pain as a penance for our shortcomings and, second, to learn something from the accident so we didn't repeat it. If time allowed, such little disasters would lead her into a teaching story.

Mama could create a tale of magic for her kids while bandaging a skinned knee, canning beets, or turning the hand-cranked clothes wringer beside the washtub. She was our singer of songs, reader of fairy tales, maintainer of the conviction that we children (despite drought, Depression, and the poverty that engulfed Pottawatomie County) had nothing to worry about except maintaining our purity, being kind to others, saving our souls, and making good grades. With Papa's help, she persuaded us that we were something special. We weren't just white trash. Great things awaited us. Much was expected of us. Bumps, bruises, and winter colds were not be complained about; whining and self-pity were not allowed.

"Offer it up," Mama would say, hugging us while she said it. When life seemed awful, cruel, and unfair, Mama would remind us that it was just a brief trial we had to endure, a race we had to run, a test we must pass as best we could. We were born, we'd live a little while, and we'd die. Then would come joy, the great reward, the Great Adventure, eternal life. So, children, never, never be afraid. Not of spiders (avoid the black widow, and she avoids you), not of lightning (avoid standing under trees during storms), not of storm clouds (see the beauty in them, the majesty; but if you see tornado funnels, we'll have a little picnic in the root cellar). Not of drowning (God loves you but He expects you to use common sense). Not of snakes (they were our allies in humanity's war against rats and mice).

Papa's instructions were more specific. Our kind of people never lie, never steal, never cheat. And maybe most important of all, Hillermans never judge others. We're all God's children and we'd leave the judging to God. That meant we couldn't be racist. But he never gave us a specific prohibition. For example, the autumn before he died he called Barney and me in, told us he had been hearing some disturbing reports about the pool hall in Konawa. "I'd be disappointed if you boys went in there," he said, and I didn't go into a pool hall until years after he was dead. Or, when he discovered I had been missing the school bus and making the two-mile walk down to the South Canadian River to while away the hours daydreaming in the shade, telling me I might be happier staying home and helping with the work. I tried that one day, and never played hookey again.

Mama was a Nebraska-born Anglophile. Her mother died and Mama rode to Oklahoma as a baby in a covered wagon with her father (Grandpa Grove, the only grandparent I ever met), a sister, and two brothers. Her next adventure came when she was farmed out to a neighboring family of German extraction to be cared for until her big sister became old enough to be mother to her. Mama was restored to her family in good health but speaking only German—a situation that caused confusing problems to be laughed about years later at family gatherings.

As a teen, Mama and her brother Christopher took two teams of horses, a wagon, and a buggy and headed northwest to the Oklahoma Panhandle to become homesteaders. In Beaver County, each of them staked out 160 acres of prairie, built the residences required by the Federal Homestead Act, and settled down to live the time mandated to win title to the land. They cut squares of sod out of the prairie grass, stacked and roofed them to make their dirt-floored homes. They hauled their water in barrels from a creek miles away, lived off the staples they'd brought in the wagon with them (flour, salt, sugar, etc.), augmented by what they could raise or catch. Rabbits were plentiful and prairie grouse could be trapped. (How? Take the top out of an empty flour barrel, replace it suspended on two nails and carefully balanced. Sprinkle on corn kernels. The grouse lands to dine, tilts the top, is dumped in, the top swings back into place, he can't get out.)

Their "soddies" were typical of homesteader housing on the high plains—partial dugouts walled with earth. Mama recalled hers as relatively cool in summer and warm in winter, fortunate because neither coal nor wood was available on those vast treeless plains. The fuel for cooking and heating was provided by "buffalo chips." These dried droppings left by the huge herds of bisons that had recently roamed those prairies burned with pretty fair heat, as Mama recalled it, as well as a distinctive aroma.

It sounds like tough going but Mama's memories of it (at least the ones she relayed to her children) were full of fun and happiness. For example, I remember her laughing about their yearning for shade—and the day her brother came by her soddie in their joint-use buggy. Chris reminded her they'd seen trees growing along a creek that drained into the North Canadian River. They packed some food, headed ten miles or so over the prairie and spent a day enjoying both shade and having someone to talk to.

Mama still maintained that taste for shade and quiet places while mothering three kids. She'd pack a basket, we'd head out for the creeks and woods for picnics, and she would use the time to show us what out there was good to eat and what wasn't. For example, the wild mushrooms she collected had to pass three tests. She showed how they looked (pinkish white), how they smelled (delicious), and finally how the thin skin on the cap had to peel back. We learned how to harvest the wild poke greens, which grew along creeks so they would return next summer, and never, never, to chew on them until they were cooked. We learned about poison ivy and poison oak, to be careful about where we put our hands when climbing creek banks in snake season. Above all, we learned that it was a lot better to have a skinned knee than to go through life afraid of falling.

One of the songs Mama sang was a celebration of homesteaders, which involved blowing dust, fleas, frozen mud, bedbugs, etc. "Good-bye to Greer County," she would sing,

where the blizzards arise,
where the sun never sets
and the flea never dies,
where the wind never ceases,
but always remains,
til it starves us to death,
on our government claim.

I'm not sure how long she lived that lonely life on the high prairie, but it was long enough to gain legal title to her quarter section of land. The price she got when she sold it bought the forty-acre farm on which I endured adolescence.

Mama loved music (not "wangdoodle" Bob Wills western songs or "trashy honkytonk" tunes) and her favorites came from World War I. "It's a long way to Tipperary," Mama would sing, in her sweet, perfect-pitch voice, "It's a long ways to go."

The only pieces of furniture of any value we owned created music. One was a large, black Victrola in which a hand-cranked spring motor played 78 rpm records—mostly of operas and music hall stuff. The other was an upright piano. On that Mama made a musician of Margaret Mary (who is still a first-rate organist) and tested Barney and me on the keyboard until confident we had neither talent nor motivation. Barney played the tuba briefly in the St. Mary's Academy orchestra. I had my dreams of being a guitarist and entertaining the world with my ballads, but the best I could master was the bass drum.

I have many embarrassing memories of that musical period (being in the band branded one a sissy) and one happy one. I persuaded (or thought I had) a cute Potawatomi flutist that if she stuck her finger in the little hole through which air escaped when the drum head was pounded, her fingernail would fall off. This caused a lot of booming and giggling during practice until Sister Gregory put a stop to it.

But back to Mama.

Sometime after her homesteading period she followed her big sister to nursing school at St. Anthony's Hospital in Oklahoma City. She joined the American Red Cross nursing service in World War I and was sent to Camp Travis, where she cared for the wounded returned from the battlefields of France and those dying in the great black iwnfluenza plague that accompanied the war. It was a little after that when romance flowered between Mama and Papa. They married at Sacred Heart in 1920. He was a forty-seven-year-old widower caring for two teenaged daughters, his ailing mother-in-law and his aged father. She was thirty-five. If homesteading in the high prairie on the Oklahoma Panhandle didn't qualify Lucy Grove as a brave and adventurous woman I think that marriage did.

If the notion that writing is a good way to spend one's time is inherited, that gene came to me from Mama. Her love of music spread over into the same sort of love for poetry, of stories, of the world of the imagination. She told me once that she had written poetry when she was young but stopped because she had trouble with spelling.

I inherited that spelling flaw from her, too, plus her tolerance of empty spaces and lonely places. While she laughed a lot about the discomforts and inconvenience of life in a sod house on the prairie, I never heard her complain of the month after month of silent loneliness that homesteading in Beaver County entailed. It was an adventure.

Remembering that has helped me understand why, when I turned eighteen and notice came from the draft board, she was willing to set me free for my own adventure. By now Barney was in Texas, training to fly Waco CG4A gliders, and as the last available son of a widowed farm woman, I was exempt from military service. I was supposed to stay home and farm. She knew I yearned to go and signed the necessary release. I say with shame I didn't understand the nature of that sacrifice until I had children of my own. I climbed upon the inductees' bus at Maud, Oklahoma, nervous and joyful—oblivous to everything except that I was headed for a real war and my big adventure.

Mama was fifty-eight years old. She packed her clothing, said good-bye to the house she'd loved and the farm she'd bought with her homesteading money, and moved into a rooming house in Oklahoma City. There Margaret Mary was finishing her nursing education at St. Anthony's Hospital and Mama's older sister was Sister Monica, the superintendent of nurses. There she supported herself with a job in a hospital sterilizing room.

Two decades later Margaret Mary, Barney, and I brought her back to Sacred Heart to bury her beside Papa in the cemetery on Church Hill. I remember a mild early summer day, the Zoeller pear orchard below still in bloom, mockingbirds performing in the old cemetery cedars, and the songs of meadowlarks accompanying the graveside prayers. I remembered how Mama had loved days like this. And a host of other things about her that I was now old enough to begin understanding. Such as how she knew I was the sort of kid who needed an adventure.

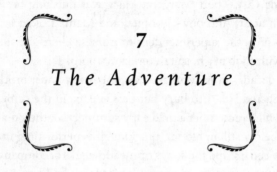

7

The Adventure

The real war, which was to be my adventure, had to wait a bit even after I signed up.

First there was the medical examination center in Oklahoma City, which for some reason was called "The Shrine." There one received a physical examination that preceded the inoculations the Army required. Those ruled healthy boarded a bus for Fort Sill. There we were yelled at by the cadre, issued a pair of regulation brown U.S. Army high-top marching shoes (at last) and a duffle bag full of clothing, and were introduced to what the Army called "military courtesy"—saluting, marching commands, and the other stuff I'd already learned in my semester of Reserve Officer Training Corps. It was there I came to understand what was going on back at the medical examination center when I was led into a room and questioned by a captain. Do you like boys, the captain asked. I said sure, a lot of them. How about girls? Did I have a girlfriend? I said I wasn't sure. What did I mean by that? I explained that I had a girlfriend named Carol who lived in Ada and I had a date with her just last night, sort of to say good-bye before marching off to war, but when I appeared at her address right on time, her aunt came to the door and said Carol wasn't there. Why not? The aunt said she couldn't say. But her expression was sympathetic, causing me to suspect that I no longer had a girlfriend. There was more to that story but the captain had lost interest and hustled me out.

On the ride down to Fort Sill I met Bob Huckins, who was destined to become a lifelong friend and to be wounded trying to give me a hand when I was blown up at Niefern. Huckins was from Sasakawa, only slightly larger than Sacred Heart, where his father was a merchant and mortician. Yes, he said, the captain had asked him the same sorts of questions. He'd asked the captain what they were about and the captain said it was to determine if we were queer. I had never heard the term. Huckins had, but wasn't sure what it implied. Need I remind you that we were country boys.

The Army promptly sent Huckins and me and a trainload of other teenaged Okie recruits to Fort Benning, Georgia, there to learn how to be soldiers in the infantry. We were housed in the ramshackle barracks of an abandoned Civilian Conservation Corps camp, in an area called Harmony Church far from the fort's regular Infantry School Center. Except for the barracks floorboards, which were as warped as in our Sacred Heart house and through which scrub water poured when we tried to mop them, this was indeed a strange world for me.

Our training unit was filled with draftees sent South from New York, New Jersey, and the Boston reception centers—all earmarked for the Army Specialized Training Corps. Four of us from Oklahoma, one from Kansas, and two from the West Coast, having posted the same sorts of lofty scores on some test or other, had been added into the mix. This was my introduction to cultural diversity. These were city boys right off the streets of East Orange, Queens, and Scully Square—urbane and sophisticated. They spoke a harsh Northeastern version of English, fast and without the Okie drawl, described strange and exotic customs, and—so it seemed to me—were wiser in the ways of the modern world. On the other hand, few of them knew how to drive a car or harness a horse, understood that milk didn't originate in the bottle, or had hunted squirrels. Thus our sense of ignorance and inferiority was offset when we got to the firing ranges. All seven of us off the turnip wagons qualified the first time through as marksman or expert and we posted four of the top rifle scores in a thousand-man battalion.

This isn't the place to discuss the joys and rigors of getting through infantry basic training. I will linger on it a bit only because it was here I first began to better understand the connection between the real world and the one I had known through novels and magazine stories. The fierce mess sergeant who starved us so relentlessly was right out of Dickens. Sidney Jablonski, the plump kid from the Bronx who bunked below me and yearned endlessly for battlefield glory, needed only an upper-class Anglo Saxon name to be one of P. C. Wren's heroes. (He lived the Wren plot idea, too, volunteering for the paratroops and drowning when the tow planes jettisoned their gliders off the coast during the invasion of Sicily.) Our drill sergeant, a survivor of the Aleutians battles, was exactly the sort of cynic Cervantes had in mind as Don Quixote's assistant. The raw material for fiction was all around in the piney woods but I collected it only for jokes and anecdotes with no idea then that I would have a more serious use for it. For that matter, few of the memories I accumulated there would fit into plots. For example, while Army Jell-O could be stretched and refused to melt it wasn't useful in fiction. Nor did the faces of the German prisoners of war we used to trudge past on our marches through the Georgia woods. Veterans of Rommel's Afrika Corps, they studied us, exchanged sardonic remarks, and gave us the feeling goats might have when walking past a pack of caged wolves.

Useless memories, but they stick with me.

Phase two of our military career took Huckins and me back to Oklahoma A&M—told we were being sent to college to prepare for our roles in the new high-tech Army. No more dreams of glory. We sewed on shoulder patches that featured the lamp of learning ("The Flaming Pisspot") and the catch line of our marching song was:

> *Take down your service flag, mother.*
> *Your son's in the ASTP.*

On the bright side, the barracks adjoining the campus were much improved from the decaying CCC camp we'd left and the food was better. The shame of our shoulder patch was partly offset by the fact we were veterans of the infantry basic, which meant we could wear the musket on a slim blue badge of the Queen of Battles if we ever managed to join an Infantry unit. We were salty enough to be skeptical. Our commandant, for example, was old (at least forty), he was a West Pointer, and he was only a captain and should have advanced at least to colonel. What terrible deed had he done? It couldn't be mere stupidity. Citizens drafted out of the real world knew stupidity was no impediment for advancement for West Point grads. Had he seduced a general's wife or what?

Whatever, he was an amiable commander. When bed check showed we were violating curfew, he was willing to believe—time after time and without checking—that we had been studying in the A&M library and not hanging around the downtown movies trying to meet girls as had been repeatedly reported to him.

My memory holds little of any significance from the ASTP phase of the real war. My classes were pretty much the same stuff I had studied—the big difference being I now had money, shoes properly Army brown, and wasn't assistant dishwasher, janitor, and ditch cleaner as well as student. I actually was making A's in my physics and math classes. Another difference was in the gender field. I had learned in my first tenure on the A&M campus that starved-out civilian freshman boys were simply invisible to coeds looking for more promising males. Now we were visible, but were looked upon with scorn. Patriotism had replaced social caste among the coeds. Why weren't we out there with their big brothers defending the flag?

That scorn may have been more imagined than real, a product of the way we felt about ourselves. We told each other that ASTP actually stood for Always Safe Till Peace. How could we escape nerfdom and resume our pursuit of glory? Huckins, always full of risky ideas, talked me into joining him in applying for a transfer to the paratroops. We applied to the captain. Don't worry, he said. You're out of here any day now. And we were—sent to fill the ranks of the 103d Infantry and get ready to join the battle. But before entering phase three of the real war, what is there in any of this that bent me toward writing fiction? Not much. No romance. No halls of ivy here. The groundskeepers of this Aggie school had prepared for the future arrival of spring by fertilizing the campus with literally acres of manure from the cow barns, pigpens, horse stables, and (most aromatic of all) the poultry grounds. When the winter sun warmed this bizarre landscape of animal excrement, the aroma was pervasive and I talked myself into one up-close-and-personal encounter with it.

We were walking back from the gym after our daily workout. (Why did the Army think its selected scholars need muscles? We'd soon know the answer.) I was regaling my friends with my remarkable ability to endure cold. A kid from Chicago scoffed at the Oklahoma version of winter, noting Polar Bear Club members break the ice of Lake Michigan for a swim. I pointed to Theta Pond. "I'd swim across," said I, "if it wouldn't get me in trouble with the Army."

No males need to be told how that worked out. A challenging bet is made—five bucks against my honor. I accept, hoping that with payday far behind they won't have the fiver. They did. I dive through the skim ice in my exercise togs, a sensation still vivid. Everything works except lungs, which refuse to inhale. I splash to a tiny island that decorates the center of the pond and is crowned with a thick crust of fertilizer. I sat there on that mountain of frozen chicken droppings getting my lungs working again and deciding that I preferred freezing on the island to completing the swim. Alas, the taunts and jibes of my friends drove me back in the water. They signed the fiver for me and I carried it for more than a year until my wallet fell into the hands of medical personnel when I was wounded.

The only concrete contribution here to my future efforts as a writer involved an odd friendship of a fellow I'll call Jack McKeen. He showed me a side of humanity I hadn't known. I remembered him while I was trying to make a creditable baddie in *People of Darkness*.

McKeen was the only son of a banker, and was tall, handsome, charming, and witty. If he had sisters (or a mother) they were never mentioned. In McKeen's worldview humanity fell into two segments—the prey and the predators. The prey included all women and most males; the predators Jack's dad, Jack, and a handful of other males. We got acquainted at a music store near the campus, where I was having a Bach recording played for me by a skeptical clerk. Jack came by, said Bach was okay but for real music I should be listening to Wagner. Since Jack had been actually buying records the clerk made the change. We listened to Wagner. Jack was taking the ASTP even less seriously than the rest of us. He'd done his high school in an expensive military academy and was awaiting a pending appointment to West Point to come through.

Since Jack eschewed library work he had a lot of idle time and I'd often find him in the music store listening booth, headset on and Wagner booming away. He appealed to me as a Martian might have. He was interesting. He was a year older (big deal when you're eighteen) and he'd been around. I think I appealed to him as the only one in the barracks willing to listen to his philosophical and political theories. I'd been reading Plato's stuff. He said Plato preached nonsense. Teaching morality and ethics is useful, Jack would say, only because it helps keep the majority placid in its role as prey for the predator class. The philosophers worth reading were Nietzsche, Zeno, and Hedon—the apostle of the Superman and the two disciples of living only for self-gratification. Why was I a Catholic? Nietzsche taught that Christianity was the greatest curse ever imposed on humanity but his dad said it must be supported to keep the working class calm. Never ever think that social rules apply to you, said Jack. They apply to the gazelle, not to the lions; to the goats but not to the tigers.

Pretty heady stuff, and Jack McKeen practiced as well as preached. For example, one day he showed me a diamond tiepin his uncle had sent him as a birthday present, along with the jeweler's documents appraising it as a flawless 2.2 karats. Jack suggested we get a pass to Oklahoma City. I'd take the pin and pawn it. He'd report it stolen and if the police didn't locate it, he'd go to the shop, pretend to be shopping for a diamond stickpin, recognize it, call the cops, and reclaim his property. Then I'd keep half the pawn money as payment for taking the risk.

The Army separated us by abolishing the ASTP and shipping us down to fill gaps in the 103d Infantry Division at Camp Howze, Texas. I went to Company C and Jack to Company D. Weeks later, I was ordered into the office of Captain Curtis C. Neeley, commander of Charley Company. Neeley told me Private Anthony G. Hillerman had been arrested in Oklahoma City the previous weekend without the required pass. Before he pronounces sentence, do I have an excuse for this? I do, having spent the day in question far from Oklahoma City cleaning grease traps in the Charley Company kitchen for Sergeant Carl Pohlad, our mess sergeant.

The captain reads my serial number off the report. Is that mine? It is. We look at one another. Will the captain call Pohlad to confirm my story? Will he ask me who did this to me? Will I answer him if he does? The captain decides not to test me, nods, says I'm dismissed. He goes back to his paperwork. I go looking for Jack McKeen.

Does he deny it? Of course not. Predators don't apologize to their prey. But why me, I ask. Because mine was the only serial number besides his own that he knew.

(If any baseball fans are reading this, Mess Sergeant Pohlad survived the war as an officer and became owner of the Minnesota Twins.)

It was about then I gave up on the idea of converting Jack to Christianity and I only saw him again on three occasions. Once was just a few days before we shipped out to Camp Shanks, the staging base for our boat ride to Europe. Jack told me he was not going because his transfer orders to become a West Point cadet had finally come through. He wished me well, reminded me that the prey were the dead heroes, the predators survived. Next I saw him at a truck park somewhere up the Rhone Valley, still with Company D. The class at West Point had been filled, canceling his transfer. But the senator friend of his dad had arranged an appointment to Annapolis—always his first choice. Weeks later I saw the machine gun section of D trudging up a rainy road in the Vosges Mountains but I didn't see Jack. I slid down the muddy slope to inquire. Shot in the fighting at St. Dié, I was told—a machine gun bullet in the head.

I don't know what finally has become of Jack. I know he survived the head wound because he showed up at the University of Oklahoma. It was January 1946, when the waiting list for cars was at least a year long. Jack was driving a shiny new sedan. He removed his golf cap and showed me where a metal plate was replacing missing bone. He called my attention (without introduction) to the lovely girl waiting in his car. He asked about my eye patch and my limp. He'd enroll at the university, join his dad's fraternity, and become a lawyer. We'd get together.

I never saw him again but for me he lives on as B. J. Vines. McKeen made it possible for me to create this character. Papa tried to teach us not to judge others, but McKeen made what Vines did in the *People of Darkness* plausible and his death justified. I pray for a happier ending for the bona fide Jack McKeen.

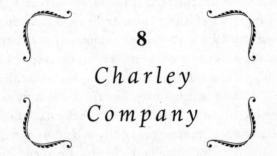

8
Charley Company

At last! At last! At last! Herded off the train at Gainesville, trucked to a sprawl of shabby barracks on the rolling North Texas plains, down the gravel battalion streets, dumped off in little bunches at various company headquarters buildings, depending on what our orders said. Mine said "Company C, 410th Infantry, 103d Division"—finally a genuine, bona fide combat outfit.

Up the wooden front steps, through the door, into the company clerk's office, hand my orders to a corporal who glances at them, unimpressed. "Another quiz kid," he says to the first sergeant. "Get him back to supply," says the First.

I trot back to the supply room, where a six-by-six truck is parked, its driver unloading bundles of clothing. I report to another corporal. "Another quiz kid," says the corporal. "Just in time," says the supply sergeant, who is standing checking a list with the driver. The driver climbs back into the cab, starts the engine. The supply sergeant points to the truck bed, says: "Hop on, soldier, and toss out stuff."

I hop on, confused. The truck is rolling down the alley toward the battalion street—supply sergeant and corporal running behind, motioning me to start tossing. I toss. As the truck turns up the battalion street, the door of company headquarters opens, two men dash down the steps and join the sergeant and the corporal, picking up the bundles I'm tossing and encouraging me to toss more. One of them is wearing captain's bars. The truck slows, turns up the alley next to Company B headquarters. I bail out, walk back to Charley Company to resume my efforts to report for duty at the supply room. The four bundle collectors are there, including Captain Curtis C. Neeley, our company commander, doing his duty, taking care of his own.

Neeley's own was an oddly mixed bag who could be roughly classified in two groups, the standard US and THEM division of American society. THEM were the cadre, those who had survived the Louisiana Maneuvers, most of whom were officers and noncoms, but some were privates who had managed to be overlooked when the division was looted to provide replacements for the riflemen being killed in Africa, the Pacific, and Europe. US were those who hadn't endured the horrors of the Louisiana war games— mostly replacements poured in from the aborted ASTP projects and would-be flyboys dumped into the infantry grinder when the Army noticed it was training more flight personnel than it needed.

We called the cadre "lifers"—the insulting term civilian soldiers applied those days to regular Army personnel. Some were regulars, but many were Arizona National Guard troops of the 103d's original life. That didn't matter. Nothing mattered except The Maneuvers. They produced a treasury of anecdotes—tales of heroic exploits, drunken foolishness, endless bug-infested food, notable Army stupidities, and unspeakable agonies endured. Those

Maneuvers also produced the bonding that only shared misery seems to cause. We quiz kids and the flyboys were outside this fraternity—apparently forever.

We made the first crack in that Iron Curtain one sweltering August day, thanks to another outsider—a newly commissioned second lieutenant just out of Officers Candidate School at Fort Benning. He had been a halfback on the Georgia Tech football team. He was in superb physical condition, but he hadn't done the Louisiana thing. He gets the job of leading the company the required ten-mile, end-of-training forced march that would demonstrate to the Inspector General, or whoever judges such things, that we were ready for combat. I've always suspected our new lieutenant volunteered for this as an opportunity to demonstrate to The Maneuvers fraternity that he was every bit as tough as they were.

Alas, he did.

This ten miles is supposed to be completed in two hours carrying full field equipment. In my case that was sleeping bag, a "shelter half," which when combined with the other half formed a pup tent, two tent stakes, a blanket, a day's rations, a canteen of water, an envelope of salt tablets, and everything else you owned, plus your weapon, a ration of ammunition, etc. For the average grunt it worked out to about sixty pounds, not counting one's steel helmet. In my case, as the gunner in my mortar squad, the burden also included a leather box containing the sight, the mortar barrel, one of those .45 caliber pistols designed to knock down berserkers at point-blank range during the Philippine Insurrection, and a couple of extra clips of pistol ammunition. I never learned to like that pistol but one day it would save my life.

It is axiomatic in the Army that wherever you are it is the hottest summer, dustiest spring, coldest winter, deepest snow, etc., in the memory of man. Thus the temperature was to rise that day to one hundred and eight degrees Fahrenheit. Add a blazing sun and high humidity. Away we go down the dusty trail, warming up on the first mile with the infantry's standard three-miles-in-fifty-minutes pace, getting us ready for mile two. That mile we run. We rest in the roadside ditch, butts down, feet up the embankment, steel helmets (too hot to touch) set aside and the plastic helmet liner used to keep the sun off our faces—a technique we'd learned in basic. Our lieutenant walks up and down the row, warning us to take it easy on the canteens and to take our salt pills. I still remember thinking with foreboding that he looked fresh as a daisy.

During mile three the first man takes a dive—a buck sergeant in one of the rifle squads. We pass him sprawled in the ditch. Several more fall out doing the mile-four run. On mile five it gets serious. Charley Company had always been notorious in the 410th Infantry for singing while marching. No songs left now. We trudge along in stony silence looking for the telltale tilt to the right in the man ahead of us, which signals he's about to tumble. Soon the roadside ditch is well populated. During the break before mile six, the word spreads among us that one of the loftier noncoms has fallen out, gotten back to company headquarters, and reported to Captain Neeley. Ambulances have been dispatched, we hear, and Neeley has called off the exercise.

If he actually did, our lieutenant didn't get the word. Off we go on the six-mile run. More dropouts, more canteens being drained, more fellows leaning to the right and then following their rifles in the tumble into the ditch. During the break before mile nine, Bob Lewis and I discuss whether our sense of manhood would be too badly damaged if we join the fainters. Before we can decide, we are trudging away on mile ten. Finally the end is in sight and it is too late to do the sensible thing.

In the latrine showers after the ordeal a huge truth dawned on us. Those of us who had finished the ten-miler were almost all quiz kids. Nearly all of the fainters were the Louisiana Maneuvers tough guys. Captain Neeley noticed this. Everyone had. The only formal and official notice that the ten-miler was behind us was the handing out of a second copy of the little blue bar with the musket device to pin on uniform shirts certifying us as infantrymen. More important, we were being accepted as soldiers by the old hands. Some kidding still, but no more blatant disrespect.

I'm sure the same was true for the rookie lieutenant. It developed that he had misread the map and our ten-miler had gone thirteen, but trouble with maps seemed to be no handicap for officers in the 103d Division. He became leader of one of the rifle platoons.

The last time I saw him was on a much colder day in the outskirts of Villa, a smallish French town we were wresting from the Germans. He'd been knocked off the street by the blast of a mortar shell, part of his face chopped away by a fragment. The snow was blowing over him and one of the aid men was kneeling beside him, trying to stop the bleeding. But the mortar rounds were still whistling in and we were running for cover. No one stopped to say good-bye.

That epic ten-miler also marked the end of training. We were now battle-ready. A division review was done so the top brass could look us over, we were trucked south to parade through the streets of Dallas with bands playing and regimental flags flying, we scrubbed the floors and whitewashed the rocks at Camp Howze so it could be abandoned shipshape to the wind and weather, packed our gear for the train ride to the seaport, and got passes for a final good-bye.

9

The Sentimental Journey

I walked out to the highway and hitchhiked north, en route to Oklahoma City and a farewell visit with Mama and Margaret Mary. And this, I think, requires a digression for those young folk who won't remember how hitchhiking was in the olden days. The Depression had made it socially acceptable to be out on the road without bus ticket money. With the unemployment rate about 30 percent, those fortunate enough to be driving certainly had friends or relatives uprooted and homeless drifting around in the hope that they'd find work over the horizon. Then came the war, further uprooting, gasoline rationing, jam-packed public transportation, and millions of men trying to get home or back to camp. Failing to pick up someone with his thumb out was antisocial. Passing up one in uniform was akin to treason. For servicemen hitchhiking became so common that a protocol was developed. If others were seeking rides on your stretch of highway you moved down the line past them. They were expected to suggest to the driver who picked them up that you, too, would appreciate a ride. The point to the above being that hitchhiking was easy, orthodox, sometimes exciting. Exciting? On my way back to camp after this very leave a LaSalle limo driven by a middle-aged woman and already occupied by three girls and a private with red artillery braid on his cap stopped to pick me up. The young ladies said the driver was the madam of the place where they worked in Tulsa—moving them to Dallas where business was brisker. Why didn't I come along? I said my pass was expiring. The girls suspected my reluctance was due less to duty than to fear (the hygiene movies the Army showed recruits were far more terrifying than the best Stephen King has produced) so they showed me the needle marks left by their anti-VD inoculations. But my moral standards clicked in. And we were about to ship out to the real war. I couldn't risk missing it.

The first driver who picked me up on this three-day pass wasn't as memorable. But the second ride was with a World War I veteran full of stories of trench warfare, mustard gas, and lice. He said he could get me twenty miles up the road toward Oklahoma City but then was turning eastward—headed for Ada. Ada is only about twenty-five miles from Sacred Heart. I decided to detour, take a nostalgic look at the home place, and then go visit Mama. Two rides later and a little after midnight, a truck driver dropped me off at Higdon's Corner—less than a mile from home.

I have an unsatisfactory chronological memory, marked by great year-long gaps and vacancies. The few hours that follow in the summer of 1943 take up more space in my subconscious than the ten long years of the 1980s. It was a mild night, three-quarter moon lighting the front of the house, the familiar smells of a hot, dry summer, a mockingbird on the roof ridge producing an imitation of a blue jay's call. The front door was locked. I have no key and need none. I slide up the sash on the bathroom window and climb through—into those smells of dust and emptiness one finds in deserted houses, into dark rooms where the electric switches are inoperative and where I need no light. I open windows to admit the night air, sit at the kitchen table remembering the supper when Mama, Barney, and I sat here deciding I'd be a scholar, remembering the meal when the odd grinding sound we couldn't identify proved to be the sound of the injured pup Papa had brought home chewing the leg on Mama's Victrola, remembering hugs, happiness, and huge dreams.

I went into the front room and sat in the chair where Papa had rested in those last weeks until he could sit no longer. Moonlight through the front window was now illuminating the couch where he'd spent the days when he could no longer remain upright—and where he had died Christmas morning.

Margaret Mary, home from nursing school, had driven us to the monastery to see if we could find a priest who wasn't busy with Christmas services to come and give him what we then called "The Last Sacrament." We couldn't, but it was too late for that anyway and we both knew it. Papa was already dead. I think we both also knew that he didn't require that terminal blessing. He had fed the poor, clothed the naked, carried his cross, and somehow persuaded us kids that we were special and the same sort of conduct was required of us.

That's not the sort of thinking one needs after an exhausting day of hitchhiking. I climbed the stairs into the room Barney and I had shared, opened the windows, and sprawled on our dusty bed. The mockingbird was gone now but the whippoorwill was singing his sad, lonely song in the woods on Old Man Mann's farm, just as it had done every summer. With that in my ear, I fell asleep. I was feeling deprived, lonesome, sorry for myself. I intended to do great things in this war. Damn it, Papa should be alive to know about it.

I remember awakening the next morning with the sort of hunger fast-growing teenagers feel when their last meal is eighteen hours and a lot of walking behind them and there is absolutely no prospect of even a drink of water for breakfast. That, and the reality of submarginal farming poverty I was seeing, cut short my inspection of the home place. If I was writing fiction now, I'd describe a stop at the top of the hill, a backward look, and a lot of emotion. I didn't stop. I had a mile to go to the major gravel road where I'd have a chance to catch a ride. Besides, I didn't need to look back. I remembered every bit of it (and still do). It had been a happy place but I sensed I would never live there again.

My first ride that morning was the truck of the cattle dealer named Davis who'd bought our little herd when my call came from the draft board. We talked about that a little, about how the price of beef had shot up in the year since then, about how we'd have a hard time buying back in when the war was over. But mostly he wanted to tell me about Papa. He delivered a series of anecdotes, how Papa had gone and got old Agnes Brown and took her up to the asylum at Norman when she went crazy, how Papa had talked a Potawatomi family into holding out for more money when a lease buyer was trying to cheat them, rattling off names of families Papa had helped feed when the price of cotton dropped to four cents a pound at the gin. I don't remember many of them but I do recall the exclamation with which he concluded each of them. He'd slap me on the knee and say: "Gus was a goodun!"

Davis dropped me off at the village of Asher, on the paved road toward Oklahoma City. No café there, but I drank about a gallon of water from the hose at the filling station and the next ride was with a woman who worked at the plant where Douglas Aircraft was churning out C-47s for the Army. It was nonstop to Oklahoma City. There I received food, the farewell advice and instructions younger sons get from mothers with the good-bye hugs. Margaret Mary wasn't there. She'd married Frank Chambers, an artillery forward observer in my regiment, and had gone to Texas to see him off.

Our next stop was Camp Shanks, New Jersey, and our troop ship. While awaiting the ship, we were allowed very brief leaves, long enough to get into Manhattan via ferry and back again in time for the morning wake-up bugle, and long enough to teach me two memorable lessons. One of our four-man patrol claimed enough big city experience to know how to meet girls. He had us clustered around a sidewalk grating, and staring into it as if fascinated. As he promised, it soon collected a small throng of the curious. Although these quickly left after deciding we had nothing interesting to look at, we eventually gave pause to three girls, teenagers like us, who asked us what we were doing. When we confessed we were simply trying to meet girls, they agreed to go to a Fats Domino concert with us.

The second lesson came after delivering the girls to their subway stop for their trip home. At a bar/grill passed enroute to our ferry we paused. I ordered a Singapore Sling, advertised to contain eight kinds of rum. I drank this, plus some other stuff, and a bit later was advised by the waiter that the waffle on which I had poured syrup and was trying to cut was the photographed waffle on my menu. The subsequent hangover was a terrible thing.

After subjecting us to the most foul-smelling spring in Oklahoma A&M records, following this with the hottest summer in Texas history, the U.S. Army capped it with the stormiest Atlantic crossing since C. Columbus. Captain Neeley had made this more onerous for his Charley Company wards by drawing the short straw when the company commanders decided to assign shipboard cooking and dishwashing duties by lot—sentencing Charley Company to scrubbing those vomit-covered trays (almost everybody was seasick) and saving us from the on-deck crap games. And for the first time ever, I was loaded with cash.

Ever since basic training at Benning, I had dutifully set aside three or four dollars a month as my contribution to the payday crap shoot. While gambling was prohibited by the Army, it was Charley Company tradition that officers stayed away from the enlisted men's latrine on payday evening—thereby avoiding the knowledge of evildoing. I always played. I never won. Not ever. This changed at Camp Shanks.

On shipping-out eve, we were required to turn in all cash over one-dollar bills and coins in exchange for phony-looking script the Army had printed for use wherever we were going. This left us without much for investment in the farewell game. All those sevens and elevens that had eluded me now appeared. I cleaned out the game in Charley Company, accumulating a pocketful. A friend suggested that this run of luck shouldn't be wasted and we drifted across the street to the Baker Company latrine. There my lucky streak continued. When I struggled up the gangplank the next morning, carrying every thing I possessed, my pants were sagging with untold pounds of coins and every pocket of my field jacket was abulge with wads of ones.

On the ship and in France this wealth was utterly unspendable— and illegal as well. No good came of it. Months later I managed to convert the $172 I hadn't given away to French villagers into a money order made out to my mother. Pending a chance to mail it, I kept it dry in a field jacket pocket. Before that chance came it was captured, along with my field jacket, helmet, mortar, and a sack of mortar rounds, by a bunch of early-rising German ski troopers. But more of that later.

Nothing notable happened on the trip across. Our convoy veered northward, which lent weight to generally believed reports that we were going to liberate Norway from the Nazis. We sailed through the fringe of a hurricane, which produced waves big enough to sweep over the flight deck of the convoy's escort carrier and have us all confined below decks. When allowed up again we saw rows of landing gear still chained to the carrier's flight deck but waves breaking over the deck had swept away the aircraft.

About the time we saw Gibraltar, Axis Sally let us know Norway was not in our future. She greeted the 103d Division and our commanding general by name and welcomed us to Marseilles.

We got there a bit late. The port had already been captured and the only greeting our landing craft encountered was a Frenchman in a motorboat passing out cards inviting us to a brothel.

Exciting times, those, with the port city still smoking from the demolition projects of the retreating Germans and an occasional recon plane drawing antiaircraft fire. Grand adventure ahead, but first an exhausting march from the sea level landing area up the top of the plateau behind Marseilles followed by an extended introduction to life in the mud at the division's tent camp.

Some philosopher once described war as an infinity of boredom punctuated by occasional moments of abject terror. The only boredom I remember was experienced in this staging area. We spent about ten days living in our pup tents with nothing to do but dig the required sanitary slit trenches and be trucked down to the port now and then to help unload weapons and ammunition off ships.

Bob Lewis and I slipped away from one such stevedore detail, found a sort of makeshift bistro nearby, and there met a trio of other layabouts drinking wine and wearing shoulder patches of the famous 45th Division. Mortar gunners, were we? They shook their heads in pity and sorrow. Too bad. Anzio horror stories followed and the information that the life expectancy of mortarmen in combat was something under fifteen minutes. They made combat sound even worse than the Louisiana Maneuvers, and while we recognized it was mostly the game veterans play with newcomers, it made the staging area boredom more tolerable.

The only other memorable moments there came when Lewis and I and couple of others from the mortar section decided to slip away from the staging area under cover of darkness and see if we could find a little café we'd noticed while being trucked back from the wharfs. We didn't, but we did find a massive villa, the long driveway of which was lined with Jeeps, weapons carriers, the ugly olive-drab sedans staff officers use, a few civilian cars and a couple painted the U.S. Navy blue. What could it be?

A half dozen or so men were waiting on the porch for their time to join the crowd in the foyer. We had found a brothel, they explained. They were the end of the line. The wait was about an hour. We skirted the place, looking it over. One of us (I plead not guilty) noticed that by dumping out a rain barrel, rolling it from under its downspout to a lighted window, and hopping atop we could determine if this was actually a house of ill fame. It was, and the brief peek into the bedroom was even more antierotic than those hideous disease films we'd watched in basic training.

Then came the ride up the Rhone Valley to the forested foothills of the Vosges. What we had come for was about to begin.

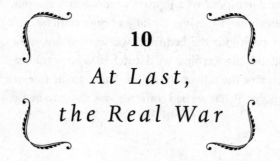

10
At Last,
the Real War

The real war began for me one mild autumn day at a farm-house beside the Meurthe River. Charley Company and the rest of the First Battalion of the 410th Regiment had sneaked down a steep and heavily wooded hillside the previous night, warned by our superiors that the least sound or glimmer of light would bring us under devastating artillery fire from the Germans on the opposing slope. We had arrived at a valley farm with only sprains, scratches, and bruises, moved into the farm buildings, and survived a peaceful first day on the front. Now, with evening approaching, my mortar squad comrades were summoned with members of a rifle squad into the farmhouse living room. There stood Captain Neeley, our platoon leader, and a stranger wearing the golden oak leaves of a Major. We were having our first experience with Army Intelligence, a term that we would learn is the classic oxymoron.

Captain Neeley told us we were about to conduct a raid. The major would explain. He did. Just across the Meurthe River from our farmhouse, the major said, ran a railroad with a parallel highway. Every night German supply trucks came down that highway delivering ammunition to German forces holding St. Dié. We were to wade across the stream, establish positions, and ambush these trucks. My mortar, obviously, wouldn't be useful on this mission and was left behind. To augment my .45 caliber pistol I was handed a "grease gun"—the crown jewel in the U.S. Army's array of ill-conceived and misbegotten weapons. The major unfolded a map and explained things to the lieutenant who was to lead this venture. Upstream we would find a footbridge but it was mined and should be avoided. However, the river was only about three feet deep, not dangerously swift, and we would wade across it below the bridge, take up positions at the highway, and shoot up the trucks when they came along. Those standing closer to the conversation reported later that the major told our lieutenant the Germans had strong positions beyond the highway, that we should expect a quick reaction, and not delay getting back to our side of the Meurthe.

Away we went, out into the darkness, quiet, well spaced, and, speaking for myself, nervous and excited—a rifle squad reinforced by mortar men. I think I can speak for the entire party when I say we were not yet experienced enough to have been as scared as we should have been. We moved silent as mice across the bare hayfield that lay between our farm buildings and the river. At river's edge we hit the ground while the lieutenant and the squad leader talked things over. The footbridge wasn't where the major's map had shown it. Scouts were sent upstream and downstream to find it. They returned. No bridge. Another whispered conference. It's about time for the German trucks to be showing up. We'll just wade across here and get the job done. The squad leader walks gingerly into the water. There follows a muffled exclamation and a flurry of splashing. From where I was sprawled all I knew was that the sergeant had gone under. He emerged briefly, weighed down by steel helmet, rifle, ammunition, hand grenades, etc., and is swept away. Fifty feet or so down the bank we helped him crawl out. Clearly the major's intelligence about the depth of the Meurthe is no more accurate than his location of the footbridge.

I presumed we would now call this affair off, sneak back to the farm, and let the war wait another day. No such luck. The lieutenant was as green as we were and has not yet understood the invincible ignorance of military intelligence. The major had assured us the river was shallow so the lieutenant thinks we can find a ford. We move slowly downstream looking for such a place, managing only to get a couple more riflemen wet. But, alas, the splashing and yelling has not gone unnoticed—not by the Germans but by Company A, which is occupying high ground downriver from our farm. An Able Company mortar fires a flare. It ignites into a dazzling light above us and drifts down under its parachute. Then another flare, and another. We lie in the hay stubble as flat as the human form can make itself—trying to crawl into our helmets. Will Company A decide it has caught a German patrol in the open and mow us down? Or will the German machine gun positions across the river handle the job? Either way, it would be a short and inglorious war for us.

But nothing happens. The flares burn out. By now even the lieutenant has had enough of this outing. We hustle through the blessed darkness back to cover.

Day two. Our squad was alerted about 2 A.M. We pick up our mortars, ammunition sacks, and containers of extra rounds. We cross the road away from the river and struggle through the darkness up the same wooded hillside we'd come down to reach our farm. We dig in. Our goal we are told is still to destroy German trucks that Army Intelligence now reports are parked under a railroad bridge across the river. Army Intelligence will tell us how to do that.

Dawn comes. The major who seems to be running this antitruck operation radios orders for us to chop down a few trees to clear a field of fire. We do this. Somewhere across the river a German notices this activity, gets on his radio, and calls a half dozen rounds of artillery fire down on us. We dive into our holes. It's scary, but no one is hurt. And now, we are no longer virgins. We have actually been shot at. As Winston Churchill said after his experience with combat in the Boer War: "Nothing is more exhilarating than to be shot at without effect."

Time to shoot back—our first volley of World War II. The voice on our radio gives us the range and direction. No problem with the direction, but the range is another matter. Apparently no one has told Army Intelligence that rifle companies are armed with little short-range 60 mm mortars used for killing up close and personal. We don't have the big, long-range 81 mm jobs weapons companies use. Bob Lewis, only eighteen but wise for his years, figures we can deal with this.

A mortar is a steel tube set on a base plate. The bomb it fires has a cone-shaped detonator fuse on one end and four tail fins on the other. Between tail fins a little square of TNT is attached. When the round is dropped into the tube, a shotgun shell in the butt end of the projectile strikes a firing pin in the base of the tube. That fires the shell, which fires TNT, which blasts the bomb out of the tube. Maximum range is about a thousand yards with all TNT in place and the tube lowered to forty-five degrees elevation. For shorter ranges, one removes TNT squares—all of them if the target is dangerously close—and cranks up the elevation angle.

For what Army Intelligence wanted us to hit, all four TNT squares and forty-five degrees wouldn't come close to reaching it. We couldn't see what we were shooting at, or where our shells were landing, but whoever was observing the shots was reporting our rounds short.

Lewis's idea was to stick a couple more of the TNT squares between the fins. So Lewis strips the TNT from spare rounds and adds their squares to the rounds he'd be firing. I sit by my mortar and watch, thinking if it works and doesn't blow up Lewis's mortar, I might try it myself. Lewis finishes his task. He leans back, grinning, an unlit cigarette dangling from his lips. He says: "Anyone got a light?"

Someone flips him a lit cigarette.

WOOOSH!!

Lewis is engulfed in a dense cloud of white smoke. The cigarette apparently hit one of the TNT squares, which ignited the fifty-three other TNT squares in the neat nine-round pyramid Lewis had arranged between his legs. End of experiment, end of Lewis's eyelashes, eyebrows, and forelock.

That's my the only vivid memory of the episode. We fired off a few futile short rounds. Someone opened his first aid kit and smeared ointment on Lewis's face. Someone explained mortar range to the major on the radio and when darkness came we carried our stuff back down the hill again.

For those who try to understand war and Army Intelligence, I should add that when our battalion crossed the Meurthe and helped capture burning St. Dié, we noticed that there was neither a highway nor a railroad across the river from our farmhouse. Our side of the river had both. Was the major reading his map upside down? Was he having us attack ourselves? Apparently so, because the only railroad and highway ran down our side of the Meurthe. That seemed incredible at the time. A bit later it would seem perfectly normal.

To illustrate this, I'll skip forward a few weary days to a hay barn in which our mortar and machine gun sections were enjoying a cozy night's sleep in the hay. In comes our platoon leader. "Saddle up," he says. "Let's go." I had violated orders by taking off my boots and still remember frantically sorting through the hay pile for the left one, which had gone missing. We straggle out into the predawn rain and head north up the road. The lieutenant tells us to load our weapons on the Jeep, a first for us, and a promising sign. One doesn't put his machine guns and his mortars on a Jeep trailer if he is preparing to fight. Sure enough, word drifts down the column that we're going into battalion reserve. Jubilation. We are going to hunker down in a little French town called Lusse long enough to get some hot food, dry out, and rest. Private First Class Tom Morick, another mortar man with a better sense of geography than most of us, mentioned that it seemed odd that we're walking north toward trouble instead of south toward the rear. But then we were still relatively innocent. Why worry?

Captain Neeley, however, has had closer contact with Army Intelligence and is less sanguine. He has us halt beside a railroad track and sends a patrol of riflemen ahead to take a look at things in Lusse, which we can see just ahead. Why? Army Intelligence said Company A had captured the place yesterday. We wait, helmets adjusted so the water dripping from them goes somewhere besides down the back of the neck. Then through the drizzle comes the unpleasant sound of ripping cloth, which we now have been around long enough to recognize as the song sung by German MG38 machine guns. The lieutenant doesn't have to tell us to extract our weapons from the Jeep trailer. Army Intelligence has neglected to notify the Germans that they no longer hold this little French village. They have our patrol, or what's left of it, pinned down on a slope below their machine gun positions.

I am tempted here to describe what happens to a rifle company in such circumstances as if I saw it all. All I saw was my friends in the Fourth Platoon grabbing machine guns, ammunition cans, mortars, ammo sacks, and so forth, out of the trailer and scrambling along the railroad and up the road, bent low, looking for positions. The rifle platoons were already doing their thing ahead of us.

It was just about now that Company A, one day late, arrived to capture Lusse. The riflemen on the Able Company point squad heard the gunfire, saw us running around in the drizzle, presumed we were Germans, and started shooting at us. I didn't see it myself, being involved with setting up my mortar and locating the spot where the German machine gun fire was originating, but legend has it that Neeley put a stop to this intramural war by running down the railroad tracks, shooting his pistol, jumping, waving, and screaming imprecations.

Our little battle for Lusse will never rate mention in the military histories but it had a permanent effect on us. Neeley became a sort of hero to all of us, and we never again trusted A Company. (The lyrics of our marching song became:

> Company A is always late, parlez-vous,
> Company A is always late, parlez-vous,
> Company A is always late,
> they stay in bed and masturbate.
> Hinky-dinky, parlez-vous.)

As for me, it was here that I began thinking of myself as a bona fide and skillful mortar gunner. As I remember this affair, my first round exploded directly on line, and just a little behind the machine gun position on the slope above the railroad. A twitch up of the elevation, and the next three rounds fell right into it. We captured Lusse, losing five of our men and bagging twenty-seven Germans, including fifteen prisoners. (Not very glorious ones, since they were goof-ups left locked in the town jail when their unit withdrew.)

Lewis claimed his mortar bagged the machine gun but neither of us wanted to walk up the hill and inspect our handiwork. Unlike riflemen we could usually keep our war impersonal—thinking of knocking out machine guns and not of killing the fellow teenagers behind them.

A few years ago a social historian released research findings suggesting that soldiers from the early nineteenth century through World War II didn't seem to enjoy killing the enemy. I recall neither the book title nor the author's name, but he provided a wealth of interesting statistics. For example, a high percentage of those engaged in the battle at Waterloo hadn't fired their weapon and most of the muskets collected from the battlefield at Gettysburg were still loaded. Research following World War I showed the same pattern. The U.S. military had become aware of this shortcoming among combat soldiers and we were taught at Fort Benning the value of shooting if only to cause the bad guys to keep their heads down. The lesson seemed well learned when we were shooting at targets. Now, however, things have changed. I had seen that demonstrated dramatically on our fifth day in combat. That day saw the first of us killed.

By the clock the episode that converted me from boy to soldier lasted about forty hours or so, but I think of it as a seamless unit because it lacked the usual time out to eat, sleep, and get dry. It began a little after midnight. We formed on the road outside our farm with our full load of gear, were told to stay well spaced and keep it quiet. Going where? We'd learn eventually that the First Battalion was making a flanking attack on German units holding St. Dié and the hills around it, and Charley Company was the point. But to ask one's platoon sergeant whence we were marching was not GI. The officers probably hadn't told him. So off we went in the dark, both literally and figuratively.

The cold rain fell. The road was muddy. We walked at the standard pace—three miles in fifty minutes, a ten-minute rest, another three miles, another rest, on through the night. About two hours before dawn we stopped at the edge of a forest. Word came down the line that the company kitchen Jeep would show up with hot food. We wait. No Jeep. No food. Unfed, we descend from the high ridge we'd been climbing much of the night, slipping and sliding down the slope. We reach the level ground again—hearing artillery now. Some is ours outgoing, some incoming German, near enough to cause uneasiness, not near enough to cause fear. We hear the river, the Meurthe again we presume, noisy now with runoff and flooded far out of its bank. We march into the water—four or five inches deep—and stand in it. After perhaps an hour the word comes down the line. The German artillery had knocked out the pontoon bridge we were scheduled to cross. We wait as the water rises toward our boot tops while the Engineers repair it. Relentless rain drains off our helmets, off our ponchos, down the backs of our hands, our necks, our backbones. We are shod in snowpacks—boots with rubber bottoms and leather tops. Each boot comes with two felt insoles, one worn, one carried inside your underwear to be dried by your body heat and ready for tomorrow. But even these wonderful boots couldn't cope with standing in deep water. Nor can our ponchos deal with the wind-driven rain. Dawn comes, still we stand. But not all of us. It's axiomatic in the infantry that anything can be endured if you keep your butt warm and dry. Many of us haven't managed that. Some of us admit it and rest our cramping legs by sitting in the muddy water.

Full daylight comes and still we wait. Finally the blessed shout of "Move out." We splash through the water, run across the bobbing pontoon's tracks, trudge up a long muddy slope into a cluster of small stone houses. Our platoon leader points to one, tells us to get inside and try to get dry. He tells us food is coming but not to take out our bedrolls because we'll be moving right out again. We sprawl, dream of rest, warmth, dryness, but most of all we dream of hot food or at least C-rations, which are one step up from the usual K-rations. Instead, a Jeep driver from headquarters dumps a pile of D-bars on the floor.

The D-bar lurked at the absolute bottom of the military's culinary scale—the nourishment of last resort. It was a cereal mixed with a protein concoction (possibly soybeans) and chocolate. This was compressed into a block the size and consistency of a flattened brick and wrapped in multiple layers of waxed paper. Given time, water, and a source of heat, one could soften this enough to bite it by boiling it in your canteen cup. Otherwise, you had to hammer it into fragments and let it dissolve in your mouth. The D-bars we received seemed to have been made in 1918 and stored since the end of World War I. About a third of them had been partially digested by mold, which made them much easier to eat with no noticeable effect on the flavor.

The good news was that we finally had something to eat. The bad news was that the sack contained exactly enough to provide two bars for each of us. That told us we'd go two days without real food—and for me it produced one of those oddities that proved I could be wrong even when I was right.

Our mortar section had just received two replacements, filling gaps in the mortar section caused by injury and illnesses. They knew each other, apparently having become acquainted in the replacement depot, but they were still total strangers in the unit. After one and all had managed to consume their D-bar for the day, these two fellows unwrapped their second one. Having had previous D-bar experience (and wanting to impress these recruits with my saltiness), I warned them that one would be all the stomach could tolerate for a good many hours and that if they ate the second one now, they'd be starving tomorrow. Good advice, but I noticed later they were both finishing off tomorrow's ration. So much for unsolicited advice.

An hour later we are moving down a narrow trail on a grassy slope. Our dream of rest, warmth, etc., remains unrealized but the rain has finally stopped and the clouds are lifting. A German artillery forward observer sees us now and decides we are worth a few rounds. They were low-velocity howitzer shells, not the dreadful 88s, which arrive before you hear them coming. By the time these exploded on the slope just above us everybody has his face in the grass except the two replacements carrying sacks of mortar ammunition just behind me. Shrapnel got them both. Did they survive? They looked dead but I don't know. I never learned their names and the company's Killed in Action roster lists many such replacements—strangers among the men they died with. Whether they lived or not, clearly their idea of when to eat their D-bars in combat was sounder than my own. Tomorrow might never come.

We resume our walk. Fog lifts from the mountaintops. The sun is out now, warm enough on our backs to make our soggy field jackets steam, my own D-bar digesting happily in my stomach. Those endless hours of cold and hunger are behind me. About noon we take a break in a hillside woods. One of the scouts finds two beehives and tries to extract honeycombs with all hands furiously blowing cigarette smoke into the swarm. The bees win this skirmish. The riflemen return to the march with nothing but multiple stings to show for their effort and become the subject of humor. In rifle companies, even ones as green as we were that day, instant forgetfulness was already the policy. Walk away from the dead.

Implausible as it seems to me now, I remember the afternoon that follows as my happiest hours of the war. I am dry now, warmed by the sun, walking along a grass slope through beautiful landscape. The Alsatian version of meadowlarks are out, singing their farewell to summer. A disorderly little gaggle of crows fly out of the woods, having characteristic crow disputes exactly as they did over our alfalfa field in Oklahoma. Having been missed by shrapnel a couple of hours earlier has confirmed in me the knowledge that I am invincible.

Even better, I am making history. It is clear now that Charley Company is the point of this advance to wherever we are going and I am with the point rifle platoon. Thus every step I take affects the military map of Europe—moving back the margin of Nazi conquest a tiny fraction of a millimeter. The grass ahead of me is occupied territory. The grass I have just trod upon is free. Adventure at last.

Joan Didion told us in one of her essays that memory is often an effort to get acquainted with the stranger that was you a long time ago. That is approximately what I am doing right now, as I try to re-create that day in my remarkably vivid memory of it, and my reaction to the brutal fate of the two boys behind me, and to what happened next.

A STRANGE ENCOUNTER WITH THE ENEMY was the headline it received in *Reader's Digest* when I wrote about it forty years later—and strange it was.

"It was early afternoon," I wrote then, "when our platoon neared the ridge where we were to await the two trailing platoons. Our two scouts moved cautiously through the granite outcrops, stopping to see what lay ahead, then motioning us forward. Suddenly one signaled 'take cover.' "

That remains now just the way I remembered it then. We scattered among the boulders. Our platoon leader hurried up to join the scout. I hear the sound of a harmonica drifting up through the still autumn air. I look down the steep slope into a narrow, grassy valley and see beside a small stream a stone hut. Smoke from its chimney was forming a blue haze across the meadow in front of it and drifting into the dark fir forest beside it. The lieutenant was scanning this with his binoculars and the scout was pointing at something below shielded from my line of vision by the trees.

"Then two men came into sight below us, strolling along a cow path toward the cabin. One was bareheaded, his blond hair looking almost white in the sunlight. The other wore the cap of a German enlisted man. Both were draped in the long gray overcoats of the German infantry. The blond was tapping what must have been a harmonica against the heel of his hand, talking and gesturing . . . He played his harmonica again—a tune I now recognized as 'Lili Marlene.' The soldier with the cap walked with his hands clasped behind his back. He looked young and small, perhaps a teenager like ourselves."

As the long paragraph above suggests, the point platoon of Charley Company did not spring into the instant action this situation required. Twenty or so young men carrying M1 rifles and two Browning automatic rifles stood looking down on these representatives of the enemy for a long, long moment. The lieutenant gives the hand signal to fire. We fire.

This was not a job for my mortar. I popped away with my pistol—comfortable in the knowledge that the two were out of the range of this ridiculous weapon even if I aimed at them. For the riflemen it was another matter. Each had qualified as marksman to win his infantry badge. Most of them qualified expert. Any one of them could have killed both of the young men below us with one shot each. Fate has made each of them a one-man jury in the death sentence case. They blaze away. But they were still young then, not yet soldiers.

The Germans run frantically up the path to the cabin. The boy with the cap falls, scrambles to his feet, and runs again. A bullet clips a limb from a birch. Bullets scatter the yellow leaves beside the path. Splintered shingles fly from the cabin's roof. The enemy disappears through the cabin door. The shooting stops. In the sudden silence I hear the BAR man chuckling. Moments later, we see the two dash from the back of the cabin, disappearing among the firs through another flurry of rifle fire.

Was the blond boy carrying a machine gun from the house? Some of the riflemen said he was. I couldn't see but judging from German tactics we would repeatedly encounter later I guess he was. The two were probably "harvesters" left on an outpost with a MG42 machine gun, a can of ammunition, and orders to kill as many men in the attacking unit as feasible, and then escape to fight again.

Another rifle platoon soon replaced us on the point at that ridge and ran into a firefight in the woods across the valley. I have only one clear memory of that, in which I am sprawled on my stomach behind a fallen tree with rifle bullets snapping overhead and a wounded German soldier behind me repeating alternate cries of

"Wasser, Wasser," and *"Mutti, Mutti,"* which we guessed meant "Mama."

When the shooting stopped we give him water despite instructions that this was not a good practice for men shot in the stomach. But this man had also taken bullets through the lungs and elsewhere. His gray tunic was soaked red and he was far, far beyond being hurt by a sip from a canteen.

In that little battle skirmish the first man I had personally known became a Killed in Action statistic and the war also ended for five other members of Charley Company. Sergeant Adolph Lucchesi was killed trying to get close enough to a machine gun position in the woods to throw a hand grenade. Lucchesi worked in a little bar in Chicago, an amiable, kind, and fun-loving man. I wondered then, and wonder now, if the machine gunner who killed him was the blond boy who played the harmonica. After that skirmish we were no longer quite so young.

That forty-hour longest day of mine had a few more hours to run. Before it was over it produced a sort of "rite of passage" for me in which I had to decide—without really understanding how crucial that decision was—what sort of fellow I was going to be.

We had cleared the wooded ridge where Lucchesi died. On the slope above St. Dié we again waited in vain for rations to arrive. We found a partially harvested field of sugar beets, dug some, and found they're edible if you're hungry enough. It is twilight now. We stumble down the slope into the edge of the smoky city and settle into a warehouse, wet, hungry, cold, and exhausted. Rest at last, I think, and untie my bedroll—which has reverted from soggy to merely damp. "Saddle up," the platoon leader shouts, and we're off again—up another hill and down it and away to lend a hand to Able Company in a fight it was having.

The route brought us to a steep embankment above a narrow road—a matter of slipping and sliding. It was raining again. I was hungry, filthy, miserable, aware that war was not what I'd expected, at the absolute end of my endurance. The ankle I had torn up as a kid in a jump out of our barn loft to demonstrate how paratroopers did it was still weak. I remember standing at the top of that slope, looking down at the road below, aware of the weight I was carrying and knowing that all I had to do to escape this nightmare, to get food, rest, a warm bed, etc., was to jump and land with that questionable ankle turned in. It would break and I'd be out of there.

This business of soldiers making their separate peace wasn't unheard of. Morick told me one of our comrades had handed him his rifle and asked Morick to shoot him in the hand ("I told him to do it himself"). Our company had at least two cases of men court-martialed for self-inflicted wounds, but a broken ankle wouldn't provoke punishment. Why didn't I do it? It had nothing to do with patriotism, or how badly it would hurt. I think it was because I didn't want to miss whatever lay ahead, or I didn't want to go through life knowing I was a sissy.

The author, sitting at left in the wagon, with big brother Barney holding handle and big sister Margaret Mary hiding eyes. Other participants are cousins Joe, Elizabeth, Emma, and Monica Grove at Uncle Arthur's farm.

(*Above*) Family picnic at Sacred Heart, with author (crying because he didn't get to sit on the tricycle) showing talent at getting the front-and-center spot when pictures are taken.

The author displaying skill at holding fish closer to camera to augment size. *Left to right:* cousin Joe Grove, the author, Barney, and cousins Monica and Johnnie Grove.

What was left, in 1990, of the Sacred Heart store
Gus Hillerman operated during the Great Depression.

The entire senior class of Konawa High School, with the
author seventh from left in the front row.

Konawa High owned
twelve baseball uniforms,
which went to nine starters,
two relief pitchers, and a
utility infielder. The author
(*top row, sixth from left*) was
substitute right fielder,
where the damage done by
his inability to judge fly
balls was minimized. World
War II took a heavy toll on
the team.

Part of Fourth Platoon, C Company, 410th Infantry, looking uncharacteristically tidy, in a French village during its conquest of the Third Reich. The author (grenade in lapel) is on the jeep hood at the center.

A rainy February 9, 1945. Hillerman receiving Silver Star from Gen. Anthony McAuliffe. The general had just become famous for his one-word ("Nuts!") response to German demands that he surrender his forces in Bastogne during the Battle of the Bulge. Unknown to the general, the soldier he was decorating was Absent Without Leave, having slipped away from the army hospital at Saverne the previous day to rejoin his platoon.

HE STOOD *fearlessly*

Pfc. Anthony G. Hillerman

By BEATRICE STAHL

ONE brave man honored another on the day Pfc. Anthony G. Hillerman received his Silver Star. For Hillerman, a fighting man of Oklahoma, was decorated by the hero of Bastogne, who punctuated history with a word.

On the morning of February 12, at an unnamed spot within the Reich, Maj. Gen. Anthony C. McAuliffe, who answered the Nazi demand for surrender with, "Nuts!", pinned a Silver Star on the borrowed blouse of Private Hillerman who single-handedly beat off a vicious counterattack on his company's right flank, in another and later engagement.

Tony Hillerman is 19. He was born in Pottawatomie county and has always called Sacred Heart his home. He had finished Konawa highschool and entered A&M college when his older brother went into service, and Tony quit school to manage the family's 140 acre farm.

Then came Tony's eighteenth birthday and he decided the army needed him, too. So he landed in France with a glider battalion ground crew on D-Day and later transferred to the infantry. Now both brothers serve in Europe.

It was to his mother, Mrs. Lucy Hillerman and his sister, Margaret Mary, of 709 NW 9, that he wrote on the evening of that big day, Feb. 12.

"This morning I shaved, put on the cleanest clothes I could borrow and they took me back to the rear. There they had a lot of troops in review, a band playing, and a platform with lots of brass on it.

"I went up on the platform and the general, our division commander, (103rd. Inf. Div.) pinned a Silver Star on me, shook my hand, and I went back to the company. . . . It was for something that happened back in January. I'm getting a lot of kidding now, but I'm kinda proud. . . . Don't let the citation worry you. I was just in the right place at the right time."

THE order for the Silver Star, read by General McAuliffe that morning, cited this private first class for "magnificent courage" and told a story of daring action during the early hours of 19 January, near an undisclosed town in France.

In the dimness of that dawn, Hillerman, a mortar gunner, was with his company in the midst of battle when a severe enemy counterattack struck on the company's right flank. The concentration of German small arms and mortar fire was so terrific that Hillerman's mortar was knocked out of action at the very beginning of the fight.

His was an important position. Quickly he realized the imminent danger that confronted the whole company, should the enemy break through that spot. So he forgot his own danger, and stayed at his post—armed only with a pistol and hand grenades.

The Nazis came pouring toward him, supported by all that they had. He couldn't tell how many. But it didn't matter now. Somehow he knew they must be stopped. And it was then that Hillerman no longer crouched beside his broken gun. He stood up.

The citation picks up the story: "He stood fearlessly in the face of enemy fire, simultaneously shooting his pistol and throwing hand grenades into the midst of the onrushing foe.

"His utter disregard for his life . . . his gallantry and accuracy of fire, resulted in four enemy dead and the complete disorganization of the hostile attack. Private Hillerman's magnificent courage was in accordance with the highest traditions."

SOME of Tony Hillerman's letters give a graphic description of how the boys from home get along over there in what he calls a "strange kind of war." On December 18, he wrote:

"Tonight I'm sitting in an expensive apartment in an overstuffed chair and I've got a deep featherbed waiting in the next room. Of course, I'm plenty dirty. I haven't had my pants or shirt off in over a month. But we're all the same, so it doesn't matter. Tomorrow night I may be sleeping in a foxhole, but tonight I've got a silk bedspread."

December 23: "It looks like we're going to have a white Christmas after all, and it's a lot like living in a Christmas card. Narrow cobblestone streets, peaked roofs with snow on them. Chimney pots, etc. Everything you could expect to find on a good Hallmark edition.

"We're even living in a manger at present. It's not bad, though, stove, plenty of straw. We've been singing a lot of Christmas carols and so forth. It's not like being home for Christmas, but we'll have that next year—all of us.

"In the last town the man of the house came into the kitchen where we were gathered around the stove and sang carols with us. In German, of course. He had a nice looking daughter, too. I liked it there but we had to move on. We always do. So we shook hands with old "pop," kissed Josephine goodbye, put on our packs, and moved on down the road.

"This is a strange life. Today we have a manger, tomorrow perhaps a hotel suite, perhaps a foxhole."

IN March he wrote from a hospital bed in France, where he recovers from shrapnel wounds, sustained on a volunteer patrol.

"I'm plenty proud of my outfit. They're the bravest bunch of men in the world.

"I hope you haven't worried about me. I hope you don't feel sorry for me, either. I don't. I've gotten more out of this war than my scars. I found out just how good a man I am. I learned a lot, and I gained a good deal of self-confidence and self respect.

"I didn't have to go on that patrol, and I didn't go because I wanted to either. No one does. I can't find words for why we do go on. It's something we learn from watching others we love, do things for us.

"Every time I was in danger, I thought of you praying for me, and you can't realize how much it helped. I wish I could let you know how much I love you all. Tony."

This article gave Hillerman a wonderful display of the magical, mystical powers of the journalist (and the Army citation writer) to convert grubby reality into high drama and it led him right to the University of Oklahoma Department of Journalism. However, his own account of featherbed and silk bedspread (see paragraph 16 and following) remind him that he himself was already adept at gilding lilies.

Form B
To: 7th Army PRO
From: 103d Div. Press Section, G-2   for immediate release

WITH THE 103d DIVISION OF THE SEVENTH ARMY IN GERMANY--

__Pfc__   __Anthony G. Hillerman__ of 709' N.W. 9th,Oklahoma City,Okla
(grade)   (name)   (street address, city, state)

has recently ~~been promoted from~~   ~~to his present grade~~   .
              been awarded the SILVER STAR for _____.

He is the __son__ of __Lucy M. Hillerman__   , who lives at
         (relationship)   (full name)

   __same address__   , and has been in the Army
(street address, city, state)

since __2 Aug,1943__ . He sailed for overseas duty __6 Oct,1944__
         (date of entry)   (date)

and is currently serving with __410th Inf Regt__ of the 103d Infantry
                                    (unit)
Division.

               Condensation of citation (if an award)
For gallantry in action.During the early morning hours of 19 Jan,1945,in
the vicinity of *** France,Hillerman,mortar gunner,was with his company i
the attack when a severe enemy counterattack was launched on the company'
right flank.The concentration of enemy small arms & mortar fire was so
severe,Hillerman's mortar was knocked out in the initial phase of attack.
Realizing the danger to his company if the enemy broke through his positi
he,with utter disregard for his life,gallantly remained at his post,armed
only with a pistol & hand grenades.He fearlessly stood up in the face of
enemy fire,simultaneously shooting his pistol & throwing grenades into th
midst of the onrushing foe.His gallantry & accuracy of fire resulted in
four enemy dead and the complete disorganization of the enemy attack.

            Other decorations held by the soldier are:
Expert Infantry Badge
Combat Infantry Badge

-30-

It is interesting to note that the author's mortar was not in fact disabled; Smith and he dashed off and left it to the oncoming foe (minus the sights). Also left behind were their shovels, his helmet, his field jacket containing a money order ready to be mailed off to Mama, and some emergency food he'd been saving in the likely event rations didn't arrive. And the multiple grenades the author is credited with fearlessly hurling at the enemy were actually one grenade borrowed from Pfc. A. J. Shakeshaft. Military public relations are a wonder.

Tony in role of caddy in photojournalism class at the University of Oklahoma after the war. The golfer is Dick Wharton, who accompanied the author to Mexico. The guy improving his lay is Bill Shelton, later a noted journalist.

August 16, 1948: The author marries Marie Unzer, the greatest coup of his life.

Summer 1951: On the night shift in the United Press bureau in Oklahoma City.

Winter 1954: The author in uncharacteristically double-breasted attire, photographed by the governor's press secretary while covering politics for the *New Mexican*.

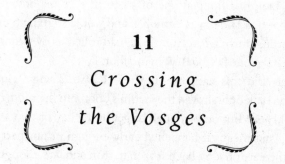

11
Crossing
the Vosges

Of what lay ahead in the dying days of that autumn I have only an episodic memory. Some weeks are almost totally blank while some days come flashing back vividly with full-color details, complete with sounds, smells, and even that perpetual sense of soggy clothing and cold feet. Mostly I recall endless walking, endless cold rain, and occasional dives into roadside ditches when we received harassing fire from German artillery and the brief but exciting flurry of shooting when we ran into roadblocks.

Among my clear memories is trudging up a narrow and very muddy dirt road, the night made darker by the rain and the dense fir forest. A Sherman tank was clanking up the road, doing maybe four miles an hour—lights off of course. A BAR man was two men ahead of me, too far for me to see exactly how the accident happened. But suddenly he produced an ear-shattering scream and the rifleman behind him began pounding on the side of the tank with his rifle butt and yelling for it to stop which—if you understand how tank treads operate—was the worst thing it could have done. The screamer's boot had slipped into the path of the tank and the tank had flopped one of its tread sections down on the boot. That tread now was immobile and would so remain until the tank, putting down tread after tread, had rolled its own length and picked up the one on the BAR man's foot.

Where did this happen, or when? I have a single clue. The thirty-ton tank only shoved the victim's boot into the mud, causing painful bruises but only enough to get him a day or two at an aid station. That means it happened early enough in our part of the war so the earth hadn't been frozen to iron and late enough so we knew the BAR man would have been luckier if he'd had some foot bones broken. That would have given him at least a long, warm, well-fed hospital rest—perhaps even a trip home. (Vietnam war policy sent one home after twelve months in combat and World War II Army Air Force flight crews earned a transfer home after flying twenty-five [sometimes thirty-five] combat missions. In the infantry in World War II, the only way to get home alive was to be wounded seriously enough to be no longer repairable for return to combat.)

In the later months of the war a point system was devised for time overseas and decorations earned (a purple heart was worth five points and so were the "gallantry" decorations). I never heard of anyone in a rifle company staying healthy long enough to earn the eighty-five points required. On average an infantryman in a line company lasted about five months before he was killed or wounded badly enough to be shifted into a safer environment—such as a rear echelon unit.

Another of those indelibly vivid memories came on a sunny morning—worth remembering if only for the lack of rain. We were in the east slope foothills of the Vosges Mountains, a grassy open slope, a narrow dirt road with a rock wall on one side. We were sprawled beside it, waiting, listening to the sporadic sound of small arms fire up ahead and salty enough now to know that B Company was on the battalion point that day and happy to let B Company deal with it. We were content to simply rest.

Then we hear the cloth-ripping sound of a German machine gun very near. The sound seems to come from a stone house—the top of which we could see down the slope a couple of hundred yards from our road. We're covered by both roadside embankment and the wall. No sweat. Somebody who gets paid to decide what to do about such things will either tell us what to do, or won't. We wait. Time passes. More firing from up ahead. Another burst from our nearby machine gun. A man from one of the rifle platoons trudges up the road past us, carrying a BAR. He turns off the road through a gateway in the wall, down a path which leads toward the house, and disappears. We listen. We hear the machine gun again and the slower pounding of the BAR. Then silence. The word comes to saddle up, fall in, and move out. As we do we see the BAR man trudging back up the trail toward the road, his weapon over his shoulder. It was an odd incident, weird in fact, but so much else was going on that I didn't think much about it at the time. In fifty-plus years of quieter times I've wondered what happened at the house and what provoked this man to take that lonely little semi-suicidal walk in the sun. Had he reached the same slough of despondency which had once caused me to considered escaping the misery by breaking my ankle? Perhaps he'd decided he'd rather suffer a nine mm bullet or two now than suffer through more wet, cold, weary days waiting for something as bad or worse to provide relief. But the clouds had parted and the morning was bright. On such days hope overcomes reality. Perhaps he was simply a hero.

Later that sunny afternoon we came to the point where we could finally see out of the mountains and into the great openness of the Rhine Valley. But before we could get there we had to get past the charming little road-junction town of Itterswiller, now one of the loveliest gems of the French Department of Tourism's wine country route.

The last time I saw it I was with Marie. It was a late summer day in the 1980s. Itterswiller's window boxes were glorious with geraniums and its streets were jammed with the cars of tourists. The first time I saw it was on a cold November morning from the wooded ridge to the west. From there you could see only its vineyards, the row of stone buildings that line the entry road, and no sign of life. It looked like trouble, and the trouble had already started.

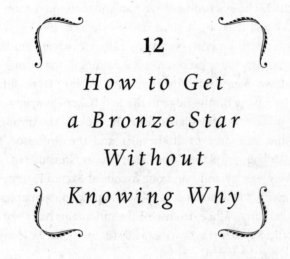

12

How to Get a Bronze Star Without Knowing Why

Having read about what U.S. Army historians call the Battle for the High Vosges, I now have at least a vague idea of what we'd been doing that rainy autumn. Itterswiller and the portion of the High Vosges we had been pushing through was held by the 716th Panzer Grenadier Division, an armored infantry unit provided with tanks, self-propelled artillery, and so forth. A grunt in the infantry is the absolute authority on the conduct of the war in a radius of about twenty yards in every direction from his foxhole, and absolutely ignorant of everything outside his line of vision. Standing on that ridge looking at Itterswiller through borrowed binoculars, I had no idea that our battalion was the point of the Seventh Army plan to drive through Saales Pass into the Rhineland, thereby cutting off four German divisions.

The thinking behind this strategy was that since this section of mountains had no roads to support tanks, artillery, and the trucks needed to haul such things as ammunition or food for soldiers the enemy would not expect such a maneuver. Thus the mountains would be, as the military historians phrase it, "lightly defended."

Which was how it worked. We had encountered mostly hasty roadblocks and delaying actions by units which, like us, had no armor or artillery support. Not many casualties except among the rifle squads, which got picked to be the point at the wrong time. And here we were, the First Battalion of the 410th Infantry, Charley Company on the ridge to the left, Baker Company across the narrow valley on the ridge to the right, looking out through the trees at the vineyards of Itterswiller and the Promised Land. Success! We had "enveloped" the 716th Panzer Grenadiers.

The way Barney and I and our friends at Sacred Heart played our war game, the 716th was supposed to pick up its marbles now and quit. It didn't. While defense of the mountains had been light, defense of Itterswiller was heavy. Luckily for us in Charley Company, Baker had got there first.

The table of organization of a German Panzer Grenadier Division shows it having two battalions of 105 mm howitzers, one battalion of 150 mm howitzers, plus an "antitank" battalion, which meant those awful high-velocity 88s. From where we sat on what we came to call Charley Hill most of these guns seemed to be established somewhere behind Itterswiller and most of them were blazing away at the hill that Baker Company was holding.

Judging from the small arms fire we'd been hearing across the little draw, Baker had run into much more serious opposition than we had on our side of the declivity. Their hill was wreathed in the smoke of exploding shells while our patch of woods was receiving only a now-and-then round—just enough to add vigor to our fox-hole digging—and we are experienced enough by now to dig them in the open, safer from the lethal "tree bursts." We hunker down and wait—knowing absolutely nothing about where we are, what we're doing there, or what happens next. Something bad had happened to Captain Neeley, the lieutenant leading our platoon. He had been wounded earlier and not replaced, and a sergeant was running things in our part of the war. We dig and wait and wonder what the hell is going on.

That wonder is soon intensified by the sound of gunfire from the slopes behind us. Who is shooting at whom? Rumors fly. My old friend Bob Huckins walks up to my hole, cool as always. Bob is part of headquarters company, Captain Neeley's runner, and—in Army parlance—his dog robber. Huckins has been dispatched to our position with instructions from our platoon sergeant to pick up a volunteer and go back to company headquarters and find out what is happening. Specifically the sergeant wants to know why we are hearing that gunfire behind us as well as from up front. Huckins suggests I go along with him. Why not? The last shell had exploded in the trees about forty yards to the right—getting a little closer. Taking a walk rearward with Bob seems a good idea.

Huckins believes that company headquarters was in a large stone farmhouse and barn back in the narrow valley between and behind Baker and Charley hills—and Huckins knew an easy route. We walk down the ridge toward the rear, where a path angled down the slope to the house. It's a beautiful late afternoon, the sun slanting through the trees, the great granite boulders lining the ridge casting long shadows. A faint breeze brings us the noise of the shellfire hammering Baker Company and the occasional crash of a howitzer round exploding on Charley Company's position. But if you are young and healthy it takes little effort to convert that noise into nothing more troublesome than, for example, a bunch of trains coupling in a railroad yard. Thus, you make the war go away.

Alas, it doesn't stay away.

Huckins stops. Points. Two Germans are sitting on the ground in the cluster of boulders perhaps forty yards ahead, their backs against the stone. One has spread out a cloth on a rock and seems to be cutting a slice from a long, fat sausage. A backpack radio is on the ground beside them—its antennae extended. Huck and I edge discreetly out of sight. Back in Fort Benning, Huck had shot an almost perfect score on the rifle range. He is carrying an M1. I am carrying a .45 caliber pistol, good to make fighter pilots and field grade officers feel like warriors but useless in combat beyond rock-throwing distance. We hold a whispered conference. Shoot them or take them prisoner? Either way we get their sausage. Huckins's time among the officers at headquarters had made him conscious of the importance of taking prisoners—especially when we have no idea what's going on. And neither one of us liked the idea of killing these picnickers. We will slip around behind them and make the capture. We begin this stealthy maneuver, rifle ready and pistol cocked. We reach the chosen position. I look out from around the boulder. The radio is there but the men and the sausage are gone. Just then a bullet whacks into the boulder, spraying my face with bits of rock. Germans are coming up the path from the farmhouse. How many? No time to count since they are shooting at us.

Churchill's remark about the exhilaration of being shot at and missed proves true. We run. One of the two radiomen reappears now and shoots at us with his pistol but sprinters racing through trees and boulders are hard to hit. By the time we reach the Charley Company perimeter our friends have surmised that maybe they are surrounded. Their rifles and machine guns now swivel to the rear. In other words, at us. But they recognize our shouts, welcome us home, and await the arrival of the trouble we surely have drawn down upon us all.

Nothing happens. With twilight the German artillery calls it a day. Rumors spread—one being the obvious truth that while we are enveloping the 716th Panzer Grenadiers, they are enveloping us. Riflemen in foxholes down the hill send up word that they have been hearing the rumble of tanks in the valley behind us—extremely unpleasant news. We hear that all of the officers in Baker Company have been killed or wounded but that what's left of Baker is holding its hill. We hear that Lieutenant Boyle, our artillery forward observer, has crossed the defile to Baker Hill and taken command of what's left of Baker. We hear that Captain Neeley had been wounded and had been taken to the aid station at company headquarters. We hear that a German panzer unit has captured company headquarters, including our captain. Twilight deepens. We guess that the Germans whom Huck and I had surprised at their lunch were forward observers for the German artillery, directing the fire on Baker Hill. That seems logical and explains why we haven't been shelled more heavily. What sane soldier would call down fire where long rounds would be hitting him? A rumor spread that we have been surrounded. It happens to be true but, being a born optimist, I scoff at it. The sergeant who has taken charge of our hill in the absence of any officers had long since had us arranged in a defensive perimeter. Then things get even weirder.

We hear a motorcycle puttering down the road from Itterswiller toward us. It stops, starts again, and rolls on below us toward our company headquarters farmhouse. Gene Halsey and George Rice, whose machine gun positions are on the slope above the road, send up word confirming that it was indeed a motorcyclist and they hadn't shot the fellow because they have no idea what's going on. That ignorance is short-lived. Again we hear the motorcycle, the sound of tanks, and shouting voices. The message is: "Don't shoot. We're prisoners." A column of our compadres is being marched down the road below us (shielding the tanks in the process) to spend the rest of the war as German POWs. Halsey, Rice, and the others dug in on the slope above the road can only watch—not that .30 caliber machine guns and rifles could dent tanks even if they'd been crazy enough to shoot.

We spend a nervous night. Dawn comes and the rumors thicken. Company headquarters had indeed been captured, or was it battalion headquarters? The German tanks and infantry we had bypassed in our rush through the mountains had surrounded

the farm buildings behind us yesterday afternoon. They had captured the battalion medicos who were patching the wounded in
the building, plus headquarters personnel, and the battalion's
Intelligence and Reconnaissance platoon. Captain Neeley, in the
process of having a leg wound patched, had jumped out of a window and escaped into the woods, sans shoes and trousers. The
tanks rolling past us from the rear during the night were escorting
prisoners, including the walking wounded, into Itterswiller.

Morning comes. Quiet. No artillery. Huckins shows up at my
foxhole again. The sergeant is sending a little recon patrol into
Itterswiller. The Germans have withdrawn, he tells us, pulled out
of the village during the night. Those in charge just want to make
sure. Come along, Huckins suggests.

Having written the above, I find myself stuck—staring at the
computer screen and reexamining my memory. What happened
next seems unlikely and irrational. How can I expect a reader to
believe it when I can hardly credit it myself—and I was there doing
it. I said okay, or something to that effect, and climbed out of the
hole and went—more or less as a volunteer although I hate to
admit it. More likely the platoon sergeant had added me to the list
of volunteers and sent Huck to give me the bad news.

We were a staff sergeant and five riflemen from the second platoon, plus Huckins and me. We walk down the hill, well spaced,
strung out behind the sergeant, staying in cover as much as we can
and aiming to hit the road below a vineyard—which allows us to
move into the first buildings of the village without being sitting
ducks until the last moment. Army Intelligence seems to have it
right for once. No one is shooting at us. But as we walk past the
vineyard, within twenty yards of the first building, we learn Army
Intelligence is operating as usual.

I remember hearing engines being started in the village ahead
and simultaneously a voice, just above and behind us, shouting
something in German. A soldier is standing among the vines,

pointing a rifle at us. A sentry, probably. He must have been sleeping or he would have seen us coming. Huckins shoots him and he
tumbles down among the vines. We sprint toward the village. Two
men rush out of the first building, looking surprised, see five or six
rifles aimed at them and stop. One raises his hands high. The other
jerks off his helmet and bounces it on the cobblestones, cursing.
Here the entry road makes a ninety-degree turn to become the
main street of Itterswiller. Pressed against a wall, I can hear more
motors coming alive but I can't see what's going on. The squad
leader sends the prisoners out across the open space toward our
company's position in the woods, tells them to go there and surrender again. Then he disappears around the corner. We spend a very
tense few moments, fingers on triggers. The two soldiers we've
bagged trot toward Charley Hill, hands atop heads and disappear
among the trees. Did they ever get all the way to Charley Company
to declare themselves prisoners of war? I never heard, never asked,
and never cared. But I doubt it. The sergeant reappears with the
happy news that the Germans (probably a rear guard at best) were
going, going, gone.

The encounter at Itterswiller was over. But it needs a couple of
footnotes—the first one to illustrate the baffling irrationality of the
military and the second to suggest that some levels of compassion
survive in our species even in the heat of combat.

About six months after the affair I learned that I had been
awarded a Bronze Star by the U.S. Army for "action on a daylight
recon patrol on 29 November 1944." Since I was only a tagalong I
presumed that everyone who went was awarded those five points
toward going home, with maybe something higher for the
sergeant. But I learned later that Huckins, the only one of us
except for the sergeant who actually did anything, got no medal, so
I presume the others didn't either. Why me? Who knows? Maybe
names are drawn from a colonel's hat.

That's the irrational example. Here's the compassion.

One of the eighty casualties Baker Company suffered that day was John Walters, who'd been a friend of mine in basic training, and had become a BAR man in B Company. I located Walters, now a retired oil man living in Durango, and he told me his story. Baker Company had run into a stiff close-quarters firefight with dug-in German infantry on that infamous hill. Walters found himself engaged in a sort of one-on-one affair in the woods, his BAR against an MG42. Walters suffered a face wound. He remembers sitting against the trunk of a tree, sort of collecting himself, then becoming aware again and discovering that the top of the tree had been blown off, that three hours have passed, and that he has a huge splinter sticking through his thigh muscle, the worst of a multitude of less important injuries. Walters hobbles toward the rear, meets Lieutenant Boyle, is put on a Jeep, and taken to the headquarters farm building. There the splinter is removed, various wounds are bandaged and Walters waits with other wounded in the basement for what happens next. He remembers hearing tracked vehicles arriving, hoping they are U.S. tanks, hearing some shooting and shouting and then a call down the stairs.

"This is Lieutenant Remington," the caller shouts. "If there's anyone down there, come on up."

"It sounded like perfect American English," Walters told me. "We thought he was an American officer."

So Walters and others able to climb stairs became prisoners and were herded through our lines to Itterswiller, thence over the Rhine, where Walters concluded his war by helping clean up bomb damage in Munich. It was standard practice to deal with questionable basements in such situations by tossing down a grenade first, and then asking questions. One stays alive by not taking chances. We did it, and I'm sure it was equally routine in the German infantry. Those in that basement owe their lives to the phony "Lieutenant Remington," who preferred to take a risk rather than kill a bunch of wounded men.

One finds humanitarians in every Army and brutes as well, but the brutes tend to shy away from danger and accumulate, like slime at the bottom of the bucket, in rear echelon units. I was sprawled beside a mountain road one afternoon awaiting word to move out when two men from the regimental headquarters came along with two prisoners they were taking to the rear. They stopped for a smoke and decided that guarding their charges was onerous. They pointed their rifles at the two—boys about my own age—and ordered them to run up the hill. The two ran and were shot in the back—the only prisoners I saw murdered. We reported the incident and were told the men from regimental headquarters were arrested and stood court-martial. I hope they were shot.

I have only vague memories of long walks and truck rides for several days after Itterswiller—moving south as part of a regimental combat team sent to help the French First Armored, which didn't seem to be doing much. My only recollection of this visit was seeing a truck loaded with ammunition blown up by a mine—producing a spectacular explosion and a gaping crater. The first week of December our First Battalion drew Regimental Reserve near some Maginot Line forts. The purpose of reserve is to give exhausted combat troops some rest. Instead we were put through a regime of close order drill—an exercise useful when troops were armed with flintlock muskets but obsolete (everywhere except West Point) since the Civil War. We also were strafed by a couple of our fighter bombers, which came in too high to hit anything. (To complete this account of our air war, the only casualty C Company suffered from air attacks was a rifleman hit in the back by an empty 20 mm shell casing, which came from a British Spitfire shooting at something far ahead of us.) On another occasion a single sneaky German Focke-Wulf flying just over the ground terrified a bunch of us into diving into an icy stream and after we had crossed the Zinzl River, two P-47s showed up and bombed the pontoon bridge our engineers had just installed, dumping a Sherman tank into the river. They made a second pass and the tankers shot down one of them.

Our holiday in reserve also produced the high point of the

winter. Two huge tents and an oil-burning water heater were installed and Charley Company took a bath. We marched into tent one by platoon, stripped off our outerwear (field jackets, helmets, wool caps, waterproofs, snowpacks, etc.). Clad in underwear and socks now, we marched down a boardwalk through a mixture of snow and sleet into the shower tent. There we doffed underwear and socks, tossed same into bins, were handed bars of soap, and marched under a row of nozzles spewing hot water. A minute or so to soap up, a minute or so to rinse off, and we were at the other end of this process. There we were handed fresh underwear and socks, reclaimed our boots and clothing, donned same and were back out in the muddy field in well under ten minutes. It was a combination of car wash and sheep dip, and the first—and the last—bath I had between getting off the troopship at Marseilles and getting out of a body cast months later in the Third General Hospital. How had we smelled? Terrible, I'm sure, even worse than one would imagine since this was also our first change of underwear since leaving the U.S.A.

Here, too, came our only formal and official encounter with U.S. Army organized religion in the combat zone. A Catholic chaplain arrived, set up a makeshift altar on a tank repair rack, and all concerned—Catholic or not—were invited. On another occasion, neither formal nor official, Bob Lewis and I saw the same chaplain's Jeep, found the priest (a captain) was saying Mass in the village church, and—with his driver—formed a congregation of three for the ceremony. Our only other chance to attend Mass came the Sunday morning before a Sunday afternoon fight to recapture Shillersdorf. We noticed villagers going into the little local church, walked in to join them, and were stopped at the door by the usher who told us in a mixture of German and gestures that we could not bring our weapons into the building—leaving us with a choice of whose rules to respect. The U.S. Army lost that one. My pistol and Bob's tommy gun waited for us at the door.

13

Life in the Mertzwiller Convent

For the Fourth Platoon our next stop after the memorable bath was a convent. We were trucked off to Pfaffenhoffen, unloaded and walked some fifteen miles to Mertzwiller and back to the war. The last miles were through a woods under artillery fire—not a heavy barrage but enough to tell us our four days in Regimental Reserve were over. We wait in the forest for darkness and move into the town, replacing an exhausted, evil-smelling bunch from the Forty-fifth Division's 160th Infantry, who looked as if they hadn't had a bath in months.

Mertzwiller is divided approximately in half by the Zinzl River. The 160th Regiment had captured the south half. The Germans held the other half and, alas, the Zinzl was only about thirty feet wide. That set up a situation which causes a mortar gunner once again to thank God he's not in a rifle squad.

We set up our mortar behind a thick stone wall that connected a large Catholic church and the convent—a perfect place. The church steeple provided a perch for a lookout with easy communications. The basement of the convent, long since evacuated by its residents, provided a convenient place to sleep dry and warm—and all this on a hill from which we looked down on the hostile side of the town. Wonderful! The only drawback was the slope of the land exposed the basement wall to the Germans, and the Germans, we soon learned, possessed a 76 mm antitank cannon and two flak wagon half-tracks armed with dual mounted 20 mm antiaircraft guns. The flak wagons were to make life miserable for the rifle squads posted in the shot-up houses along the river but were no real worry to us. The cannon, however, caused those using the basement as a dormitory to sleep light, nervously aware that at any second a German cannoneer might decide to punch one through that exposed convent wall just for luck.

The only fiction I've written about the war was based on incidents at Mertzwiller—where we lingered (a verb appropriate for those of us in the mortar section but not for the rifle squads) four memorable days before evicting the Germans from their half of the town.

The first of these short stories was stimulated by the fate of one of a gaggle of replacements sent up to replenish our depleted ranks. Huckins was taking him down to turn him over to a rifle platoon by the river, which involved crossing two exposed streets. In the "take a deep breath, pray, and sprint" dash across the second of these the replacement had dropped something. He stopped, jumped back to pick it up, and was shot. His body lay on the street until early winter darkness made it prudent for someone to drag it to shelter.

The fact that no one knew the replacement's name until they retrieved the corpse and looked at his dog tags inspired my story. I made my protagonist one of two men waiting on the back side of the town to guide the crew from headquarters, who would, when darkness fell, be carrying ammunition in from the woods. He is trying to get the names of replacements who, not knowing the survival tricks in the land of death, didn't last long enough to make friends. I have this chain of thought interrupted by the distant sound of machine gun fire, which provokes the required three rounds of retaliatory mortar fire, which is followed by silence, into which appears a man walking down the access road in full daylight, in plain view of the flak wagon that lurks in the battered buildings across the river. He interprets their "take cover" signals as welcoming waves, but the Germans are napping. He arrives safely—a second lieutenant replacing the recently deceased leader of a rifle platoon, which he is fated to be leading across the river come dawn. My story, if you haven't guessed, ends with my protagonist making sure he has this poor fellow's name memorized. That was the only one of the three ever published. Another one was influenced by the minimalist fad and dumped unsubmitted when I regained my taste, and the third one is still somewhere in my files. In it, the spotter with the binoculars in our church tower notices that a motorcyclist arrives about dawn each morning in the German side of town, enters a building, stays a while, and then putters off. A messenger, he presumes. Could our mortar reach him? Yes. So we pick a point the cyclist passes on his daily route, we establish the exact charge and tube setting to drop a round on the street there, we count off the seconds required to deliver the shell from tube to street. In the bell tower of the Church of the Good Shepherd our spotter is dealing with his end of this conspiracy, clicking off the seconds it takes the cyclist to get from the railroad crossing where he is first visible, to the place we have chosen for him to die. We test this formula one afternoon during our random "keep their heads" down shooting exercises. We have it precisely right. Tomorrow morning the spotter will signal "crossing tracks," we will count off eleven seconds, and then we will fire three rounds and wait.

But how do you end that story? In real life, when C.J. Smith (assistant gunner) and I discussed doing exactly the above, we were spared making such a life-or-death decision ourselves by orders sending Charley Company storming across the Zinzl to take the rest of the town, including the house the messenger visited each morning. In the short story, one ending had the execution performed and the protagonist walking past the cyclist's body later in the day. In another, I had him deliberately lower the tube a notch to overshoot. In still another I had the spotter describe both the cyclist and the cycle, converting the messenger from enemy to fellow human and the motorbike to one much like the machine his cousin let him ride. My question now (as a memoirist trying to get reacquainted with the who I was in 1944) is whether C.J. and I would have actually killed this fellow had fate not intruded. It was exactly what we were being paid $65 a month to do. I don't think we would have done it.

It must sound odd, but Mertzwiller sticks out in my memory as another of the few pleasant places in the winter of 1944–45. For the first time we were consistently dry, warm, and moderately clean, sleeping each night under a roof. While our platoon's machine gun section was posted along the river, providing support for the rifle squads in a series of shooting scrapes with German snipers and the prowling flak wagons, we mortar gunners were conducting our comfortably abstract sort of war.

Each of our three squads had its tube set up behind a wall—making it hard for the Germans to spot the flash and smoke that normally gave away our location. We had a spotter located where he could give us guidance, since the Germans hadn't bothered to knock down our church steeple. Our daily routine was comfortable—collecting our supply of ammunition, collecting our rations (canned C-rations here, instead of the dreary K boxes), firing occasional harassing rounds or trying to outguess one of the flak wagons when it was prowling the riverfront shooting at our rifle squads.

In contrast with this I present a bit from the notes of E.E. Reed, a rifle squad scout, who spent those days in the basement of a house beside the Zinzl bridge. The night before we attacked across the river Reed was one of six sent over to check on German defenses. They ran into a firefight and five of them got back across the stream.

"Spivak was missing, so Link, Copeland, and myself went back across to look for him. We found him badly wounded in the head, lying in a ditch, losing so much blood we thought he was a goner. We started swimming back through the icy water when the Krauts shot up a flare and opened up . . ."

I skip now to the official U.S. Army citation by which Sergeant Copeland received five points toward going home and a Bronze Star for "actions reflecting the highest traditions of the military service."

"Sergeant Copeland crawled seventy-five yards through the hostile fire, dragged the wounded man to the edge of the river, and placed him in a rubber boat. Fired on by riflemen only a few yards away, he returned the fire with his rifle and threw two grenades, killing and wounding several of the enemy . . ."

My point:

Note that Reed and the others involved in that midnight shootout didn't collect the five going-home points or the Bronze Star. Compare that patrol with my own walk into Itterswiller—which netted me the medal. Military justice was not equal then, and it has gotten worse. When we had our little scuffle with a Cuban workforce on Grenada in 1983, Bronze Stars were issued, literally, by the hundreds, many of them to high-ranking swivel chair officers who never left Washington. Or consider the affair in Kosovo, when a patrol of our Peacekeepers stopped to buy candy bars, took a wrong turn, drove into Serbian territory, and were arrested. The soldier who took a poke in the nose in that silly affair received a Purple Heart.

While the riflemen were living dangerously along the Zinzl, our only serious scare came the afternoon before we all crossed the river. As usual I blame the goof-up that preceded this crossing on Army Intelligence. Whatever the cause, a truck towing a trailer loaded with pontoons rolled into Mertzwiller in broad daylight and stopped at the road junction in front of our convent to ask directions. The vehicle got into town somehow without drawing German attention but that didn't last long. The sight of the truck parked on the street was all the warning a seasoned grunt needed to dive for his foxhole, which we did. The first German mortar shell fell right in the middle of the street and the next ones covered the area surrounding it, sending shrapnel whining all around us. One of those steel fragments cut through the cardboard tube in which my mortar rounds were packed, cut through the small individual tube that holds a single shell, cut the plastic fuse device off the top of the shell, and exited.

I mention this because the container was right behind my fox-hole, about three feet away from from my head, when it happened. Mortar fuses are set to explode at the slightest pressure. If this one had done its duty it would have detonated the other rounds in the container. C.J. and I would have been fragments. We found the fuse mechanism. The shrapnel had hit the little firing pin and severed it. When I claim to be unreasonably lucky later in this memoir I hope readers will remember this.

The combat engineers weren't lucky. Both were killed— one in a way that left me with one of those "burned into the optic nerve" memories. When the shooting stopped C.J. and I sneaked down to see what had happened. A helmet lay on the cobblestones open side up near the remains of the truck. The top of owner's head including one eyeball was still in it. Fifty-six years later I still see it.

That night we carried the pontoons and left them out-of-sight near the Zinzl. The word was we were doing the attack at dawn, and it would be preceded by a "timed on target" artillery barrage. We moved down nearer the river, waited and watched. The horizon far to the south lit suddenly with great flashes—the huge eight-inch rifles so far away that the sound wouldn't reach us for seconds. Then closer flashes of the 155 mm rifles, followed by the big howitzers, and finally our own regiment's 105s. Then the air overhead was screaming with the sounds of hundreds of passing shells. A moment later the north half of Mertzwiller erupted into a thunderous chaos of exploding shells. When the shelling stopped we crossed the river without opposition and took the town with only a few brief firefights.

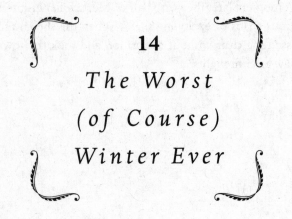

14

The Worst (of Course) Winter Ever

Now winter began getting serious. It was to prove to be the worst European winter in frigidity and snow since an epic bad one in 1902–3—fitting the pattern all World War II draftees remember of always being where legendary records were being set for heat, cold, humidity, mosquitoes, fleas, and general random environmental unpleasantness. I remember mostly endless walking, being cold, occasional skirmishes with no sense of who, where, when, or why. We understood finally that those mid-December days were occupied on a drive toward Wissembourg and the Siegfried Line because we eventually captured a small city with that name on its entry road. We took one prisoner in a brisk little fight at Walburg, slept in a genuine bed with a goose-feather comforter, ignoring occasional mortar fire. Entered Eschbach without resistance. There B Company replaced us at the point and we got eight hours of rest.

The house in which I spent those eight hours in Eschbach was a mansion with lavish grounds, stables, and a racetrack. Its parlor walls bore many paintings, most involving horses, one photo of Joseph Goebbels, one of Reichsmarschall Hermann Goering, both autographed and inscribed, several of a well-dressed man posing with fellows wearing swastika armbands and, judging from the braid, uniforms of high-ranking officers. Behind one of the horse portraits was a wall safe, which proved flimsy when a grenade was taped to it and the pin pulled. It contained legal-looking papers, keys, and a cigar box holding paper money. Some of this was old Weimar Republic currency in the huge denominations of the devastating German inflation, souvenirs of a national tragedy. Much was Third Reich cash amounting to more than 4,000 marks, which we understood would be spendable at a rate of about 60 cents to the dollar.

Our warm dry hours ended when the rear echelon brass decided the village was safe enough for them. They moved in and we were back in the rain trudging through the woods to Walburg. The word spread up and down the column that Huckins, Hillerman, and Lewis had struck it rich and we improved our status by handing out deutsche marks to the less fortunate. That didn't last long. A battalion headquarters Jeep rolled past us, its occupant seeking Captain Neeley. Then down the line came the first sergeant, asking questions and getting answers that caused us three to be given a Jeep ride back to Eschbach and turned over to a major. He held in his hand the empty cigar box.

The major, who I presume was an intelligence officer, seemed to have looked the house owner's wine cellar. He got his eyes focused on a number written on folded paper, sat us at a kitchen table, and told us to empty our pockets and count our ill-gotten deutsche marks. We were in deep trouble, he said. Unless we returned the 4,000 plus number on his paper, it was even deeper. Each of us counted separately, and when the three totals were added it came to a little over five thousand marks—each of us trying to fudge enough to cover our charity handouts and overdoing it. The major dumped the stack of bills into the box, revised the number on his paper, and sent us back out into the rain to resume our walk to Walburg and onward to the German border at Wissembourg.

Charley Company was in reserve there—perfecting our foxholes in a hillside vineyard while the less fortunate units tried to punch a hole though the Siegfried Line. Smith and I roofed ours with fence posts, left a hole for smoke to escape, and found some badly singed rugs from a shattered house for flooring. We didn't know it but while we were perfecting this Taj Mahal of foxholes the Germans off to our left flank had smashed through General Patton's Third Army front, their panzer divisions roaring down to Bastogne in what came to be known as the Battle of the Bulge, and Hitler had ordered "the elimination of all American forces between the Lower Vosges and the Rhine." That was us. But all the platoon sergeant told us was to saddle up, fall in, and move out. We never got to build a fire to make our foxhole cozy.

We withdrew, spending the next three days and nights alternating between bumping along in the back of the truck and slogging along through the woods, all under perpetual snow. This period produced a single vivid memory. A dark, cold evening, moving fast down a narrow wagon track, a few shells coming in, one exploding in the trees some fifty yards ahead, passing Sergeant Jack Arras, a friend, the nicest non-com in the machine gun section. Arras had been blown off the road. He was slumped against the side of the roadside ditch, helmet off. His expression was stunned, but when I shouted to him he seemed to be trying to laugh. I never saw Arras again but one of his machine gun squad visited him after the war. Cared for by his mother, he was playing with toys in a back room of their home.

The rest of us climbed on trucks again, climbed off at some nameless place, and slogged over the hills to Buschbach, and another version of the war.

Ah, Buschbach!! No lapse of memory here. Home at Buschbach was a farmer's house by day, but the endless winter night was endured in a hole in the frozen earth about five feet deep and big enough for two men to stand in it. It was on the reverse slope of a hill, offering a view of leafless fruit trees and deep and endless snow. On the lip of the hole rested Gene Halsey's machine gun, white with frost. The canvas ammunition belt fed into it was frozen cracklingly stiff, the bolt frozen, ice in the barrel. Would it fire if Halsey pulled the trigger? Maybe the round in the chamber would fire and maybe that would produce enough heat so it would continue firing. Probably not.

Now I understand we'd been shifted southward to protect the flank of the Third Army—filling the huge, frozen, snow-whitened expanse otherwise left vacant. Thus Charley Company, its 212-man force reduced to maybe 140 or so by unreplaced casualties, was scattered along about four miles of frozen hills, with no support behind us except—way back there somewhere—some tank destroyers and a battery of howitzers.

I know the tank destroyers and howitzers were there because on Christmas Day, while we were standing in line to collect our rations, our tank destroyers spotted us, decided we were German, and began shooting. This interrupted lunch and so enraged Captain Neeley that he called artillery down on the armored unit (so we believed), quickly ending this intramural battle. One other frigid day in Buschbach our artillery bombarded us with leaflets, printed in German, which urged us to surrender and promised good treatment if we did.

These two incidents caused us to think that Captain Neeley had walked us into one town ahead of where we were supposed to be. This notion was reinforced early one morning, as follows:

We were occupying the last house in the village, which, typical of Alsatian houses, was half human residency–half cow barn..I was just in from one more night in my frozen hole and another man and I were in the barn relieving ourselves. There came a knock on the barn door. At it stands a German soldier, machine pistol hanging from a strap over his shoulder. He begins a question, realizes that these two fellows he is looking at must be American soldiers, spins around and dashes away, shouting an alarm to the soldiers scattered along the street behind him. Everybody runs. We race upstairs spreading the alarm among our sleeping companions. Weapons are grabbed, but the Germans have already sprinted around the corner and out of sight. We presumed they were returning from a patrol unaware that Buschbach had been accidentally occupied by Americans deficient in map-reading skills.

The German Intelligence forces thus seemed as imperfect as our own. But their planners understood it snowed in the winter and had equipped their troops with modern plastic machine gun belts, white helmets, and white camouflage suits. Our Army had dressed us for snow in olive drab. A few lucky units had stolen mattress covers (used as body bags) from Grave Registration supplies to wear over their clothing, but most of us looked as if the West Pointers who make such decisions had designed us as targets. (Incredible? Remember an earlier generation of academy alums dressed our Army in heavy wool to fight the Spanish in the sweltering heat of Cuba.)

It surprises me still that such a large segment of my memory is devoted to those nine days at Buschbach. Nothing much happened. We lost only five men in that period—four wounded and one with a nervous breakdown. The sole casualties were rifle squad members, who had the job of crunching through the crusted snow on night patrols in their olive drab camouflage to make sure that Germans weren't up to something in adjoining villages. I was tapped for none of those. Instead, each day about sundown, Gene Halsey and I would urinate and defecate (our last chance to do either for at least fifteen hours), put on every item of clothing we owned, and trudge about a mile and a half through the snow to a hillside orchard, getting there just about 5 P.M.—full-dark time in the heart of winter at that latitude. We would relieve the lucky bastards who did day shift, climb into the hole, and try to get comfortable for the ordeal.

Both of us would crawl into our sleeping bags. One would zip it all the way up, slump down into the bottom, and try to sleep. The other would stand behind the gun, watching, waiting, memorizing the shape of every bare tree in the orchard, the shape of the slope where it met the sky, noting where the stars were on the skyline so he would notice if someone in white camouflage blocked some, straining eyes for a sign of movement, imagining the worst, keeping the rifle unfrozen inside the sleeping bag since the frozen machine gun probably wouldn't work. Then, when the man at the bottom got too cramped, or the man on guard too cold, the roles would be switched. An hour would creep past, but your watch would insist it was only ten minutes. And once in a while Halsey and I would talk, voices very, very low because sound carries remarkably well in the bitter cold.

The first hours of the first night we consider our position. How far away was the next foxhole? We hadn't seen it, but what we'd been told was maybe as far as a thousand yards. If a German patrol came over the hill would there be help? Impossible. We were merely outposts. Expendable. The shooting would trigger the alarm, reserves would be alerted to the raid, or the attack, or whatever it was. Someone had to do it.

With that out of the way, we talked of girls, of the meaning of life, of the death of this friend or that one, of why two of our high-ranking noncommissioned officers were never around when serious shooting started. We talked about home, about life after death, about the difference between perceptions and reality, about Bishop Berkeley's question of whether a tree falling in a forest made a sound if there was no one there to hear it. Finally, the faint blush of dawn in the east. More waiting, then the favored ones doing the day watch would arrived, and we'd trudge through the snow over the hills to Buschbach, and food, and warmth, and time to thaw a little before repeating the process.

Finally we were relieved by the Second Battalion and walked through the snow to Diebling to become part of the reserve of the Sixth Army Corps—which put us way back there with the colonels and generals—just as safe and comfortable as it's possible to get. Nirvana at last. We stay in a house, warm and dry, eat hot food, happy as larks in paradise.

Fools' paradise, it turns out. While we didn't know it, the Germans have given up on their Battle of the Bulge campaign. They have shifted armored divisions south to launch the Nordwind offensive—intended to recapture Strasbourg. All we know is we're told to saddle up and load into trucks. We unload back in Alsace, at a pretty little town named Niederbron. We're still in Corp Reserve under a three-hour alert as opposed to the fifteen-minute alert in Regimental Reserve. The house we occupy has a grand piano in the living room. Bob Huckins plays Chopin and some show tunes for us. Then back to reality.

"Saddle up," the sergeant shouts, and within fifteen minutes we're back in the truck, driving through the sleet to God knows where, or why. We're seasoned enough to know that if the three-star general commanding the corps is committing his reserve, it isn't going to be a relaxing place.

It turned out to be the Bois de Sessenheim outside the pleasant little Rhine-and-railroad town of Sessenheim, where Goethe did a lot of his writing. Not far away today there's a beautiful military cemetery at St. Avold, its headstones bearing names of twenty Charley Company men—and scores more from Able and Baker Companies. The previous night, the Tenth SS Panzer Division had stormed into the town and driven out our Forty-second Infantry Division—none of which we knew then of course.

For this memoir, I dug up the offical reports. Our First Battalion had been peeled off from the 103d Division and sent over to the

Seventy-ninth Division to help it recapture Sessenheim; then we are peeled off again and attached to something called Task Force Linden, which seems to have been a jumble of units controlled by the notoriously inept Forty-second Division. During all this card shuffling, we hear reports that a column of trucks loaded with Forty-second Division troops has driven into Sessenheim, apparently unaware the Germans had regained custody of the town. They are captured, trucks and all. The fellows running this show then launched a tank-infantry attack against the town. After all eight of the Shermans involved are knocked out, this was called off and plans changed from offense to defense.

Alas, we had been literally lost in the shuffling. If the 103d brass told the Seventy-ninth Division colonels, the Seventy-ninth seems to have failed to tell the Task Force Linden people that the attack we were about to launch had been canceled.

Sessenheim is where almost everything went wrong. (But thanks to relentless Hillerman luck, it was also the place that involved me in an incident that put me in touch with the woman who persuaded me I should become a writer.) Having read postwar battle histories, I know now that elements of the German Army Group G had smashed through Forty-second Division positions and we were to wage a counterattack to close the gap. But when we climbed off the bed of our truck in the woods and stood in the midnight darkness awaiting orders while the sleet rattled off our helmets, we knew nothing. I recall having an unusual sense of dread as we trudged away into the forest. We were walking toward the sound of artillery fire. When we stopped at dawn to dig in, we were on the receiving end of it.

There was no place in this dense Rhineland forest to avoid tree bursts. I remember digging deep, cutting through roots with my trenching tool, and sitting huddled in the bottom, head down with my arms folded over my helmet listening to the shells coming in, estimating the distance of the explosions.

The sun rose, the sleet stopped. We moved out again, stopping where a wide strip of timber had been cut, forming a firebreak about 150 yards wide. Across this opening we could see the raw dirt of fresh German emplacements inside the tree line. Far to our left, we saw the church steeples of Sessenheim and the smoke of burning Sherman tanks. I counted seven, but the official report says I missed one—that all eight Shermans involved in that part of the attack had been methodically destroyed and that the Germans had only a single Tiger involved in the fight. Our tankers called their Shermans "Ronsons" after a then popular cigarette lighter because "they never fail to burn."

We dug again and waited, and waited, and waited. Some machine gun fire was exchanged across the firebreak. We fired a few mortar rounds. The shooting stopped. We waited, and waited.

The rumor now was that any minute we would attack across the open strip, drive the Germans out of their positions, and capture a point where a narrow one-lane road through the woods intersected with the highway and railroad running up the Rhine into Sessenheim. Captain Neeley was back in the woods yelling into the radio. We presumed he was ordering smoke to cover us when the artillery preparation began. I looked across at the enemy woods—across a flat expanse of snow devoid of any cover. I thought of the account in *Lee's Lieutenants* of Pickett's ill-fated attack across the grassy pastures at Gettysburg. On the one hand, the Yankees who slaughtered the Virginians had no machine guns. On the other hand, we would have far better artillery support and, so we were told, Able Company was to be making a flanking attack to our right.

We waited. Time for the artillery to begin laying smoke and dropping shells on the German positions passed. The dreadful word reached us. No artillery support. Why not? Who knew? No one had thought to mention to a borrowed battalion that we were to retreat instead of attack. Captain Neeley was off the radio now. The word was get up and attack.

Here you have another proverbial moment of truth. Would you

prefer to charge out of our woods into that snow field and take a machine gun bullet or fail to do so and live with the contempt of your friends and the incurable damage to your fragile nineteen-year-old self-esteem? By now you have answered that question several times. You knew you were going. The secret was not to think about it. You went and so did everyone else. (Except, as we noted when noses were counted later, a couple of our bully-boy tough guy non-coms, who became invisible in the presence of danger.) Fortunately we didn't know then that the men across the firebreak were the Sixth SS Mountain Division, about whom I quote from an official U.S. Army report of the battle.

"The Sixth SS Mountain Division was undoubtedly the best German division in the fight for the Low Vosges; in fact it was probably the best German infantry on the entire Western Front in early January 1945. It had been fighting the Russians in Finland. When the Finns made their peace with the Soviet Union, it had withdrawn through Norway and was thrown, fresh, reequipped, and rested, into the Vosges battle."

The artillery support we'd awaited didn't happen because the Seventy-ninth Division howitzers were rolling toward the rear. About the time we were charging across the firebreak, Able Company was getting the word of the withdrawal and had canceled its supporting attack. Sounds hopeless for Charley Company, right? But while not handicapped by the West Point tradition the German brass had its own supply of dimwits.

In retrospect, I suspect the Sixth SS Division commanders were well aware that the Seventy-ninth was withdrawing. Thus it was preparing pursuit instead of defense and our misguided lunge across the snowy field, sans artillery preparation, smoke, tanks, or any sort of support, must have caused surprise and amazement. Whatever the explanation, we overran German positions and made it all the way to the railroad/highway objective at a cost of only twenty-six men.

(More than forty years later Charley Company was holding its first reunion at a hotel in Hot Springs, Arkansas; we Fourth Platooners were in a bar trying to get our war stories coordinated. To solve the problem we agreed to start the story of our daring dash at Sessenheim at the moment we rushed out of the woods past the body of Vincent Thornton, who had been a few steps ahead of us. That worked pretty well. One remembered seeing Vince fall. Another remembered the concussion of a mortar shell moving his body, and so forth. I remembered giving his corpse a passing glance as I sped past him. A bit later I went to the bar to get a round of beer. The bartender told me the customer a few seats down was looking for people from C Company, 410th Infantry. I went over and introduced my self.

"I'm Vince Thornton," he said. "What the hell happened to you guys? I remember running out of the woods there at Sessenheim, and the next thing I knew I was back in the hospital at Saverne."

So much for wartime memories.)

But I do clearly remember the gray concrete pillbox the French had built to guard the junction we had taken. Company head-quarters moved into it, while we grunts were sorted out into a defensive posture, dug ourselves a fresh set of foxholes behind the railroad, and waited for instructions.

The snow began again and then turned into rain (Luckily for us because the Sixth SS Mountain Division was equipped with stark white winter camouflage.). C.J. and I had set up our mortar in a clear space behind the railroad and dug ourselves a foxhole behind it. A couple of men from the Intelligence and Recon unit had arrived after dark. They took the two Germans we'd captured and left behind the gossip they'd overhead at battalion headquarters. To wit:

1. The Seventy-ninth Division had pulled back and forgot to tell battalion.

2. Neeley was supposed to cancel yesterday's attack but hadn't gotten the word.

3. Able and Baker had gotten the word and were now entrucked and riding happily rearward.

4. Able and Baker were going to jump off tomorrow morning and would join us. The whole battalion would then push all the way to the Rhine, only two miles ahead.

5. We were supposed to withdraw as soon as it got dark enough to be safe.

6. Yesterday the idiots in the Forty-second Division had shot a bunch of German prisoners right out where the Krauts could see it happen. Remember that if you're thinking of surrender.

7. We were surrounded. Those really big shells going overhead and exploding way behind us were from German railroad guns across the Rhine.

And so forth. Take your pick. Believe what you liked, or none of it.

Meanwhile C.J. and I had inventoried what was left of our ammunition and found we had nothing to shoot except flare rounds (which, as we were soon to learn, were exactly what we needed). We devoted much of the night trying to build a little dam to keep a mixture of melting snow water, rain, and mud from draining down into our foxhole. Dawn was near. But what would the morrow bring? I had my helmet and my field jacket off, working with my trenching tool. We heard George Rice, who had his machine gun set up on the railroad track near us, shouting something in his Dartmouth College version of German. More shouting in German came in response. George's machine gun fired a short burst. Very short since the wet canvas belt wasn't releasing spent shells. A shower of German "potato masher" grenades come flying over the tracks, trailing sparks, making their ear-numbing explosions and sending fragments whistling around us. We heard one of the rifle platoon leaders shouting: "Pull back! Pull back!" A fine idea. Germans in their white helmets and snowsuits, visible even in the predawn darkness, were streaming over the railroad embankment. Much yelling, much shooting, more grenades.

C.J. and I raced away from the tracks toward the road where the pillbox stood. Neeley and a lieutenant were there, organizing a stand. We heard the characteristic "chung, chung, chung" sound of a mortar being fired. Our mortar! The lieutenant looked at me—an accusing stare. But, thank God, the only ammunition we had were those flares. These exploded high overhead and drifted down— more help to us than the Germans. The plan seemed to be to make a stand along the asphalt road and I was signaled to hustle down it. I hustled, my model 1902 pistol in hand. I scrambled up the steep road embankment, flopped on my belly. Just as I did, a German hustled up the other side of the embankment, crouching, carrying a machine pistol. He pointed it at me. I shot him.

I have relived that moment often. At first, with no particular emotion except relief, remembering him seeing me, jerking his machine pistol toward me, his body slamming backward from the almost point-blank impact of that heavy .45 slug. But soon my imagination gives him a personality. This was face-to-face killing of a man, not the impersonal killing we had done with the mortar, where the victims were an invisible enemy in a machine gun position, or some hypothetical person who might be on the street when you fired the required harassing rounds. Later, when what was left of Charley Company was back across the firebreak into the woods from which all this had started, I found myself engraving every detail of those few minutes in my memory.

The German dropped into a crouch on the edge of the single-lane asphalt directly across from me and perhaps fifteen feet away. I seem to remember his face, although the dawn light made that unlikely. I was aware that I had three rounds in the pistol, having used the rest potting at running figures in our rush away from the railroad. I was also aware this didn't matter. Luck gave me the first shot, but that's all I'd get. He had the machine pistol.

My shot hit him either high in the chest, the throat, or the face.

The heavy lead slug knocked him backward and sideways, tumbling him down the embankment. From where I lay I could hear the shouts of his squad yelling for grenades. Jerry Shakeshaft was running along the embankment below me. He heard the shouts, too, and tossed me his grenade and a word of advice: "Don't forget to pull the pin."

I pulled it.

The grenades we were using had five-second fuses. I held it two counts to get the proper arrival time, then bounced it off the asphalt and over the road. It exploded out of my sight but in the air. We lay there a few moments, Shakeshaft beside me now with a carbine, and listened to the screams of those blown away by the grenade fragments.

What happened next? End of memory. I vaguely recall recrossing the firebreak. I remember coming under artillery fire in our retreat. I remember passing a 60 mm mortar left behind by Baker Company when it jumped off in its day-late attack. I remember C.J. and me taking it along to replace our own. I remember walking through a little town with its inhabitants watching us sadly. And I recall meeting David Hubbell coming up the road from the opposite direction with a group of replacements. I remember thinking that was Dave's third trip back from the hospital and that he was getting a very unfavorable impression of the war.

The last time the hospital had sent him back to duty he'd found us sitting on a hillside in a heavy fog, burning K-ration boxes to heat water in a canteen cup to make instant K-ration coffee, killing time while Neeley organized to attack a little roadblock up the road. The rations/ammo/mail Jeep stopped down the hill and Hubbell limped up to be greeted. But we'd overestimated the fog, or underestimated German binoculars. Here came the mortar shells, breaking up our picnic. Down the hill we scramble and up the road into the attack. More shells, some shooting. Hubbell is hit. The same Jeep that brought him up takes him back to be patched

up again. And now here he is again, meeting what's left of us strag-
gling down the road in defeat.

"Fellas," Hubbell shouts, "I just couldn't wait to get back."

Shakeshaft's ironic shout to me about pulling the grenade pin is
another example of the ironic humor combat seemed to produce.
The shout originated as a jibe at Gil Rodriguez, who had joined the
platoon as a replacement just in time for the attack on Villa. In the
street fighting there Rodriguez got himself into position to toss a
grenade into a window from which a German machine gun was firing. He missed the window, the grenade bounced back to land
amid his fellow grunts, producing about three seconds of terror
before it was noticed he hadn't pulled the pin. Thereupon Gil was
greeted with that "pull the pin" shout at every opportunity. He was
one of those killed crossing the firebreak.

After that nothing much happened to Charley Company for a
week. A lot of walking from one village to another. One hot meal.
A chaplain came up from somewhere distant and held a memorial
service for our dead, and we spent bitter-cold nights manning roadblocks.

At one of these Tom Morick and I captured three prisoners the
easy way. They walked up the road waving a white towel and
shouting, "Kamarad." (The surrender leaflets our Army showered
down on us at Buschbach taught that was the politically correct
surrender word.) The fellow in charge of this peace delegation
spoke English. He said they didn't mind fighting Americans but
they had just learned their unit was being transferred back to the
Russian front. They'd been there and done that and wanted no
more of it. We swallowed that insulting comparison, searched
them for souvenirs, and turned them over to company headquarters.

The calm before another storm. Then came the wee hours of
January 29, and an order to saddle up and entruck. We'd been living
in a dentist's home and office in Ingerwiller in the quiet luxury and

bliss of Regimental Reserve. Our truck ride through the falling snow was alarmingly short. We piled off, trudged up the slopes of a wooded hill, looked down on a picturesque scene, church spires rising from a pretty village of stone houses and barns. Beautiful, but the pastoral mood was diminished by the sound of small arms fire, the zipper sound of German machine guns, and the thud of mortar shells. The Sixth SS Mountain Division, the same folks we'd encountered at Sessenheim, had smashed through Seventh Army lines and recaptured Schillersdorf, doing serious damage to our Second Battalion in the process. We grunts knew none of this, of course, only that the bad guys had captured the town and now we had to charge through that infinitely wide snow-covered hay field and recapture it.

Able Company had already attacked, captured the first two houses on the road into town, and was now pinned down. That explained all the shooting we were hearing.

I recall staring out across the field of snow with the same feeling of foreboding the Sessenheim firebreak had produced. Bob Lewis, my selection as the bravest man in the Fourth Platoon, was standing by me, carrying the Thompson submachinegun he had stolen somewhere to replace his .45. Lewis nodded at the snowy field and said: "This situation seems fraught with peril," in a perfect imitation of W. C. Fields's famous whiskey voice. Rice, my selection as our most lighthearted member, recalls joining some riflemen who were rolling in the snow, trying to apply self-camouflage to compensate for the West Pointers not knowing about snow in Europe.

"At first I thought it would melt right off and just get me wet," Rice recalled, "but then I thought: Better wet than dead."

The disasters one expects don't seem to happen. We floundered through that snow, knee-deep in many places, without losing a man. Once in the buildings it got more exciting. The Third Platoon, with Rice and his machine gun attached, penetrated deep into the town and was almost immediately cut off from the rest of the company. Two tanks, which were supposed to be supporting our attack, finally arrived. Neeley told the lead tank commander where to go to break a way open to the Third. I wasn't close enough to hear the exchange but the gestures made it clear that the tank driver was rejecting the idea. Neeley drew a pistol, pointed it at the tanker. Tanker dropped down into the turret. Neeley yelling. Tanker slammed the lid shut, slammed his steel monster into reverse, and backed away down the street.

In fairness to tankers let it be known that the Germans used an antitank rocket which, in contrast to ours, actually destroyed tanks. The *panzerfaust* looked like a plumber's helper—a large cone-shaped charge on the end of a sawed-off broomstick. It was a one-man weapon, trigger-fired, relatively short range, and with a huge punch. Ours was a long-skinny tube, with the shooter holding it and peering through his sight, and a second man sticking in the rocket, connecting wires, etc. Our advantage was longer range. Our disadvantages were: (a) unless the rocket hit just right it bounced off instead of exploding, (b) even if it did hit serious armor it didn't have enough punch to get the job done, and (c) it was too awkward and clumsy to be much use in street fighting. Thus prudent tankers tried to stay off the streets unless escorted by infantry to protect them from *panzerfaust* holders in basements, upstairs windows, etc.

With the tanks gone, Neeley tried other ideas to reach the Third Platoon. I was standing there with my mortar set up but nothing to shoot at until I knew who was where, so the captain sent C.J., Huckins, and me down the street on a recon patrol. About four houses down we noticed German hobnail boot tracks leading through the snow into a barn. We peeked in. Just inside the barn door were two of the cans that hold ammunition belts for the German machine guns. C.J. and Huckins were carrying M1 rifles. I had my .45, fully loaded again. No sign of the machine gunner but the rungs of the ladder into the hay loft had snow melting on them. We discussed this. Our man was probably an ammunition bearer.

Even if he was the gunner he probably wouldn't have hauled the gun into the loft with him and left behind his ammunition. On the other hand, he didn't leave behind his pistol. We concluded that C.J. and Huckins would cover me with their rifles, I would clamber up the ladder taking my pistol where it would be close enough to count if necessary. I crept up the ladder, took off my helmet, and poked it up on the barrel of the pistol to see if it drew fire. It didn't. Put it on again, peered over the edge, eyes at loft floor level. Nobody home. Just a great pile of loose hay against the back wall. I climbed out, pistol pointed at the hay pile, shouted the German phrases we'd memorized to encourage the bad guys to surrender. Nothing happened. I heard C.J. scrambling up the ladder behind me. I shouted again. No response. I fired a round into the hay pile.

From behind and above comes a frantic shout. Our machine gunner had climbed up into a little attic in the eaves just under the barn roof. Given the choice of either surrendering or shooting a couple of us with his Luger and being shot himself he has chosen surrender. We tell him to climb down. He does. We take his pistol and his gas mask case (as usual a treasure of food) and frisk him. C.J. extracts a pack of Camels from his shirt pocket. *"Nein, Nein,"* he says, clearly angry, and tries to grab the pack back from C.J. A discussion ensues. It seems this fellow had been reading our surrender leaflets and was persuaded that we really did treat prisoners well. He wants his smokes back and, despite having three cocked weapons pointed at him, seems to be reconsidering his decision to become a prisoner of war. C.J. shrugs and returns his Camels. I take him back up the street to give him to the captain. C.J. and Huckins return and report Germans holding positions around the corner about two blocks away. We get other assignments.

Mine was to be part of a five-man patrol to find another way to reach the Third Platoon. Our leader was my very own sergeant, Walter Hitz, the boss of what was once a six-member mortar squad. He'd been badly wounded in our first days in combat and had just returned from the hospital a day or two earlier. Our plan is to skirt through an opening behind some battered houses into an apple orchard, then slide along a high stone wall of the cemetery beside the village church, and keep going until we either find the Third Platoon or run into Germans. Before we get to the houses we are spotted. Here comes the mortar fire. I dive into the snow beside a fallen telephone pole. I hear a round coming in, hear it hit, get some snow splashed over the pole onto my neck. The round is a dud. The next two explode with Germanic efficiency, reducing our five-man patrol to four as we scramble for a safer position. Sergeant Hitz now has Bob Lewis with his Thompson, a bazooka man from the First Platoon, and me. We reach the apple orchard and the cemetery and begin moving down the wall.

Oops! The muzzle of a machine gun suddenly juts out from around the corner of the wall ahead of us. Its owner hasn't seen us and is simply setting up for action. Lewis blazes away with his Thompson. The German jerks the gun and himself safely back behind the wall. We scurry for the only available cover—which is a large, snow-covered manure pile. What to do? The muzzle of the gun reappears with its owner trying to edge it around enough to get a shot at us without exposing himself. Hitz pops away with his carbine, me with my .45, and Lewis with his Thompson. The muzzle vanishes.

Hitz decides the gun is probably still there, just waiting for an opportunity. We will see if we can hit the inside of the wall with a bazooka round, blowing a bunch of rock into the gunner. The bazooka man stands, tube on shoulder. Hitz inserts the round, Lewis and I providing cover. The bazooka man fires. The rocket soars over the cemetery wall, hits the inside of the wall as planned, neglects to explode, and bounces away. Time to try again. The process is repeated but the machine gunner has been alarmed. Just as the bazookaman fires the second round the gunner sticks his head and his hand out and snaps off a shot with his pistol. The bullet hits the bazooka man in the right shoulder. The bazooka rocket hits the inside of the wall, neglects to explode, and bounces away.

The bazooka man, looking woozy with pain, sits on the manure pile, confirms the bullet has broken his shoulder at the joint, and hobbles off through the snow toward the rear, with Lewis and me firing a few rounds to keep the German from doing more damage. Time to try again. We load and wire the bazooka. Hitz stands behind the manure pile, aims. Before he can fire, the machine gunner sticks his pistol out and fires off another round. This strikes Hitz just where the tendon connects at the point of the shoulder, doing substantial damage to bone, tendon, gristle, muscle and morale. Hitz drops the still-loaded bazooka and sits bleeding on the backside of the manure pile.

The plan now is to forget the bazooka idea. Hitz will stagger back through the orchard to safety and medical attention. I'm out of pistol ammo and will use his carbine to help Lewis provide cover fire. When Hitz is safe Lewis will cover me while I make a run for it. Then I'll snap off carbine shots, Lewis will blaze away, and then he'll run for it. Hitz makes his escape unmolested. Lewis signals *Go!* to me. I go.

Anyone who has tried to begin what he intends to be the fastest sprint of his life through deep snow wearing rubber-bottomed snowpacks can predict what happened. About five yards beyond the cover of the blessed manure I slipped, landed belly down, couldn't find the traction to get up, and had panicky visions of the German setting up his machine gun in the open and shooting me multiple times. But he didn't. Lewis fired off the last of his final magazine and we both made it.

We cleared the rest of Schillersdorf the next day (killed ten, captured twenty-five) and went back to Itterswiller, got three truckloads of recruits to replace men lost the past few weeks, enjoyed a couple of indoor days, and then trucked through a blinding snowstorm to relieve troops in foxholes above Rothbach. A most unpleasant place.

Since I developed a fever, and have hazy memories of Rothbach, I will quote from a chronicle I borrowed from a friend.

"On line at Rothbach within fifty to two hundred yards from German positions. Receive mortar and artillery fire. Lose eight men. Weather warms, ice melts, foxholes fill with water. Lots of trenchfoot cases. Sniping back and forth. We claim ten. They had tanks. Night of sixth we walk back to Itterswiller and through it to Obersultzbach. Go into Division Reserve."

I was feverish because I was catching pneumonia. I recall being issued a new model mortar by some clean and fresh-faced captain from ordnance and lugging it through the mud to a hillside hole where we replaced other grunts who were delighted to leave.

This new mortar is worth a word for those who seek to understand the military mind. It was produced by sawing about 70 percent of the tube off an 81 mm mortar and then replacing the big knob on the butt cap with a little knob that would fit into our little 60 mm mortar base plate. The only other revision was modification of the bipod to fit the fatter tube. Since the tube was now only an inch or two longer than an 81 mm shell, one fired it at real risk of serious burns and total deafness for the gunner. The shell tended to come out of the barrel wobbling, which made it totally inaccurate, and the tremendous increase of impact on the little base plate drove it into even frozen earth. We only fired it a few times, endangering no one but ourselves. When I returned from the hospital it was gone.

The hole we occupied had been dug deeply into a hillside above a narrow valley. The village of Rothbach was below if we cared to look—which we rarely did because German foxholes were dug into the hillside right across from us. We could see them. They could see us. We could hear their tanks rumble along the road; not always a reliable sound because the Germans sometimes played recordings of tank sounds to amuse us over their loudspeaker systems. But here we could actually see the long 88 mm barrels of their Panthers.

My fever was climbing and I only had a couple of days in this hole. The second evening when our relief came and we climbed down to company headquarters I found Otto Mittag, our aid man, and told him I was sick. Otto ushered me into a room with two other miserable-looking grunts and took my temperature. It was 102. That won't cut it, he said. Last month they raised the temperature level and now it has to be 103 before I can send you back. He loaned me a pack of cigarettes, told me to chain-smoke, and he'd be back before the ammo Jeep arrived and retake my temp. I did, and he did. Whether or not the smoke added a degree to my body heat or Otto fudged, he put me on the Jeep with his two other patients and I got to visit the Army Medical Clearing Station at Saverne.

A couple of days and the lungs are cleared up and the fever down. Hot food, clean sheets, a *shower*, total luxury. The young fellow in the bed to my right had a lot of skin burned off him. He was swathed in bandages and too doped up for conversation—just waiting to be well enough to be shipped to a regular hospital somewhere for skin grafts. The occupant of the bed to the left wore a variety of bandages but talked endlessly about his missing right hand, which had been chopped off by shrapnel. He knew it was gone, he told me, but he could still feel it. He would hold up the bandaged stump for me to see. "I can feel the thumb moving," he'd say, moving the stump as if to show me, "and I can close the fingers like a fist." And so on for two days until one morning he was gone; back somewhere, I presumed, to get himself fitted for some sort of artificial hand.

Both of these neighbors had lucked out. Headed for the Zone of Interior with the Million-Dollar Wound. Their beds are filled by someone else. For me, no more fever now. I'm back in uniform, with fresh, clean underwear. Feeling fine. Walking around outside. Every hour or so, a huge shell roars over and explodes somewhere out of sight. An orderly tells me it's from a railroad gun hidden in a railroad tunnel back in the hills, rolling out now and then, trying to hit the railroad bridges in Saverne. When am I going back to the company? No one seems to know. Or care. I walk down to the

railroad station and find the "Re-po-dep-o," the Replacement
Depot where new arrivals are taken off the trains, sorted out, and
entrucked for whatever rifle companies are being brought up to
strength. There I find a truck heading for the 103d Division, now at
Obersultzbach, and climb in the back with about twenty or so nervous replacements. The hospital will list me as Absent Without
Leave. So what? The recruits are full of questions and I enjoy the
prestige of being a battle-hardened vet. Not a worry in the world.
Once at division headquarters, it will be easy enough to get a ride
to Charley Company. We pull into Obersultzbach and I find the
Company is there.

Charley and the entire bruised and battered Second Battalion is
in Division Reserve, having its gaps filled with new men. We even
have a new division commander. General Anthony McAuliffe, ex of
the Eighty-second Airborne Division, who had made headlines
with his "Nuts" response to German demands that he surrender
Bastogne. The general has ordered a little review, complete with
band, to hand out decorations won by various folks. George Rice
was getting a Silver Star for his derring-do with the cut-off Third
Platoon in Schillersdorf. I'm getting one, too, they tell me for my
one-shot, one-grenade defense of the road outside Sessenheim. I'm
issued a clean shirt, paraded out onto a rainy field with the other
winners, and our new general pins a ribbon on each of us while his
photographer records it. Then we entruck, and drive back to
reality, Obermodern, and the war and I am wondering what the
general would have done had he know he was pinning a ribbon on
an AWOL.

But we're still in reserve. Able and Baker are dug in on the hills
outside of town overlooking the tiny eleven-house village of
Niefern and the roads that intersect there. We are comfortable in
houses with occasional artillery fire coming in but no casualties.
Someone arranges to have a movie shown in a school auditorium,
a very dark, depressing film about a murder in the Louisiana

swamp. Occasional shells passing overhead add a special element to the suspense but the sound track is as bad as the lighting.

February 26 arrives. Captain Neeley, wounded again at Schillersdorf, is back from being patched. The platoon sergeant calls me in from my kitchen police job. He tells me that Sergeant Hitz has been Z-I'ed and won't be coming back—leaving the squad leader position open. He reminds me that I have been sort of running what's left of our mortar squad most of the time and instructs me in the duties of a buck sergeant. He stops, studies me for a long moment, and says: "Hillerman, I don't think you'd be happy as a sergeant," and tells me to report back to the kitchen.

Thus died my chance to go into the records as having the shortest tenure as squad leader of any man in the Army—approximately ten hours. I returned to my pot scrubbing chores and Dave Hubbell was called in and handed the stripes—in a rare example of military astuteness. Hubbell was a lot better at it than I would have been.

However, had the tech sergeant not had his astute change of mind, I would have been collecting sergeant's pay, instead of $65 per month, for half a year in hospitals. Because Army Intelligence was about to do it to us again, heading me for my cherished Zone of Interior wounds. We were about to run a patrol into the little town over the hill, into Niefern.

To quote from the chronicle:

"Feb. 27—Bloody NIEFERN!! Unsuccessful night raid by 3rd platoon and part of 4th."

A half dozen of us survivors of that nocturnal walk into Niefern returned in 1986 with our wives in tow to take a look. Nothing much had changed. It was still a little cluster of farm residences at a junction with a stream running along the main road. A farmer came out of his barn to satisfy his curiosity, then invited us in to sample his schnapps. He, too, had been an infantryman, he told us, and took off his cap to show us the evidence. About at the high hairline on his forehead was an indentation large enough to hold a golf ball. He told us he had joined the Waffen SS and was with a German infantry unit fighting the Russians. He'd been hit in the battle for Kiev. We shook hands and embraced him. The infantry makes brothers of all who have done their term in the valley of death. War historian Stephen Ambrose called service in the combat infantry "the most extreme experience a human can endure." It's something that transcends politics.

Unfortunately ethnic politics among Alsatian villagers certainly affected our "unsuccessful raid" on Niefern. The occupants of Obermodern, just over the hill, spoke German fluently and French very little—as did most of the Alsatians we'd met. We'd seen pictures of their sons in German uniforms on farmhouse walls, and heard tales of how residents had pointed the way for German units in their recapture of Schillersdorf. We'd heard on February 26 that we'd be raiding Niefern the following night. So had the local folks. Many of them must have had relatives in the German Army, and relatives over the hill in Niefern. Even we grunts were smart enough to figure that the people in Niefern would know they had visitors coming—and twenty-four hours to prepare for us.

Army Intelligence had it all scouted out. Only a small outpost group occupied the village, maybe four or five men. Our assignment was to take the village and come home with two of those poor fellows as prisoners. To do that, one Third Platoon rifle squad reinforced by four men from the mortar section would wade across the stream below the village, cross the fields, and move in from the back, cutting off escape. The other two Third Platoon squads, with a machine gun squad attached, would move in from the front. All very neat and simple. The rifle squads in theory had twelve men each but actually were down to about six or seven due to unreplaced dead and wounded. Even so, with add-ons from the Fourth Platoon, we'd have them outnumbered five or six to one. Or so it seemed to Intelligence. Plus, so it seemed to Intelligence, we'd have the element of surprise.

If we had any doubts that our surprise raid would surprise anyone but us they disappeared at the top of the hill overlooking the village. We stopped there among the foxholes of Baker Company to wait for a darker jump-off time. One of the mortarmen in Baker was an old friend who went all the way back to Fort Sill, Fort Benning, and the ASTP.

"They're expecting you," he said. "They zeroed their mortars in on the road this morning and they've been putting out mines all day. If you guys go down there, then we'll just have to go down tomorrow and rescue you—like we did at Sessenheim."

But of course we went. Quietly through the dark woods and down an open hill, splitting up at the road with two squads moving toward the village and our group crossing a fence, wading the knee-deep creek, and making a parallel approach, pretending we didn't know that they knew we were coming and were awaiting us.

(I had a bit earlier climbed upon an unattended tank hoping to find a box of Ten-in-One rations on which soldiers in armored units feasted. No such luck in this one, but I did find myself a Thompson hanging in the turret—which I needed far more than a tank jockey. At least one of the tank crew seemed to agree. When he saw me carrying it a bit later he asked me if I needed any extra magazines and handed me a couple. I mention this because in the version of this raid glamorized by my memory I was a sort of John Wayne figure carrying that Tommy gun. Many years later, when my path crossed that of David Hubbell again, he told me my role was more like Florence Nightingale. I was actually carrying a stretcher. Dave finally stopped getting wounded, became a hydraulic engineer of some repute, and had his profession's tendency to have his facts and figures right. Whatever I was carrying, we were sneaking through a muddy field toward the back side of buildings when the silence was broken by a series of explosions, screams, machine gun fire, and general chaos in the part of the village the other two squads had entered. At almost the same time, someone began shooting at us. We had been seeing poorly concealed antipersonnel mines here and there, presumed others had been buried more carefully, and were threading our way cautiously. Now we ran. I was just behind Hubbell, buck sergeant since midafternoon. I was trying to run in his boot prints.

I'm told severe trauma causes short-term memory loss. I remember being engulfed in silence—no more sound of the mines exploding down on the road or of gunfire. Just an incandescent flash, sudden silence, and knowing that I am in the air, face down and falling. My next memory was my face hurting, of being on my back in the mud, of knowing that I must have stepped on an antipersonnel mine, probably one of the shu mines we had been trying to avoid, of remembering that these things were designed to blow off the lower leg and, judging from the victims I had seen, usually did. I was aware that I was probably bleeding from this stump (although the only pain I felt was from rips, tears, and burns on my face). I was conscious how quickly hurt men died in the cold.

My most vivid memory of all this is something I have since read about in the recollections of folks who skirted awfully near death. No more pain. Just warmth, comfort, an incredible sense of peacefulness, or moving slowly through a passageway. Of being welcomed. Of God, or one of His delegates, welcoming me.

But I also remember things happening that caused this wonderful sense to fade in and out. I remember being rolled onto a stretcher. Then I fade back into warm, loving peace. Second, Joe Christopherson, carrying the front end of the stretcher, stepped on another mine. His leg was blown off, the stretcher broken, and I'm on the ground again. Next I remember Lyle Kniffin, a Third Platoon rifleman, and Bob Yager, a friend from the machine gun section, talking to me and getting me organized in a "fireman's carry." Next memory, I am dropped in the icy water of the little creek. Next memory, I am being arranged across the hood of a Jeep. I can see nothing at all, but some of my hearing is back and I pick up the voice of Captain Neeley, getting things organized, saying undecipherable things to me. (Probably advice about watching where I put my feet.) The blissful warmth and peace goes away, replaced by reality, a sense of disappointment mixed with resignation. Life apparently is not yet over. That last great adventure Mama had promised must wait awhile.

Back at Obermodern I get a shot of morphine and am slid into a bottom rack of an ambulance. My only memory of the ride to the clearing station is of warm blood dripping down on my chin and neck from Christopherson, who was dying in the rack above me. Then morphine brought blessed oblivion.

When I awaken it must be a day or so later. I am strapped into a bunk, jolting and rocking. Both legs are in casts, eyes covered with bandages. I remember exploring with my hand, noticing that bandages are also taped across the back of my other hand and that my head is wrapped like a mummy. And I hurt, big time. I recall thinking Mama would have told me to "offer it up. Get some good out of it in heaven. Build up your endurance. Whining doesn't make pain go away." But Mama wasn't there. I whined. I heard the voices of others around me calling for an orderly. Next a man was getting my arm bare, sticking in the needle. He told me I was on a medical train headed for the Third General Hospital. He told me my legs were broken up and my face had been burned but otherwise I was fine.

How about the stomachache?

That brought on the bedpan. No luck. An enema. No luck.

How long had it been? Several days, I say, having no idea of the present date. More help is summoned. The bedpan is placed on the floor. Another enema. I am lifted, one orderly supporting each cast leg and a third gripping me under the shoulders. I am suspended over the pan. Shouts of encouragement come from the bunks up and down the railroad car, cheers and exhortations. Having been raised a modest fellow and not cured from that even by barracks life, I found this humiliating. Finally, relief! A loud "boing" from the metal pan, applause from the audience, and the ordeal is over. Even better, I now know I am among understanding friends.

The Third General Hospital occupied what had been an insane asylum on a hill overlooking Aix-en-Provence, a beautiful little city in Southern France. Thanks to more morphine, I don't remember getting there, only awakening in a bed encased up to my rib cage in a body cast. No more bandages on my hands now, but my eyes are still bandaged shut and I'm wearing other patches on face and under my chin.

A most pleasant woman's voice, the first one I've heard speaking English since the previous autumn, tells me she is Lieutenant Weeks, that all is well now, and all I have to do is heal. How about details? They will come from the major when he makes his rounds. Major arrives. Asks me about pain. I ask him about my feet. Do I still have them both? Of course, he says, but the orthopedic people will tell me about that. He's interested in my eyes. He unwraps bandages. Removes pad from my left eye. Tells me open it. I can't. He pulls up the lid. Can I see anything? I can't. He repeats the process with the right eye. Can I see anything? Another negative.

I am blind.

When you are nineteen and that realization hits, it's good to have that jolly, jolly morphine in your bloodstream. The major is telling me that both of my eyes were burned and the eyeballs penetrated by small fragments. Most of these have been extracted. Some are yet to be removed. Both eyes are infected. The first priority is to stop the infection. The major thinks this will be accomplished and that probably I will be able to see again, at least some, and at least with the right eye.

I had become aware a long time ago, I think when I was trying to make the Konawa High School football team, that the things you worry about tend not to happen and the troubles you haven't considered bring the unpleasant surprises. (I thought I'd be a benchwarmer because I was skinny. It was because I was slow.) When released from the gentle bliss of sedatives, I had been worried about my foot. I had been in combat long enough to know it was probably gone. While I hadn't been able to see since I was wounded it hadn't seemed to occur to me to worry about vision. That would correct itself. I devoted my thoughts to how one got along with the artificial replacement. For example, did one have to buy a special shoe? I had presumed that once my face healed and the bandages came off my eyes would be good as new.

Now a different focus was required. My optimism was partially overcome by the enlisted man's natural skepticism of any information received from an officer. The major is lying, of course, cheering me until I'm healing and better able to handle the bad news. He actually thinks I'll be blind. But I will see again, no matter what he says. Maybe not very well, but some. At least enough to see the sky, storms forming, the patterns of lightning, the incredibly beautiful cumulus formations building, and building and building on summer afternoons until the stratospheric winds blow the shingles from their roofs. And I'll see the stars again on those winter nights when the moon is down and the constellations glitter. I will see enough sky to have it remind me, as it had since childhood, of how God loves us enough to give us all this grand beauty.

The major comes five days a week, asks me questions, removes the left bandage, asks what I see, and the answer is always nothing, followed by a second nothing for the right eye. With each visit the eyes are bathed in a solution and the bandages returned. Every three hours a nurse or an orderly arrives and gives me a very large shot of some liquid. Penicillin, I'm told. New experimental stuff some Brit invented. After a couple of weeks I run out of unused shoulder and arm veins for the needle and the nurse does her needlework on my back and buttocks. Reality is modifying my optimism. Blindness won't be all that bad. I'll have some sort of pension. I will find a seeing-eye dog, I think, and have a white cane. I have a fine sense of direction. My hearing is now fairly well restored. I am good at memorizing. I can learn Braille.

The major comes again, unveils left eye. Anything? No. Unveils right eye. I don't wait for the question. *I see him!!* At least I see something. Light and shadow, the shape of a face. Then my eye begins watering furiously. Jubilation. I am not blind.

A new phase of life begins. A few days later I can make out shapes fairly well with that good eye. Within a week I am seeing light with the left one. Now the focus of my thinking shifts to itching. The nurse assures me this is a sign of healing. Another doctor shows up, the part of the cast involving my right leg is sawed off, and the knee inspected. The doctor doesn't like what he sees and I am scheduled for another trip to surgery.

This doctor is a mere captain, not a lifer but a civilian in for the war who looks upon me as an interested participant in what's happening. He tells me that when the mine exploded under my left foot most of the damage was done there. But it also blew off the sole of the left boot and slammed it through three layers of pants and two layers of underwear into my right knee, dislocating same and making a rip about fifteen inches long down to the bone. Cloth, rubber, dirt, and etc., had to be dug out to close this wound, not enough skin and flesh was left to cover it properly, and healing wasn't going well. Therefore some skin was going to be borrowed off my buttocks. It would be used for a skin graft covering the knee and a smaller gap where the flesh had been blown off the heel of my left foot.

This ward had a tradition that no patient would be sent off to surgery without his fellows gathering at his bedside to hold a wake. The commissioned medical staff forbid this custom as insulting to them and contrary to good medical practice. However virtually everyone in the ward was a combat infantryman (the two exceptions were a tanker and an artillery forward observer) and the wakes went on anyway after the nurses had left. At these wakes, ambulatory patients would gather around the bed of the fellow due to go under the knife, discuss his character, and regale him with awful stories of ineptitude in military operating rooms (wrong organs tinkered with, arm removed instead of leg, and so forth). They would also establish "dibs" on his various possessions in the event he didn't come back alive and compose a letter to his family describing his sins and shortcomings. The only nurse who didn't consider this tradition barbarous was an old-timer captain. She thought it an antidote against self-pity—the worst danger in any ward full of badly damaged young males.

April came and hurried the healing along. The cast of characters in the ward became friends. The poker game that began after breakfast each morning on the next bed engulfed me in a fog of tobacco smoke. Except for chain smoking once to work my fever up to hospital levels I was a nonsmoker. I bitched and whined about the secondhand smoke, was persuaded that it wouldn't bother me if I smoked myself, was provided free Luckies, and quickly got myself addicted. I was welcomed into the game (a one-franc limit affair) and became even more quickly addicted to seven-card stud. (I am proud to report that I financed my stay in the Third General by that game—the Army payroll people having lost track of me— and had almost a hundred bucks accumulated before they sent me home.)

Eventually the body cast came off, replaced by a left boot cast and a soft cast on my right knee. I have two memories of that day. The first was the escape of my remodeled left foot into fresh air and daylight. Months and months of endless walking had produced a layer of callus on the bottom of my foot about as tough as a horse's hoof. Weeks in the cast had caused this to detach. The surgical tech fished out this remarkable artifact and held it close enough to my good eye so I could admire it. It also drew a crowd of ambulatory patients, interested in a size ten-and-a-half foot that was as pink and puckered as a newborn babe's butt and missing much of the meat on the side of the heel. This had been sort of rebuilt by the surgeon and covered with a skin graft. I couldn't really focus on that distant foot as yet but my friends rated it a good job. They didn't notice, and neither did I until I bought my first pair of civilian shoes, that the Army surgeon had rebuilt it to Army specifications. That gave it a loftier arch than my normal foot and problems for shoe salesmen.

The second memory is of the loudest scream ever heard in that hospital ward. Free at last from the body cast and the safety it provided, I allowed the still wet and heavy-as-lead boot cast to slip off the bed. It fell, bending a knee that hadn't been bent since the explosion dislocated it months before. Hurt? You bet!

But now I was mobile—the operator of a wheelchair. I would roll it outside, sit in the soft spring sunlight of Provence, and dream my dreams. One phase of life was finished for me. Boyhood was behind me. What lay ahead? I didn't have a clue. If I was blind and partially crippled the government would probably provide something. I don't remember worrying about it. The left eye still registered nothing but light and shadow but the right one was clearing. Maybe I would have one good eye. What more did you need? One happy day I looked down at the new edition of *Stars and Stripes* the orderly had dropped on my lap and saw METZ FALLS. True, the type was huge, but I had deciphered it myself. (Forty years later in Paris my editor at Rivages asked what cities I'd like to visit on a book-signing tour. I said Metz, told him about the day I knew I'd be able to read again, and he sent me to a bookstore there.)

The next step forward came with crutches.

If the wheelchair opened the ward door, crutches opened the world. Late spring now and my right leg is in good shape except for a sometimes unreliable knee. After breakfast, Alex, Dino, and I would don our blue bathrobes and head down the hill to Aix, sit on the benches under the plane trees that lined the boulevard, watch the French go by, and talk about the meaning of it all.

Alex was big, strong, extremely angry, and perfectly mobile. He had been a high school footballer at Louisville, Kentucky, went into the infantry, was sent as a replacement in a Forty-fifth Division rifle squad, and lasted about six weeks as a rifleman until he lost a close-range duel with a German in a Alsatian village, looking over a windowsill to get a shot and being hit in the mouth by a five-round burst from a machine pistol. Three of the 9 mm bullets had exited through the back of his neck, a fourth had been dug out of the neck muscle by the surgeon, and the fifth, and part of some of his teeth, were still there—too close to the spinal column to tinker with. The bullets had done havoc to Alex's gums and tongue and his anger may have been principally the product of frustration—trying to teach himself to talk again. However, I suspect it went deeper than that.

Dino's family ran a three-truck moving and storage company somewhere on the nether side of Patterson, New Jersey, and Dino was full of funny stories. Some involve the misadventures of his dad as a mover, and some the weird events of the previous December, when a German panzer army came smashing through the green 100th Division (in which Dino was a rifle squad leader), en route to Bastogne. The one I remember best was his account of trying to get what was left of his squad to safety. Coming down the safe side of about the third hill they'd been chased over by German armor, they saw four U.S. tank destroyers parked, with their crews sitting around a fire cooking bacon from ten-in-one boxes. Dino and the two riflemen remaining came puffing up, shouting warnings—which were greeted with scorn and derision. So Dino and his companions continued their flight up their hill, heard cannon fire, looked around to see German panzers rolling down the road below and the tank destroyer crews running frantically in the opposite direction. Although Dino lost his right leg from the hip down in a later phase of this encounter, he treasured his memory of the tank destroyer crewmen running for their lives.

Dino had an advantage in this pastime of observing French culture flowing past our boulevard bench. Missing most of his tongue, Alex could comment on what he was seeing only by indecipherable grunts, sighs, and groans. And I was working with a patch over my left eye and a peculiar problem with tear ducts involving the right. I could see fairly well while looking down, but a moment or two after I looked up, that eye would be flooded with tears. My companions dealt with this by counting down when something well worth seeing was approaching, so I could time my three seconds of clear vision for maximum benefit. Thus I saw many a pretty French maiden strolling past, and thus we passed the time waiting for healing to happen and a hospital ship to arrive to haul us home.

I spent March through July in the Third General and accumulated—though I wasn't aware of it at the time—some of the sort of knowledge of human behavior in stressful circumstances that writers need. Some wise but unwritten rule barred any sign or sound of sympathy from that ward—as witnessed by the presurgery wake tradition. You never saw anyone flinch or turn away when a new arrival checked in with half his face shot away. When the sergeant two beds down came back from surgery noticeably missing the right arm he'd hoped could be saved, he was welcomed back with shouts of "Lefty" and told where to buy single-hand glove sets. The tank gunner with part of his nose and all of his ears burned off was called "Jug" by everyone. From each side of his neck protruded what seemed to be a jug handle but was actually a fleshy tube of skin, which had been pinched up from the flesh of his neck and stitched off. When healed, the lower end of these appendages was cut free, bent upward, and grafted on again, a couple of inches closer to the ear hole where, eventually, they would provide the skin and flesh for substitute ears. Jug received endless warnings. The surgeon intended to walk both of these appendages to the top of his head as anchors for a wig (his hair was burned off). The surgeon had miscalculated, the loops would come up short, and new ear holes would have be drilled. And so forth. Jug seemed to enjoy this.

Under this determined callousness there lay an odd kind of

love. I think of Corporal Delaney, whose bed was just across the aisle from mine—foot to foot. A shell fragment had gone through one of Delaney's eyeballs and into his brain. It had left him paralyzed and speechless, unable to even squeak or groan, and able to move only his eyelids and his eyes. (Eyes up and down equaled yes. Eyes left and right equaled no. Eyes looking right equaled need something. Eyes looking left equaled discomfort.) Through that system one of the ambulatory patients who read to him discovered Delaney was a smoker and that he liked to watch our poker game. So Delaney was propped up so he could watch, and cigarettes were lit for him, with someone keeping an eye on it, extracting it from his lips to knock off the ashes and disposing of it when it had burned short.

Delaney played an essential role. No matter the pain or loss another felt, his plight made complaining impossible. The rifleman hit in the groin by a shell fragment and left crippled and emasculated could look at him and thank God. Even Alex, struggling with his anger and trying to teach his butchered tongue to speak, signaled us to pray for Delaney.

Pray, I'm sure, some of us did—if not in any organized fashion—and one day we were rewarded by a sort of a miracle. The game was seven-card stud. One player had two pair showing, another had a possible straight, a third had aces paired with a flush possible. The pot had become the biggest of day with the final down card yet to come. Everybody was watching, including the fellow who should have been watching Delaney. First we heard a tiny squeak. Then something louder carrying a note of protest came from Delaney's bed. Everyone jumps up. The cigarette has burned to Delaney's lip.

Delaney was calling for help!

The cigarette was extracted, nurse summoned, doctor called; for the first time Delaney managed something with his facial expression, which we decided to call a grin. And then he produced another series of squeaks for us. Whatever the end result of this, it excited the neurologist. When I bade Delaney farewell at the end of June, he had regained a little hand motion and making sounds had become easy for him.

Since the subject has turned to prayer, this seems the appropriate place to mention the lack of it. If any sort of religious service was held at that hospital in the months I was there I can't remember hearing of it. Once or twice when we were in reserve too far from the fighting to hear artillery fire we saw a chaplain—but never closer than that. I eventually located a priest at the hospital and asked him to hear my confession. He did, listening to a recitation of those violations of morality I might have committed had the opportunity permitted. I also told him of killing the German soldier on the road at Sessenheim. Somehow it didn't seem necessary to mention those I might have killed with Shakeshaft's borrowed hand grenade, nor the unseen victims of countless rounds of my mortar fire. He granted me absolution without comment—tired I'm sure of such accounts.

I always wondered who invented the absurd lie that proclaimed there were "no atheists in foxholes." Where else could atheism better thrive than in the killing fields where homicide was honored? In the Third General Hospital at Aix, the poker game was about as religious as things got.

Incidentally, if records are kept on such sports events, that poker game might hold the longevity crown. It was going on when I first gained consciousness in my body cast sometime in March and operated without interruption until the day when the senior nurse walked in and announced that President Roosevelt had died. She instructed all who were ambulatory to report up the hill for a memorial service. She looked in later, found us still engrossed in a hand, and repeated that order with emphasis. When she peeked in a third time with the game still going she impounded our cards.

About the time we obtained another deck and got the game revived under a more lenient nurse the good news came. Jubilation swept through the ward. A hospital ship was due to take home those well enough to make the trip.

Well enough? Anxiety replaced joy. Who would be on the shipping list. We got the word more or less one by one—from the enlisted medical corpsmen who got a peek at our charts. I was due one more trip to surgery for some work on my left ankle joint, which made me doubtful. But the joyful word came down that this would be left to stateside surgeons. Private First Class Anthony Grove Hillerman was going to make the list. Good-bye, Third General. Hello, home. (Wherever that was going to be.)

I had made good friends at Third General and I would miss them, but I wouldn't miss what we called "Night Music." A shout would jerk you suddenly awake. Tense, sweating, all those well-honed combat survival instincts demanding action, but now hearing only the usual breathing, snoring, coughing, and occasional moan produced by a room full of injured men. Then a shout again. "Get down! Get down!" Then "Go. Go. In trees. Over there." Dino, the perpetual squad leader, screaming at his men, getting as many as he could out of mortar fire or something. Then Dino would be silent, but the sound of combat had spread like a ripple down the double row of beds—bringing troubled dreams to the surface. Startled yells, whimpering, someone summoning his mom in a hoarse whisper, someone praying. And you'd lie in that noisy darkness, knowing that as long as the body cast encased you, you were safe, happy to be rescued from your own nightmare, listening and thanking your loving God for rescuing you from the horror with your Zone of Interior wound.

Another scene printed on my brain before I left beautiful Aix-en-Provence came the day I was ordered to mount my crutches and report to the headquarters building. There I was put in a room with three other eye patients, waited the usual hour or so, and then was called into another room in which a large number of well-dressed, well-pressed, well-fed captains, majors, and colonels were sitting. My own doctor (a major) removed the little pink plastic patch I was then wearing over my left eye, explained to the assembly what had been done for me at the clearing station, the process of removing as much debris from the eyeballs and sockets as practical, and the treatment decision.

He told the group that the plan was to delete the left eyeball because it was considered beyond salvation and so badly infected that it represented a threat to the right eye—which then might be salvaged. However, said this major, he had decided that this newly available penicillin had been proving so effective in killing bacteria that he would try to save both eyes. And indeed, it had worked. The assembled brass were invited to come up to take a look at how well this gamble had paid off. I was halfway back to the ward before it occurred to me how I had been used, with neither my knowledge nor consent, in a medical experiment. Two eyeballs the prize if it worked, a life of blindness the price if it didn't. Even then, at nineteen, it seemed to me that this was betting a minor inconvenience against an almost total disability. Now, having gotten along very well for fifty-six years with useful vision in only one eye, it seems to me the major might have at least asked my opinion. But no son of August Alfred Hillerman was conditioned to bear a grudge. Papa wouldn't tolerate it.

Papa was just as opposed to us bearing grudges as Mama was to us being afraid of anything and I can understand why I was used as a guinea pig. While the war in Europe was almost over Army medicine faced the prospect of the invasion of the Japanese mainland. The military expected a million American casualties as the price of that. Thank God for the atomic bomb and President Truman's decision to use it. It spared us and the Japanese from that dreadful slaughter, but my eye doctor had no way of knowing that would happen. He had to be ready to deal with more burned eyeballs.

If I hadn't been conditioned against grudges, what happened when the hospital ship arrived gave me ammunition for one I could have brooded over for years. The chief ward orderly trotted in after breakfast, shouted for attention, announced those of us ruled fit to travel were about to be hauled down to the docks at Marseilles. He would now read off the names of the departees. No surprises were expected. We had already heard by then that all of us were going except a poor fellow who had just come down with some sort of fever.

The orderly read the list. My name wasn't on it.

As Mama had said those who expect little are seldom disappointed. I wasn't exactly disappointed. I was crushed. Devastated. Watching the ward empty out provided the bleakest moments of my life. Even the guy with the fever went, the beneficiary I learned later of the careless clerk-typist who stuck his name in instead of mine. For about a week the only nightmare noises disrupting sleep in the ward were my own, but soon shipments of wounded came in from the final breakthrough battles. Germany surrendered, another hospital ship arrived, and I was homeward bound at last.

Many years later it dawned on me that this fortuitous typo changed the direction of my life. The three-week delay put me exactly on a collision course with two Navajo Marines just back from the Pacific war and with the Enemy Way ceremonial their family was holding to return them to harmony with their people. That put me in contact with the people I would love to write about. As every traditional Navajo understands, all things are connected, every cause has its destined effect, the wings of a butterfly bend the wind, the fingers tapping the wrong typewriter keys change a life.

But now I was on a list for a later ship. Now I must report to the hospital supply room and go through the process of checking out an entire new U.S. Army wardrobe from shoes to helmet, stuffing all this into a duffle bag, and getting it back down to the ward. We board a hospital bus and head for the docks. There, my crutches are taken from me, I climb aboard a stretcher, am carried up the gangplank, and deposited on a bunk in one of the ship's hospital wards. My new duffle bag is checked into the ship's storeroom, I am issued a cane to replace the crutches and away we go.

Not much need be said about the voyage. The ship was small, very slow, manned by a disgruntled merchant marine crew, and its age was suggested by a brass plaque mounted in a passageway. That declared it had been recommissioned in 1917 but gave no clue of when it had been originally commissioned. One of the crewmen claimed it had done its first duty sailing up the Missouri River during the Indian Wars. He said he had signed on in 1942 when the vessel was being refitted and a sign in the dining space said:

> PASSENGERS MUST REFRAIN
> FROM SHOOTING BUFFALO
> FROM THE PORTHOLES

The crewmen told us they had brought the ship over to serve those wounded in the North African fighting and stayed for the battles for Sicily and Italy and hadn't been home since. That didn't provoke any sympathy among their boatload of wounded grunts. But, alas, it seemed the last restocking of the ship's pantry also dated back to 1942. The principal menu items were entrees based on overaged powdered eggs. We were also warned that while the Third Reich's Army had surrendered, the German submarines hadn't got the word and we puttered out past Gibraltar and into the Atlantic with great floodlights illuminating the red crosses painted on our sides. For the voyage home the Atlantic was as placid as it had been stormy on the outward journey—good because our crew assured us that this boat would sink without a bubble in any kind of rough weather and they all intended to jump ship as soon as we got within swimming distance of land. I can't remember any of this worrying anyone. What the hell! We were going home. We lolled in deck chairs in the sun and watched the porpoises play.

Home proved to be an Army hospital on Long Island, where my cane was exchanged for crutches and I was handed back my duffle bag. I lugged this to the hospital supply room and checked in all the brand-new soldier gear, and got a new set of pajamas and blue robe to replace the ones worn on the hospital ship. The stop here was brief but produced two memorable incidents. I made my very first telephone call and the Army gave another demonstration of the truth behind the axiom: "There are two ways of doing things. The right way and the Army way."

The telephone call happened because the Red Cross handed each of us a voucher entitling us to one free long distance call any-where in America. It was my first call because there was only one telephone in Sacred Heart (at Papa's store, which was also the post office) and I had never had cause to use it for the simple reason I knew no one who had a telephone.

I still didn't know anyone with a telephone, but I did remember the name of the operator of the rooming house where Mama was living. I called her and asked her to tell Mama I was back in the States safe and sound and would be seeing her as soon as I could get a pass. Then I was almost ready to experience the Army's special way of getting its troops home.

The Army first checked us all out health-wise. Then we are sent back to the supply room, issued a fresh barracks bag in which to stuff a complete new set of soldiering clothing and gear identical to the one we'd checked in when we got off the ship. That done, we were sorted by place or origin. Nothing now but wait for an avail-able hospital train. One arrived. Residents of Texas and residents of Oklahoma were segregated. We lugged our duffle bags to the bus, were hauled down to the tracks and put aboard an engine-and-three-car train. Texans were placed in the front car and Oklahomans in the second car. The third car housed the kitchen, infirmary, pharmacy, medical personnel, and our duffle bags. Off we went, and rarely has a group made a more leisurely and luxuri-ous journey from Long Island to the Mexican border.

The cars were new, with their hospital bunks lined along great glass windows. Lots of space, air conditioning, and the best food we'd tasted since our draft boards put us on buses. Naturally such trains had bottom of the list priority on a rail system jammed beyond capacity by efforts to get millions of European Theater of Operations troops across the nation and sent off to invade Japan. So we wandered across the midwest, spending hours on sidings, and more hours in city rail yards watching the important trains roar by, playing cards, getting acquainted, discussing what we'd do when we returned to the real world (young women were heavily involved in this), swapping war stories, trying to top one another's tales of Army ineptitudes. This was not the place for accounts of either horror or heroism. These guys were almost 100 percent combat infantry. They been there. Done that. Didn't want to hear about it. Save the baloney for the rear echelon troops, the flyboys, and the civilians.

Long stop at Pratt, Kansas—home of my original squad leader, who had assured us that the sign on the highway declared that his town was: THE ONLY PRATT IN KANSAS. See neither that nor the sergeant. An orderly comes in and tells us one car will soon be switched to go to the hospital at Chickasha, Oklahoma. The other will continue to William Beaumont General at Fort Bliss, Texas. This sounds wonderful to me, an Okie. Chickasha is not only fairly close to Oklahoma City it is the home of Oklahoma College for Women—a known hotbed of young ladies. We stop again in Oklahoma City, some switching takes place, and we roll again, now missing our car full of Texans. It shouldn't be long now, I think, Chickasha is just an hour or so south. But, alas, it was not to be. The Army has again done it the Army way. We are heading southeast toward El Paso, Texas. The Texans are being deposited in Oklahoma and we Okies in the far and furtherist corner of the immense Lone Star State.

William Beaumont is a nice old hospital. I got Mama on the phone that evening, told her I'd be seeing her any day—just as soon as I could get a furlough—and the word was combat disabled people were getting sixty days. I get to keep my duffle bag this time, am issued a cane, and try to walk without a limp—hoping to persuade those who make such decisions that any additional surgery needed can be delayed. The Red Cross is teaching a typing course. I take a lesson, get acquainted with the clerk in our building, and practice on her typewriter. The officer of the day summons me and hands me a stand-by ticket good for Army aircraft with room for hitchhikers and a thirty-day furlough. I tell him I'm combat wounded, should get the sixty-day version. He tells me thirty days are now the maximum. I leave full of resentment.

On the way to the OD's office I paused under a tree to watch a Medical Corps lieutenant deal with a problem. He had been marching a dozen or so patients down the street. He halted them, left them "at ease" on the street, and disappeared into an adjoining building for a couple of minutes. His charges then sprawled on the grass in the shade. The lieutenant emerged, ordered his group to fall in. A couple bounced up but most of them took their time. The lieutenant must have felt challenged by this and raised his voice. Wrong decision. These guys were not regular Army. They were citizen soldiers, just back from the foxholes, thoroughly sick of West Point ways. They sat back down again. The lieutenant yelled some more. They ignored him. A staff sergeant going by in a Jeep stopped, watched this minor mutiny for a moment, then got out, walked over, saluted the lieutenant, chatted awhile, then squatted in the shade with the mutineers and chatted with them. They got up, fell in, and marched off with the lieutenant. End of mutiny but a wonderful expression of good old free American citizenry.

With that example in mind, I took my furlough papers to the ward office, borrowed the secretary's typewriter for a moment, erased the "30," typed in "60," and went on my way.

Bus ride to Okie City and great reunion with Mama and Margaret Mary, whose husband was still in Europe with his artillery unit. I learn Barney had volunteered out of his glider unit when gliders were no longer needed and volunteered into the infantry, thinking he had a deal made to join me as a replacement in my unit. It didn't work, of course, and he landed in the Forty-fifth Division—busy preparing for the Japanese invasion. (Years later I learn that when he got word I'd been wounded, he tracked me down to the Third General, went Absent Without Leave, hitch-hiked without a pass across Europe, and actually got to the hospital only to find I'd sailed away. Quite a big brother, I had.)

It took about three days to begin wondering why I wanted the sixty-day furlough. The only two humans I knew in Oklahoma were my mother and sister—both of whom were working through the day. Mama's landlady let me sleep on a sofa but I had no place of my own to hang my hat. The family's old sedan still ran and I bought six gallons of gas with a couple of Mama's hoard of gasoline ration coupons and drove down to the farm. August is not the season to see any farm—and an abandoned one looks even worse than most. I drove into Konawa and confirmed what I expected—my peers had gone to war. I had a sad, sad milk shake at the soda fountain in Bates Pharmacy. Then I left that empty, lonely town, finally facing the fact that nothing would ever be the way it had been. I drove back to Oklahoma City and started looking for a job.

In the United States in August 1945, not finding a job would have been downright impossible. The state employment office told me to report the next morning at a small neighborhood garage not far from the state capitol. To kill time until then I called the news-room of the *Daily Oklahoman* and introduced myself to Beatrice Stahl. Ms. Stahl, a feature writer, had received one of those press releases the Army sends out to regional papers when someone in their circulation zone is decorated. She had called Mama, who told her I had since been wounded, that I had also been awarded a Bronze Star in addition to the Silver one, and gave her the kind of reports mothers give about sons. Mama seems to have also recited a few paragraphs from some of my letters. Ms. Stahl borrowed them and said she'd like to talk to me when I got home.

Thoughtful readers must have been wondering how the events in the Sessenheim Forest could have caused the Army to honor me with a Silver Star. They may also wonder how Beatrice Stahl's arti-cle could have inspired me, who had never seen a writer, to decide to become one. Therefore I will include it here. Please note the difference between the action as described from my memory on pages 122 and 123 and the way an Army clerk imagined it back in regimental headquarters when he typed up the citation. Ms. Stahl's use of this to convert me into a sort of Horatio at the Bridge was persuasive evidence of the power of the pen.

So we talked. Ms. Stahl said what she'd seen in those letters suggested that I should be a writer. A writer? I'd never known one, seen one, even heard of an actual live one. How did one go about it? One went to journalism school, she said. And thus the seed was planted.

But back to the garage. The owner looked at the cane I was leaning on, the pink plastic patch over my bum eye, and assigned me to change the brake linings on a LaSalle sedan. I told him I didn't know how. He told me anyone can change brake pads, and showed me how it was done. I did it, and started doing the same sort of job on a Ford. The LaSalle owner reclaimed his vehicle, drove away, returned within minutes with all wheels smoking and began screaming at the boss. The boss told me he was having a hole dug under his house for a basement and the men he'd hired to dig had just quit. Was I better with a shovel than a wrench? Bad leg, I said, and just out of five months in the hospital, but I'd try. So I shoveled, got a day's pay, and came back the next day to continue. But the bells, whistles, and sirens sounded. Japan had surrendered. The war was over. Everyone quit work and I caught a ride downtown to join the celebration.

Not everyone was celebrating. I joined a Marine corporal sitting at a Main and Broadway bus stop and we talked about why we didn't feel happier. We didn't solve that so we talked about what we'd do now. Neither one of us knew but I spent a moment or two trying to imagine myself as a writer—whatever that might be.

That night I went downtown again to see what was happening. A band was playing at the USO center and when a very slow tune came along I limped over to a girl sitting by the wall and asked her to dance. Her name was Barbara, she was tall, had freckles and very long, very shiny red hair. She asked me about my leg. I told her, and she told me she lived with her father and was enrolling as a freshman at the University of Oklahoma. When the USO shut down for the evening I took her home on the trolley and we made a date for the next day. Her father was home when I came to pick her up. He said he had a bunch of drill stem and other oil field equipment he needed to get out to the Navajo Reservation for work on a shut-down oil well he was trying to revive. Could I drive a truck? I said I could learn. Could I go tomorrow? Why not?

Those of you who remember Jack Kerouac's classic *On the Road* and its madcap 110-miles-per-hour race across the American West with crazy Dean Moriarity behind the wheel should begin imagining the exact opposite. We formed a caravan of two worn-out trucks, credible only to those old enough to remember the days of gasoline and rubber rationing when vehicles were kept running with bailing wire and hope. I'll call Barbara's dad Roger, a burly short-tempered Irishman. He drove the first truck, pulling a flatbed trailer overloaded with pipe and steel drill stem. I drove something smaller, carrying odds and ends, with Barbara as passenger. We didn't drive fast, because Roger's truck would barely creep up long hills and one of my duties was to pull over, jump out, and serve as a sort of human emergency brake, limping along behind his vehicle on the steeper slopes, ready to slide blocks behind his wheels when his tired old engine demanded a rest. One of Barbara's jobs was to keep truck number two rolling along behind while this was being done. Another was to keep me awake when exhaustion set in. Because while Roger couldn't drive fast, he drove consistently. We stopped for gasoline, to refill radiators, check oil, grab a loaf of bread and baloney. No rest stops. One relieved oneself at gasoline stations and one slept a few minutes here and there when something stopped us.

Oil field people seem good at this postponing sleep until next week when duty calls. Barney developed the skill when he worked as a petroleum geologist and well-logger. One of my future wife's uncles could go sleepless for days. I never developed that ability, and I certainly didn't have it in August 1945, after spending month after sleepy month in hospital beds. The point of this paragraph is that while creeping up Nine Mile Hill, which runs from the Highway 66 bridge over the Rio Grande in Albuquerque toward Grants, I went to sleep.

I had been tagging along behind Truck One at maybe eight miles per hour. I dozed. Barbara was snoozing on her side of the seat. Truck One slowed. Truck Two didn't. Whammo!! Luckily Truck Two had drifted far enough to the right so that the pipes sticking rearward from the Truck One flatbed missed the windshield and the only serious damage was done to Roger's opinion of me—diminished at an earlier fuel stop when I forgot to restore the dipstick after checking the crankcase oil. Barbara and I had already run out of things to talk about and she (did I mention she was an intelligent girl?) seemed to be wondering what in the world had ever caused her to find me interesting. We finished the U.S. 66 part of the drive mostly in moody silence, turned off at Thoreau onto what was then a dirt road, and headed north toward Crownpoint, the Chaco Canyon country.

And fate.

Just south of Borrego Pass, a dozen or so horsemen emerge from the piñons up the slope. I stop and watch them cross the road ahead and disappear down an arroyo.

We had been driving through Navajo Reservation land for hours, seeing Navajos who, to no surprise to a kid raised among Indians, dressed just like rural folks everywhere else. But these riders were obviously dressed for a ceremony, and the leader of the group was carrying what looked like a flag of some sort on something which, had he been a Kiowa or Comanche, I would have called a "coup stick." I was immensely interested and curious.

The well site where we eventually unloaded our cargo was near (five miles is near out here) the place of a white rancher. He rode up on his horse to find out what's happening. I ask him about the group of horsemen. He tells me the delegation I saw was the "stick carrier's camp" bringing some necessary elements to an Enemy Way ceremony. He's heard this was being held for a couple of Navajo boys just back from fighting the Japanese with the Marines. The ceremony was an Enemy Way to cure them of the evil influences they've encountered being involved with so much death, and to restore them to harmony with their people. I keep asking questions. He says why not go see it. They last about nine days and if the stick carrier was just getting there today it would be still going on through tomorrow night. Would I be welcome? Sure, he says, if I don't drink whiskey and behave myself.

Thus I got to see a wee bit of an Enemy Way without knowing what I was watching nor that the memory of it would provide the best section of my first novel. (I named it *The Enemy Way* but my editor for reasons beyond my ken changed that to *The Blessing Way*.)

The next day, Roger's opinion of me was again diminished when I dropped my end of a pipe we were unloading, causing his end to bounce out of his hands and land on his toes. He paid me my salary and sent Barbara to drive me back out to Thoreau. From there I hitched back to Oklahoma City to while away what was left of my self-esteem and furlough time.

In the final week of that period Larry Grove made it back from the Pacific war and was deposited in the Navy hospital at Norman—about twenty-five miles south. I hurried down to see him.

Larry was my cousin, the youngest son of Uncle Chris Grove, the good buddy of my adolescent years and a dedicated romantic. He played end on the Konawa Tigers football team, first base on the Tiger baseball team (I was second-string guard, and substitute right fielder respectively), and we understood each other. From grade school days each of us would read anything we could get our hands on. He had considered becoming a priest but dropped that idea. After high school, he got a job in a plant at Pryor, intending to save enough to get himself started in college and eventually become a surgeon.

My first look at him in the hospital ward saw that idea wasn't going to work. Larry had responded to Pearl Harbor by joining the Marine Corps. In one of those back-and-forth struggles for high ground on Okinawa a Japanese "knee mortar" shell had hit his foxhole buddy on the helmet, blowing off the fellow's head and riddling Larry with shrapnel. It cut away part of his hand, mangled his wrist, and caused other less crucial damage here and there. Of all my boyhood friends, Larry was the wittiest and his wit tended toward self-deprecation.

For example: Larry shows me what remains of his hand. He notes where a finger had been and tells me the morning before the jump-off to recapture some hill for about the third time, the company commander tells everybody to quit being such sissies and stop calling for a corpsman if they can take care of the wound themselves. So Larry, slammed into the bottom of the foxhole by the explosion and covered with pieces of his buddy, decides he will convert himself from sissy to Marine Corps Semper Fi hero. He starts inspecting his own wounds. "I hold up this finger to see why it's just hanging down," Larry tells me. "I turn it loose. It falls off. You could hear me screaming for a corpsman all the way to the beachhead."

It was a fateful meeting. What are we going to do now? Not a clue beyond both of us knowing that we won't be farmers if we can help it. When Larry's finger dropped to the bottom of his foxhole his dream of becoming a surgeon dropped with it. I have let self-knowledge rescue me from my odd notion of becoming a chemical engineer. I tell him what Beatrice Stahl had told me about writing. When I left the hospital, we'd decided we will take advantage of the GI Bill, enroll at the University of Oklahoma, and convert ourselves into journalists.

Barney comes home from the war and we drive the tired old sedan to the home place. Barney is a sergeant, wearing the famous Forty-fifth Division Thunderbird patch, but he can hardly wait to be a civilian farmer-rancher. He suggests we take our military separation pay, add it to what went into the bank when the cattle, etc., were sold, buy bred heifers, concentrate on raising alfalfa and cattle feed, sign up for GI Bill programs designed to get soldiers back into farming. Then we will begin to expand our hay and grazing lands by buying worn-out and abandoned farms. More and more people will be starving out of these little submarginal places and looking for buyers. We can get credit. We can put together a substantial ranch/cattle feed operation.

Barney had a good idea. I'm fairly sure it would have worked. But it fell on deaf ears. Little brother didn't want the risk. Little brother therefore pointed to the problem. The price of beef had soared. Thus cattle I had happily sold for $12.77 a hundredweight, we'd be buying back at triple that price. That meant we'd have to start with too few cattle to make a living. The first year would be pretty much without income, devoted to repairing the damage to the property by three seasons without attention. Finally, I didn't want to be a farmer.

One of the several things I'd liked about the Army was the security. Room, board, clothing, and a paycheck every month with nothing to worry about except, if you were in the infantry, maybe getting killed. No getting up in the morning to see the worms wiping out your cotton crop, or looking at a field of sweet potatoes not worth harvesting because no one would buy them, or your berry crop rotting for the same reason, or any of those thousand fiascos that turn springtime bliss to autumn gloom among tillers of the soil.

Okay, Barney said. No problem. I see your point. No rush to

make a decision. So we walked down the section line to the eighty Papa had bought to take a look at how time had treated three of Barney's projects. The fence was still there, built to last. The other two hadn't fared well.

The creek we were straightening had returned to its old crooked ways, with floods from torrential rains cutting it deeper and ruining more bottomland. The Johnson grass we'd spent a hot summer repeatedly plowing out had come back with a vengeance. I think it was that, more than the creek, that finally dampened Barney's optimism.

When the Army discharged him, and we huddled with Mama and Margaret Mary to make family plans, the decision disconnected us forever from agriculture and, sadly, from Sacred Heart. Mama sold the farm and bought a little frame bungalow in Norman. We'd live there while Barney and I became two of the millions of G.I. Bill students flooding colleges.

Before that could happen I had to get back to Fort Bliss, the William Beaumont General Hospital, turn in my furlough papers, and get through the ankle operation I was scheduled to undergo. I go to Tinker Air Force Base, show the proper people my free ride ticket, and get the word that no aircraft coming through there is going to Biggs Air Force Base at El Paso until the next day. So I come back the following day, a bit nervous now because this will make me a day late, which will cause the sentry to call the officer of the day, who will actually look at my questionable sixty-day furlough. I board the plane with two other returnees. It's a C-47 cargo plane and it lands at Dallas. Some more cargo has to be loaded and our trip to El Paso will be completed on the morrow. The next morning we reboard (now two days late). We fly southwestward— the right direction—and land at something called Coyote Field. There some of the boxes and bundles we've been sitting on are unloaded and replaced with other larger boxes and pieces of machinery. We take off again, and fly, and fly, and fly. Our knowledge of the geography of West Texas, while limited, finally tells us three hitchhikers that even at the lumbering speed of an overloaded C-47 we should have been at Biggs Air Force Base long ago. No way to find out what's going on because our way to the pilots' compartments is blocked by stacks of cargo. Finally we land at Phoenix.

Sorry, the pilot tells us. The cargo loaded at Coyote had higher priority than three grunt hitchhikers. He has to take it on to an airfield near Los Angeles. He'll drop us off at Biggs on the way back. When? He shrugs. The other two hitchhikers, who presumably had legal furlough papers to turn in, decide they'll fly along to California. I climb off, take my bag, bum a ride out to the highway and start hitchhiking—now about a hundred miles farther from the hospital than when I started the journey. When I finally arrive at the sentry post at the hospital gate I am guilty of being Absent Without Leave for four days. Or sixty-four, depending on how hard you look at my furlough papers.

The sentry asks me how I managed to get a sixty-day furlough, tells me I'm late, and sends me over to report to the officer of the day.

The OD is sitting behind a desk. He looks at my furlough, at me, and says: "Sixty-day furlough?" I shrug. He says: "Four days AWOL, then. What's the excuse?"

Perhaps the Army has changed by now, but at mid-century there was only one proper answer when an officer asked an enlisted man if he had an excuse and I knew it. I said: "No sir."

He is pleased to hear that, a good sign. I have already noticed two other good signs. He is not wearing a West Point class ring and he is wearing a Combat Infantry Badge. He says: "How'd you get a sixty-day furlough? They quit giving them." I shake my head, look baffled, shrug again—all correct answers since enlisted men aren't supposed to know such things.

"Well," he says. "You're four days late anyway. We can't have that." And he marks through the sixty I'd typed, and writes in "sixty-four," hands me back my papers and tells me where to take them to get four more days of rations money. Once again the brotherhood of the combat infantry has transcended Army foolishness.

Nothing left now but to check in with my doctor. He looks me over and schedules my ankle surgery. I'm sent down to the presurgery ward, given the presurgery sleeping pills. I doze off, happy in the knowledge that when I awaken it will be tomorrow, the knifework will be finished, I'll be in the recovery room, bandaged up, healing, and finally on the slippery slope toward civilianhood and home.

But I awake with a medical service corporal standing there, telling me to get dressed and report to headquarters. What's happened to the surgery? No idea. I report to the headquarters building. A Medical Corps officer tells me I am being discharged. He gives me a bunch of papers, sends me to another building, where I get some accumulated back pay, my discharge money, a manila envelope holding the necessary documents, and the "ruptured duck"— the little faux-gold lapel pin representing an eagle and identifying wearers as honorably discharged from military service. The last stop was in the office of a weary-looking captain wearing the blue braid of the infantry. He looks at my eye patch and my cane. Did I want to sign up for enlistment in the Army Reserves? I said I didn't. He makes a note of that and tells me I am his eighty-seventh consecutive negative. Thus, a few minutes after noon on October 16, 1945, I became a bona fide twenty-year-old unemployed civilian with a notion that I'd become a journalist— whatever that might prove to be.

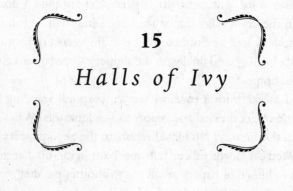

15

Halls of Ivy

The spring semester at OU didn't begin until late in January and the $90 per month largesse from the G.I. Bill didn't begin until one was legally enrolled. Meanwhile I need a job. Back in Oklahoma City, I called the employment office. This time I was sent to the owner of a little engineering company and became part of a surveying crew—another example of the effects of severe labor shortages on hiring practices.

I arrived with no idea of what I was applying for. The interviewer asked me how much experience I had running a transit. I said none. He said that's what we're hiring—a transit man on a surveying crew and the employment office told us you'd studied engineering. One semester, I said, but we hadn't got to surveying. Well, said he, I guess you could learn. So he gave me bus fare, a hotel address in Chickasha, and the name of the project chief to whom I should report. At the hotel, the project boss and I repeat the scene above. He takes me out on the street with a transit, spends a few minutes explaining how the thing works, decides I'm a slow learner and a poor risk. He will handle the transit himself and I can replace one of the chainmen who'd just quit.

Surveying crews, I learned, are a team of four. The transit man, the brains of the operation, peers through the telescope, fiddles adjustment knobs, and makes hand signals to the "pole man," who holds a long pole with a target on it. He moves the pole around in obedience to hand signals from the TM and when TM is satisfied, the PM marks the spot. (Since we were surveying a Rural Electrification Administration power line, these spots marked the places where a high line pole would be planted to support the electrical cables and are a long way apart.) The duties of the remaining two on this team—the chain draggers—require less skill. The lead man picks up one end of the chain and trudges (limps in my case, since I was still using a cane) off in a direct line from the last marked pole location to where the next pole is being located. The last man holds his end of the chain at the last pole site until the lead man runs out of chain. That point is then marked, and the process is repeated, thereby giving the transit man information about precisely how far it is between each pole.

Despite the limp (and partly because of it) dragging a chain through the cold autumn winds of central Oklahoma was the perfect job for me at the time. While it lacked the warmth and love represented by the healing ceremony for the wounded Marines I'd had a glimpse of on the Navajo Reservation it was what the psychiatrist would have ordered for a fellow who needed to do some forgetting. When the transit man stopped to work on his math, we'd gather dead wood, build a fire, warm ourselves, and talk. But the talk on this frozen ground wasn't of war and before long, back in bed in the walk-up Chickasha hotel, the dreams that came were simpler ones produced by honest fatigue. They no longer jerked me awake, sweating and yelling. Now and then I'd pass Sergeant Arras face-up in the ditch with the shells whistling in, or find myself standing on the cobblestones looking down into the helmet with the hair, brains, and eyeball in it, or trudging past the piles of dead horses still wearing their harness that the strafing P-47s had caught, but it didn't happen often. The brain was growing scar tissue over all that nonsense, and the legs were regaining their tough teenaged basic training muscles. Better still I could now usually eat breakfast without losing it within minutes to overpowering nausea. When I came back to Norman in January to enroll for the spring semester at OU I had slammed the trunk lid shut on most of those ghosts of bad moments and dead friends. I was ready for the University of Oklahoma and whatever was going to happen next.

The little frame house bought with Mama's farm sale money was on the wrong side of Norman's main street and about two miles from the campus. We moved a trailerload of stuff from the farm and established ourselves at this new address. Mama resumed her roles as family manager. Barney, his dreams of resuming farming demolished, decided to study geology. We became two of the flood of young men overwhelming America's campuses.

For a very short while classroom fashion was heavily olive drab skivvy shirts, field jackets, and combat boots. That lasted only until the vets had funds to match their hunger for slacks, sport coats, neckties, and the whole costume of upper-mobility. Years had been used up by the war. No time to waste now. Hurry, hurry. Find a spouse, get a job, start a family, get on with life. I had given myself five years to find a wife. Who? I didn't have a clue. I'd located my pre-Army girlfriend, we met and talked things over. Nothing came of that. I found the red-haired charmer from Oklahoma City, also now enrolled and living in an OU dorm. She had found another boyfriend. I was back to square one. Why worry? I intended to stay single until I put my twenty-fifth birthday behind me.

As statistics of the baby boomer years show, most vets were less patient. Surplus barracks buildings were hauled in by the hundreds to provide married student housing and the campuses swarmed with single men looking for wives—and outnumbering the coed prospects by about four to one. On fraternity row the Greek letter houses were taken over by squad leaders, tank commanders, and swabbies off the destroyers needing a place to sleep and lacking tolerance for the adolescent frat-hazing rituals. Classrooms occupied mostly by young women a year earlier were now crowded with men fresh out of the services. They brought a change in attitude.

The goal now was to maintain the "Gentlemanly C" and get that degree fast. (The C gave two grade points per credit hour, compared to three for a B and four for an A. If you made nothing but C's you had the 2.0 average needed for a bachelor's degree. If your average was higher than that you were "pushing up the curve" and making it tougher for your comrades.)

Two practices grew out of this attitude. The university prohibition against taking more than sixteen or eighteen credit hours per semester was commonly bypassed by enrolling in "correspondence courses" either at OU or at another university, with the credits earned transferred to your record. This could cut a semester or two off the 124 hours needed to get a degree. Those who had surplus grad points often enrolled in appealing courses for which they lacked the required prerequisites learning what they could and not worrying about flunking.

This was how I became acquainted with Morry, secretary-treasurer of the Communist Party of Oklahoma at the time, a former Navy yeoman and the son of a sharecropper in Oklahoma's most impoverished county. We enrolled in an upper-level philosophy course, skipping both the prerequisite courses and the exams. Morry wanted to get a better handle on the 1946 version of Marxism as seen by academia, and on Hegel, the other apostle of socialist statism. I hoped to get my own thinking sorted out on the subject of young men killing one another to the applause of their elders. But we weren't interested in credit hours.

I learned more from Morry in that course than I did from the professor. He droned through the roll call, seeming totally unaware that many students were answering to multiple names and never noticing that half the chairs were empty. No harm in that, but he also droned through his memorized lectures. From Morry's I learned something of pure pragmatism and political motivation.

Morry considered Hegel and Marx no brighter than our professor. However, the men who ran the party used their language and their slogans as the official jargon. These fellows had reached the top by knowing the theory and the buzzwords. Morry had joined the party while in the Navy, impressed with the Red Army's skill at killing Nazis. He said he thought communism had about one chance in eight to triumph in the United States. If it did, he would be an important person—the first one in his family as far back as he could trace it who had been more than an impoverished serf. If the Communists didn't make it, so what? He'd be no worse off than he would have been otherwise.

Aside from his frankness, he had other good qualities. He was remarkably good at auction bridge in the endless tournament underway in the Student Union basement and he had an unflappable sense of humor. When one of his party members was arrested for carrying two pistols into an English Lit class a reporter called Morry for a comment. Morry said the fellow had been granted party membership on the strength of being an Eagle Scout. "Tell the public that I said this undermines our confidence in the Boy Scouts."

After Morry's public emergence as the university's most prominent Red we persuaded him to write a short story for *The Covered Wagon*, the campus humor magazine, of which I had become assistant editor. He did a funny piece about a depth charge exploding prematurely under the fantail of his destroyer just as the watch officer was relieving himself in the head. We outlined the story with American flags as a political decontaminant, nobody complained, and the last I heard of Morry he was being kept busy flying back and forth between Oklahoma and Washington to take the Fifth Amendment before the House Un-American Activities Committee.

The *Covered Wagon* was my only emergence to any prominence in an undistinguished academic career. It was a moribund monthly—a repository of off-color jokes and "cheesecake" art. It had been taken over by Lew Thompson, who had survived the bloody Pacific battles from Guadalcanal all the way to the recapture of Manila and came out as an artillery captain. (Lew's best contribution to campus war stories told how General MacArthur sent out maps to artillery units prohibiting shelling of his famous Manila brewery or his various other business buildings in Manila.) As his staff, Lew recruited fellow journalism students in whom he sensed potential and got the *Wagon* rolling again. No pay for the staff except seeing your credit line under photos or your byline on what you wrote. However, whoever was willing to be assistant editor and do the office work could be editor when Thompson's one-year term expired. That made you a "Big Man On Campus," if only in your own imagination. The editor received $50 per month, which Thompson used down at Red's and Ed's buying the beer for our post-publication celebrations. In theory, the editor also received a slice of the profits. There had never been any.

However, Thompson hadn't gone from grunt to captain and to editorship of this humor mag on the basis of wealth or social position. Why not promote this new campus environment—and the *Wagon*? Get this swarm of vets to read it and make it attractive to advertisers. We made the *Oklahoma Daily* (two doors down the hall from our office in the grimy old Journalism Building) aware we were changing the magazine. I drove up to Oklahoma City and did a cover article feature on a social breakthrough—the opening of Oklahoma's first strip joint night club. Under another of his several hats, Thompson was the campus "stringer" for *The Daily Oklahoman*, which made it easy for him to give the state editor of that terrible old Oklahoma City paper a hint that scandalous things were about to happen at OU, which was already sort of politically and socially suspect. OU's famous president George Cross thus received an inquiry from a reporter asking what was going on at the campus magazine. I got a call from the president's secretary asking me to come over and talk. This was leaked to both the *Oklahoma Daily* and the *Oklahoman*. I don't recall the *OD* headline but the *Daily Oklahoman*'s said OU PRESIDENT CALLS EDITOR ON CARPET. The interview with the president was mild. He asked what this was all about. I told him we were dumping the dirty jokes and aiming at the older audience. He had no objections. Mild or not, the edition featuring "Culture Comes to Okie City" sold out, the *Wagon* was rolling again, and I had observed firsthand an example of how easily the press can be manipulated. (In years to come as reporter, editor, etc., I often saw it practiced with myself in the role of victim.)

My memories of those campus days are an oddly mixed bag of new friendships and loneliness. The loneliness was rooted in part, I suspect, in missing those dirty, disheveled brothers from the frozen foxholes. You come to love those who shared that great adventure and you never stop missing them. But part of it came from the natural urge of young humans to find their mate. I had been making no progress on this front. One of the tiny minority of girls in my "Speech and Rhetoric" class attracted my attention by being pretty and sounding smart. Her midterm speech concerned flying a Piper Cub, a happy change from the lectures we were getting from male students about techniques for maintaining torpedoes, how to clear jams caused in your machine gun by wet canvas ammunition belts, proper treatment of frostbitten feet, and so forth. She took me for a ride in her Piper Cub, I became airsick, and that ended that. I dated a young lady with glossy black hair, a dazzling smile, and a sardonic wit, whom I had recruited as a model while taking a photography course. We were friends, nothing romantic was developing, and our terminal date involved her meeting me at the *Covered Wagon* office. There I introduced her to Thompson and the next thing I knew they were scheduling their marriage.

While all this was afoot, there was also the business of learning to write—and the star character in that was a woman named Gracie Ray. Professor Ray taught us to organize. Good writing was not just a matter of blurting out the right words. It required deciding precisely what we wanted to tell, to whom we wanted to tell it, and how to arrange this message to get it told without wasting the receivers' time or testing their patience. The course was News Writing and Professor Ray used the time-tested journalistic formula. We were handed facts and sorted through them for the What, Who, Where, When, and Why (or How)—the famous "five W's and the H." Which one (or ones) should we lead with as the most important, the most interesting, etc.

A drunk jumps to his death. That's a What. He takes his dry dive off the top of the Washington Monument. Clearly a Where. But he is J. Edgar Hoover!!! A Who—but wait. The Why now struggles for the lead and the How clamors for attention. Learning such elements was the beginning and anyone can teach that. Professor Ray's great contribution was her skill at inoculating us with her passion for precision.

Every word in a sentence we wrote for her must be a necessary element in the message. It had a job do and it must be the right word to do it. Often she suggested a better one, but such failures she treated gently. She was less tolerant of "useless verbiage," of those words that could be deleted with no effect on the meaning. "Cornstarch" words, she called them—with the same contempt a five-star chef would apply to such a filler dumped into his recipe. "Like barnacles on a boat's bottom," she said. "They slow down the sentence, reduce its force, make you sound like an English major."

Students of News Writing quickly learned to use modifiers sparingly if at all. "The adverb is the enemy of the verb," she said. "If you need one, you used the wrong verb. You put 'slowly' after 'walked,' when you should have said 'trudged' or 'strolled' or 'ambled.' " Professor Ray thus produced a swarm of men and women who "wrote tight," who fit neatly into the format of the Associated Press, United Press, and International News Service. They were rarely accused of being flowery.

My other life-altering prof at OU was H. H. Herbert, a former newspaper editor. He taught Journalistic Ethics, the lack of which being Herbert's primary interest. Whether or not it's legal, constitutional, or fair, a career in journalism carries power, Herbert told us. If you are preempting the advertising revenues and the readers you have an ethical duty to use that power to serve their community. The newspaper has the power, so does the reporter. That power is used whether you like or not. When you decide to cover a marginal story, or skip past it to the next one. Whether you use a name or skip it. If you use the power irresponsibly you'll hurt a lot of people.

I had reason to remember that oft-repeated homily too often. Once, covering state government, I learned a tax stamp shipment had gone missing and traced it from printer, trucker, revenue bureau, to warehouse. I used the names of those who signed receipts. The story ran December 21. On December 24 my phone rang. The voice said: "Merry Christmas. You just cost me my job." His boss had seen his name in the paper, told him the auditing firm couldn't stand even a hint of suspicion, told him to find another job. Not easy, my victim said, when you've been fired under a cloud of suspicion.

I can't recall who taught us the skills and duties of a newspaper slot man—the person who takes the raw material turned in by reporters and photographers, prunes it to fit, deletes libel (and colorful writing), and lays out the pages. I do remember that he must share part of the blame for the most humiliating moment of my journalism studenthood.

This instructor stressed his formula for writing the ideal headline to describe the story below it—a job in which every letter in every word counts (and W's and M's, being fat, count double, and take up twice as much room as skinny little i's and l's). You look for the specific word first. Use the specific "pistol" and switch to the general "gun" only if "pistol" is too long for the line.

I took this dogma with me to the newsroom of the *Daily Oklahoman*, where we were sent to get practical experience under fire. The slot man handed trivial stories destined to be buried on about page 27 to interns, with a note on the type of headline he wanted. One handed to me reported a woman filing suit against a doctor who had operated on her eleven years earlier. A subsequent surgery had revealed that the first surgeon hadn't extracted one of his forceps before stitching up the abdomen.

I wrote:

SURGEON'S FORCEPS
LEFT IN WOMAN
ELEVEN YEARS

The slot man told me the top line was too long and tossed it back to me to revise. Forceps is specific of what? It's a tool, right? The first line became Surgeon's Tool. That fit. Hours pass with more headlines written. The bulldog edition comes up from the printing plant. The night city editor scans it. Reaches page 27. Shouts: *Stop the press,* glowers at the slot man, and says, "Who wrote this!!" I am identified as the culprit, but a night city editor would no more waste words on a student intern than a general would on a private first class. He studied me a moment, deciding whether stupidity or mischief was involved, picked up the phone, got the Journalism Department chairman (H. H. Herbert himself) out of bed, and chewed him out.

That *Stop the press* shout is often heard in old movies, but that was the only time I ever heard it in real life. Professor Herbert called me in, asked what happened. I told him and Herbert seemed perfectly satisfied that I could be blamed only for innocence in a world full of night city editors with dirty minds. I got a "B" in the course.

End of the semester also brought my twenty-first birthday, the day of being old enough to vote, of full legal citizenship, and looking back. I took a walk that evening, stopped in a coffee shop beside the highway, and drank a cup or two while assessing my situation. Barney was off on a date with his girl of the moment, Larry had married his high school flame and was living in married student housing, my various other male associates were otherwise occupied and of female associates that May I had none. One of the fellows who sometimes took the walk with us down the hill from the Third General Hospital to sun ourselves in Aix-en-Provence was from Sharps Chapel, Tennessee. He'd entertain himself with a Civil War ballad.

> *Oh, I'll never be married;*
> *I'll never have wife.*
> *I'll always be lonely*
> *All the days of my life.*

Exactly the way I remember thinking that May evening. I was feeling way down and blue, rejected by young women, looking back at a wasted youth, looking forward into an infinite unknown of unpromising blankness. But Mama's philosophy kicked in. Just a test, after all. Something to endure. Make the best of it. It doesn't last forever. And then comes the Last Great Adventure.

Later that week Dick Wharton, a fellow writer for the *Wagon*, joined me for lunch. Our moods matched. We decided to hell with summer school. Why be in such a rush to get to the future? We'd make up for the three monthly GI Bill paychecks we'd lose by hitchhiking down to Mexico City. There we could live cheap and perfect the Spanish we'd been studying.

No problem getting down through Ardmore, Denton, Dallas, Waco, San Antonio, etc., to Laredo, because Americans were still conditioned by war and Depression to picking up hitchhikers. At the border, our policy came acropper. We walked across into Nuevo Laredo and bought a ticket to Monterrey on a Mexican bus.

In Monterrey, we'd haunt the expensive hotels, meet American tourists, and bum a ride to Mexico City.

It will surprise no one who entered Mexico via bus in those days (and perhaps since) to know that we ran into a little roadblock south of Nuevo Laredo and about twenty miles from nowhere. Two soldiers armed with carbines boarded and went down the aisle checking credentials. They missed Wharton, a Choctaw Indian who might have passed as a Mexican, but spotted me. The soldier examined the visa I had obtained at the customs office and found it faulty. I would have to get off the bus, go back to the border and have the fault corrected. *"No es posible,"* I said, in my Spanish II grammar, and tried to explain there was no way to get back. He insisted. I said: *"Yo no tengo culpa,"* hoping to communicate that it wasn't my fault. Wharton, his Spanish a bit better, corrects me. He says: "You mean, *La culpa no es mio."* While correct, that was a mistake. The soldiers now spot Wharton as another gringo, recheck his visa, and sure enough, find an error and the problem broadens. The driver has sat patiently through all this, having seen it happen whenever he has gringos aboard, but the Mexican passengers want to get on with their journey. They signal us, rubbing their fingers together, that the soldiers are extorting a bribe. They encourage us by laughter, jeers, and rude remarks aimed at the military. The soldiers finally decide we are invincibly stupid, climb off the bus, and we're off to Monterrey.

Off, although we didn't know it for days, to the industrial side of town. Not a fancy resort in view of the bus station. We check into a grimy two-story hotel and hit the sack. With morning we venture out, stop a man on the sidewalk and tell him we seek hotels where the rich travelers with cars stayed. That was way, way, way down by the river, he said. His cousin would be coming along soon. He was a tourist guide. He would take us. Cousin arrives, dapper and about our age. He hails a cab (all taxis in Monterrey then were Model-A Ford sedans) and ushers us in. Our first stop was in an expensive-looking supper club—closed now of course. Cousin wants us to see it, wants us to sample a specialty cocktail mixed there. He leaves us at the door and departs to awaken the owner. The owner admits us, mixes us drinks. Wharton and I look at each other, remember the warnings our college friends had given us of perfidious Mexicans, of knockout drops, of murderous robbers. Will our fear of looking discourteous and unsophisticated overcome our common sense? Of course it does. We drink our cocktails unpoisoned. Our guide hurries us out, takes us to a magnificent old theater where a movie is now being shown. He leads us in, borrows a flashlight from the usher, and uses it for illumination while he explains the theater's famous old murals. Not a murmur of protest comes from the audience.

Back on the street Cousin tells us he must leave us to meet a customer, tells of a good place to have lunch. He will meet us there tomorrow and show us more of his city. Dick and I count our money while eating. We owe Cousin for cab fare, for cocktails, for his bribe of the usher, and for whatever he charges for his guiding time. We can't afford this. We write him a thank-you note and fold it around our guess of a fair payment and leave it with the cashier to give to Cousin when he shows up tomorrow.

We didn't return to the café for days and when we did the cashier spotted us, signaled us, frowning, and returned our note, still wrapped around our money. Cousin had refused it. He told the cashier to ask us why we had insulted him, why had we refused his friendship? Dick and I were beginning to learn.

We learned that the tourists who lived in the expensive hotels around the plaza tended to have left for Mexico City or other points south long before Wharton and I could rouse ourselves and get downtown to bum rides. Besides we were becoming fond of Monterrey.

At the social evenings when the mariachis played and the girls (with *chaperonas*) and boys promenaded in circles around the Plaza Central we had met two Mexican students (a musician who wanted to sing operas and a would-be bullfighter). They had day jobs, knew the city, and didn't object to associating with two grungy-looking American freeloaders or helping us improve our Spanish. Before we ran out of money, tired of living off bananas, bolillos, refried beans and tamales bought in the open markets, we had learned to love Mexicans and the Mexican culture. Why? Try to imagine the following happening in a major U.S. industrial city.

We board the wrong city bus. Made aware of this, our driver does a U-turn, chases down the correct bus, stops it, and sends one of his regular passengers with us to assure these gringos won't lose themselves again. It's all very educational but without academic credit hours. We hitchhike back to OU for our terminal semesters.

And for the turning point in my life.

I spent thirty months—from January 1946 to June 1948—at the University of Oklahoma in which nothing much happened except a life-changing miracle. One pleasant October 1947 evening, I put on that sports coat I had bought from Sam in my prewar existence, met Bob Huckins, also still single and at loose ends. Providence guided us to a dance at the Newman Center. Good-bye Loneliness. Hello Joy.

Those who have read my mystery novels know I'm not adept at dealing with romance when my plots require such. I'm still not but I will try. I noticed a girl dancing. She was slender, graceful, laughing, enjoying herself. She had enchanting eyes. I pushed myself away from the wallpaper, tapped her dancing partner on the shoulder, and asked if I could cut in. (Does this "cutting in" social convention survive?) I could. We danced, we exchanged introductions. I had met Marie Elizabeth Unzner.

All else that happened to me in Soonerland (or anywhere else) is trivial in comparison, and it scares me to remember that this meeting didn't happen until my senior year. (Hers, too, for that matter. I got off to a poor start by asking her if she was a freshman.) When the music is suitably slow for the only dance step I've mastered, I danced with her again. Then I stood back against the wallpaper watching her dance with other fellows. The next day I find I have her on my mind. Wharton is the projectionist at the downtown theater. He provides tickets. I invite Marie to a movie. She invites me to a basketball game. I'm unable to think of anyone else. I offer to help her with the papers she has to turn in for an English Lit correspondence course. She drops in at the *Covered Wagon* office, and we work on them. (Now, as I write this fifty-six years later, she enlightens me. It wasn't my knowledge of the course that attracted her. I had a typewriter.) Two dates later I tell her my goal is to marry her. She doesn't seem impressed, but by winter she invites me down to Shawnee to have dinner at her home. Spring comes. Wharton, who has connections, finds a ring I can afford. I propose. Marie accepts. We set the date a year in the future. I start job hunting.

The surplus commodity in the summer of 1945 was unfilled jobs. By the summer of '48 in America the surplus was unemployed young men home from the war, graduating from college, and eager to get on with it. I wanted a job as a reporter on a daily newspaper, ideally one where I could eventually become a political reporter. All my applications drew blanks. As graduation loomed in May, the best I could find was a trial opening for a copywriter at an Oklahoma City advertising agency.

The assignment was handling advertising copy for Cain's Age-Dated Coffee and Purina Pig Chow, including commercials for radio programs they sponsored. Thirty-second spots, but short was no problem for a student of Gracie Ray. The problem was Purina. The commercials were woven through an early-morning news and weather broadcast aimed at early-rising farmers. Technically, each of these programs carried three separate exhortations for listeners to feed their pigs Purina Chow, and the account executive wanted them to link, with the first one leading into the second and coming to a logical climax in the third. That was awfully hard to do. I had worried my way through a week of them when the telephone rang.

The caller was Tommy Steph, who identified himself (erroneously) as editor of the *Borger News-Herald*. He said he needed a reporter and Professor Herbert had recommended me. It paid $55 for a six-day week. Did I want it? Yes, I said. When did I start? As soon as I could get there.

Borger is about sixty miles north of Amarillo on rolling, almost treeless tundra of the high end of the Texas Panhandle. When I arrived a bit before noon on an end of May Monday in 1948, the town was about twenty years old—born when wildcatters hit a vast natural gas deposit under an empire of grass owned by the Wittenberg family. The Wittenbergs sold (more likely, leased) a strip of land along the highway as the site of the inevitable boomtown, and later two other adjoining tracts for suburban boomtowns. Phillips Petroleum built the town of Phillips on one as the site of its petrochemical refinery complex and its hired hands. The other became the home of a bunch of carbon black and rubber plants, plus related housing. All around this little cluster of occupied spots the ranch spread from horizon to horizon.

Borger, 1948. Imagine a small town in Virginia, or Vermont, or Minnesota, then take away the shady streets, the handsome old houses, the grassy, dignified town square, and the monuments to distinguished nineteenth-century heroes. Replace all this with a long row of concrete block one-story business buildings lining miles of two-lane highway, and behind them rows of the kinds of residences that members of industrial unions occupy. Cover all this with a haze of gray-black smoke produced by a multitude of jerry-built plants where natural gas was burned in low-oxygen drums to form the tons of soot from which the town claimed its title of "Carbon Black Capital of the World." Add the town's only historical monument, the bullet hole preserved in the wall of the Post Office marking the spot where Ace Borger was shot to death, leaving the town devoid of its founding mayor but enriched with its name and its claim to historic fame—the only town put under martial law by the State of Texas. (According to local legend, policemen parked their patrol car at the home of the district attorney, knocked on his door, and shot him down when he opened it, Texas Rangers were sent in to restore decorum.) The other differences worth noting include its shape, running miles down the main street highway but being only about four blocks wide, its lack of a cemetery (no one was born there), its lack of "old families" (and resultant lack of social snobbery), and a population overwhelmingly not only of my own blue-collar working-class level but of the strange "oil patch" segment of that class—folks who followed the ever-moving oil worker jobs just as whalers followed the whales.

Borger's spectacular lack of charm was more than offset by overwhelming friendliness. Everyone there was a wayfarer, moving through, headed someplace else. The *News-Herald* ran a standing Help-Wanted advertisement in the classified section of *Editor and Publisher*. For the purposes of a totally green journalist with a yen to make it in the news business, it could hardly have been better. The newsroom offered a total lack of direction or supervision, which meant you could try anything you wanted, and the town presented a wonderful harvest for a police reporter, which was my assignment. Borger had, as Fred, the newspaper's photographer told me later, "every sort of crime and violence mentioned in both the Bible and the *Glossary of Psychopathy*."

My tenure there extended from June through December, a mere six months, but in Borger one lost no time getting experience. I had risen early in Norman, driven some three hundred miles, and walked into the office about 11 A.M. I identified myself to the receptionist and was directed into the little glassed-in cubicle where the editor-publisher was working on some business papers. I introduced myself.

"Hillerman?" he said. "Well, what can we do for you?"

"I'm your new reporter."

"Oh?" he said. "Who hired you?"

"I thought it was you," I said.

He pointed through the glass out into the newsroom. "Better go talk to Brad on the news desk," he said.

Brad seemed to be about my age. He hadn't hired me, but he thought Tommy had. He explained that the editor-publisher was actually the bookkeeper who worked for the rancher who owned the newspaper but never came around and he and Tommy had neglected to tell him their police reporter had quit. Whereupon Brad told Fred to show me where to find the police station, sheriff's office, jail, courthouse, and so forth. Find him a place to spend the night later.

Off we go, Fred and I, driving down Borger's main street to be almost immediately passed by a fire truck with sirens wailing. Fred gives chase, gets on his radio, and learns there has been an explosion at the Phillips chemical plant. We join the caravan of fire department vehicles, ambulances, and police cars. Security people at the gate wave them through but stop Fred's car.

"They know me and I can't get past them," Fred tells me, "but they don't know you. Just walk right in like you have business inside." Standard reportorial thinking. I walk past the guards, join the crowd of curious workers milling around inside. I start listening and asking questions. Too many questions. Two security types grab my elbows, hustle me to the gate, and toss me out. I brush off the gravel and we rush back to the paper with a yarn about one dead and two badly burned while sandblasting a water tank. ("Workers reported that the hose to the air compressor had accidentally been connected to a natural gas line. Company officials refused to comment.") My career as professional journalist thus was launched.

At the *Borger News-Herald* those days upward mobility was fast, easy, and automatic. Brad and Tommy had graduated from Oklahoma State University in January, arrived as reporters, and were now splitting the editor's job. One would hold the post until the other one screwed up (forgot to bring home the beer, for example, or let the pancakes burn), whereupon they would switch jobs—the miscreant taking the editor's slot and the other one replacing him as general assignment reporter. They shared a bachelor apartment, shared the news editor's job because the holder of same had quit, and enjoyed a "forged in fire" friendship. When their B-24 was shot up in a daylight raid over north Germany, they limped it over the Baltic and finished the war in joyful hard-drinking Swedish internment.

As the foregoing suggests, working on the *News-Herald* was casual. We showed up at the newsroom after eight, wandered down to a lunch counter at the dime store for breakfast, and put in a couple of hours getting the paper out for afternoon delivery. Since the coeditors had fallen into the golfing habit in Sweden this situation left me to prowl the cop shops and courts as my instincts suggested. I'd read the police blotter every morning, check the desk clerk's notes on complaints, assignments, and arrests, learn who was in jail and why (as Professor Herbert taught us was our duty), then trot over to the sheriff's office, repeat the process, make a call to the Texas Highway Patrol Office dispatcher, and then conclude the tour collecting gossip at the district attorney's subsidiary office (the "seat" of Hutchinson County was not booming upstart Borger but down the road a long piece to little Stinnett). If time allowed I'd stop at the tiny office of Borger's magistrate/justice of the peace to collect historical stuff, anecdotes, and his advice to greenhorn young journalists.

A couple of decades in the future I'd find myself scavenging among my memories of this fellow to add a bit of realistic life to minor characters needed in fiction. The JP was elderly and full of lessons he'd learned in a long career as an infielder in the minor leagues. He'd started in Class D league, worked his way up to the Triple A's, failed to be noticed by the majors, and worked his way back down to the D's. Most of his customers, ushered over from the jail across the street, weren't represented by counsel and the mild medicine he administered was doled out with minimum formality. When the violation was serious enough to warrant hiring a defender, this lawyer would bring along an appropriate law book and read the pertinent passages to the JP. Whoever was representing "The People of Texas" would do the same. The judge would then solicit suggestions, ponder these a moment, and rule.

Over a posttrial cup of coffee with a couple of these barristers, I suggested that they treated the JP as if he was illiterate. They said he was. Not much to read on those minor league bus trips, but lots of opportunities to become wise.

I was also exposed to wise enforcement of our laws by the Hutchinson County sheriff, whose behavior I used, in modified form, years later when constructing Lieutenant Joe Leaphorn as a minor character in *The Blessing Way*. For example:

Two young women, probably late teens, storm into his office as I am sitting at a table sorting my notes. They demand that he go out to their place and arrest their father. Why? The older girl, who is serving as spokeswoman, tells the sheriff her little sister got their pickup truck stuck in the draw, walked back to the house, and got Daddy to come down and help her get it out. "She should have known better," she adds. Daddy had helped her dig out the truck and then had raped her. The sheriff gets a complaint form, younger sister signs it, and the sheriff says he would go on out and arrest the offender. Wow, I'm thinking. An incest rape. How do I handle this one without identifying the victim? The sheriff has been watching me jotting my notes.

Am I going to report this? I say sure. He says, "About an hour after I get their daddy locked up they'll be back telling me they won't press charges."

I say, "How do you know?"

He says, "Because that's the way it happened the last three times."

That's the way it happened this time, too. I had met a cop who tempered justice with a sort of humane wisdom. In another case involving a bank robbery at neighboring Pampa, my sheriff bagged the culprits after a chase through the network of rural back roads.

When I asked him about it, he credited the bloodless success with knowing every inch of the country and getting the job done fast before the FBI moved their urbane agents out from the city to take over and complicate things. Those acquainted with my Navajo Tribal Police books may have noticed that both Lieutenant Joe Leaphorn and Officer Jim Chee have similar traits and attitudes.

Hutchinson County jurors operated in similar fashion—and I will use the first murder trial I covered to illustrate. The defendant was a night club bartender charged with first-degree (premeditated) murder. The suspect a mailman who had arrived at the bar a bit after its 2 A.M. closing to pick up a waitress. The prosecuting attorney told the jury that when the mailman knocked at the door the bartender had denied him admission on grounds the place was closed. The mailman, indignant, had kept knocking. Whereupon the defendant retrieved his shotgun from under the bar, went out the back door, walked around to the front, and fatally whacked the mailman on the head with the gun.

The defense attorney contested not a word of this and called a single witness (the arresting officer). Did he examine the shotgun? Yes. Was the shotgun loaded? Yes. The defense rests.

In his summation, the prosecutor established that it took lots of time to get the shotgun out from under the bar, walk to the back of the bar, out the back door, around to the front to slay the still-knocking mailman. No question of who killed the mailman. No question the bartender had ample time to meditate. That made it premeditated murder.

The defense attorney showed the jury of High Plains male citizens the shotgun. "If you carry a loaded shotgun out to a man who is bothering you intending to kill him, you intend to shoot him with it. Right? You're not going to hit him with it."

The jury saw logic in that. The verdict was "Not Guilty" and the bartender was free to resume serving his customers.

The folks of Hutchinson County were also free-spirited in the world of sports—as I witnessed one Saturday when the Borger

High football game engaged our sports editor and I was sent away to Stinnett to cover its game against White Deer. The point of this anecdote is that the pulling guard in the Stinnett Rattlers single-wing offense was a girl. Actually the point is that nobody except me seemed to think that worthy of notice. When I asked one of the fans about it he said: "Well, she's little, but she's fast."

I played the same position (but as a substitute) for the Konawa High Tigers, and that remark reminded me of a comment I'd over-heard in the gym at Konawa. Our coach was analyzing our line for someone and when he came to my name, he said: "Hillerman? Well, he's little but he's slow."

I guess the double negative was provoked by the way my slow-ness had embarrassed Coach a few games earlier. We were playing Bowlegs High—an oil patch settlement without bleachers where the onlookers lined the football field on the fenders of their pickup trucks. On the fateful play my role was to pull out and lead interfer-ence on an inside-the-right-tackle charge. Alas, I arrived at the hole behind the ball carrier instead of in front of him. The Bowlegs line-backer hit the Konawa halfback, the ball squirted out and was lost to us. Coach, standing by the bench surrounded by mothers and fathers, screamed:

"Hillerman, you run like a broke-dick dog!!" It's a simile I have never forgotten, it caused the ladies to complain to the school board about obscene language, and Coach was reprimanded.

Borger was a lonely place that summer. Long distance tele-phone calls in the forties were expensive, employed by the working class mostly to announce family deaths, but I managed to use let-ters to persuade Marie that we should move up our wedding date. The original plan was for her to accept a graduate school offer for a year while I got established. We agreed to cut that to six months, getting married the following winter. By July, with much playing on her sympathy, I got that cut down to a month. We set the date for August 16.

While I was waiting, trying to keep my mind on business,

Borger was proving a fine place to learn—about being a reporter and about myself. I was talking to a young Texas highway patrolman one morning outside the Stinnett Courthouse when his radio buzzed him. A double fatality on Highway 206 about twelve miles north. He roared away. I followed. A Packard sedan had collided head-on in about the center of the two-lane highway with some sort of pickup truck. The remains of the truck was scattered in the roadside wheat field. The sedan was still on the pavement, its front end back to the instrument panel missing. The body of the driver was in his seat, his head impaled on the steering post, blood, teeth, and tissue splashed everywhere. The highway patrolman backed away from this, unable to control his nausea. I remember standing there untouched, guessing at the combined speeds, noticing how the wheel rim had gouged a rut in the concrete, collecting the details I'd need for my story, finally aware the patrolman, still pale and shaken, was looking at me as if I was something less than human. And all I could say to explain it was that it's not so bad when the dead are not your friends.

The shrinks had not yet invented post-combat trauma syndrome but I suppose that's the name for it—for the accumulation of baggage we sometimes talk about even now when what's left of Charley Company has its annual reunion. We mention a recurrence of the old nightmares, of how long it took us to get rid of chronic moments of "morning sickness," but we hardly ever discuss this incurable numbness. A deep, deep burn costs one the feeling in a fingertip. Perhaps seeing too much ghastly casual death does it to a nerve somewhere behind the forehead bone.

The impending 1948 election taught me another essential lesson—about premature bridge burning and human decency. A University of Texas law school alum was running for Congress against the right-wing incumbent. Our publisher was a proud founder of the Hutchinson County Anti-Communist League, the first such county organization in the country, and held this upstart contender's Red-hating credentials suspect. He called me into his cubicle, handed me a sealed envelope, and told me to drive out to a residence in Rubbertown that evening, pick up a fellow who would be awaiting me there, drive him to a political rally being held for the lawyer, drop him off down the street, then attend and write a story on what happened. What was all this about? Confidential, he said. I didn't need to know. Just do it.

There we have the Nike sporting goods slogan, the great exhortation for self-indulgence to its yuppie customers to accept irresponsibility. My first impulse was to hand him his envelope and quit. But that would have made me one of the indigent unemployed just before becoming a married man. Besides, I was curious about this.

I checked around about my future passenger, whom I'd met at an American Legion Post meeting. Our publisher paid our dues and required eligible hired hands to join. We quickly noticed the members were all stateside warriors and their interest seemed purely in foiling union organizing. None of the members had seen combat and none of the news staff, all combat vets, went more than once. I learned my passenger was, in AFL-CIO parlance, a scab. He had been employed as a strikebreaker for one of the rubber companies and was now unemployed. I took a peek into the envelope. Three $20 bills (more than a week's pay for me) and a list of questions. The first one asked our candidate if he was "still a member" of the Young Communist League. The others were similar. I stuck the notes and cash back in the envelope, gave it to my passenger when I picked him up, hauled him to the school where the rally was scheduled, dropped him, parked, and went in to watch. My plan by then was to report what happened, including the fact that the questions had been provided by the newspaper publisher and the asker had been paid $60 to ask them. I'd be out of work but I wouldn't be ashamed of myself.

The asker must have had the same sorts of thoughts. I sat watching him and listening to the usual political platitudes. Then he came over, handed me the envelope, money and all, and said he wanted to go home. We left. I returned the envelope to the editor the next day, told him what happened, and resumed my efforts to find a more respectable job.

I found two—one through the "good old boy network" and one the way you like to get job offers—from a competitor editor who had been reading my stuff. But before any of that happened, it was time for Marie and me to marry. It was the greatest thing ever to happen to me, but getting it done proved to be stressful. It involved a door-to-door campaign to borrow money, a head-on collision, sleeping in the Pampa jail, and other such incidents.

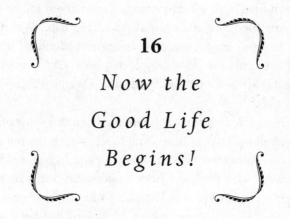

16
Now the
Good Life
Begins!

I tend to blame the troubles that led up to the altar rail of St. Benedict's Church in Shawnee, Oklahoma, on Tommy and Brad. Both were confirmed bachelors at the time (that didn't last long) and so was our photographer and our sports editor. They lectured me about the mistake I was making and the bad example it gave. Worse, they refused to allow me more than the weekend off—which ruled out a honeymoon and complicated matters. If I had a day or two off I might have avoided the following problems, which I brought crashing down upon myself.

Oklahoma requires blood tests before issuing marriage licenses. I had that done at the hospital in Borger with the results sent to Marie's brother, Charlie, who was taking care of getting the license. Friday morning before our Monday wedding date Marie called, agitated. Oklahoma didn't recognize Texas blood tests. Oklahoma required one done in Oklahoma. I dropped whatever job I was on in the newsroom and roared off toward Guymon, eighty miles north and the nearest Okie town large enough to have a clinic. I did the nail-biting wait, eye on clock, while the only doctor in town dealt with a farmer mangled in a harvest injury. When he took my blood he asked me the wedding date. When I say Monday he says "I hope you don't mean next Monday." It seems that he has to send my blood sample to a lab in Oklahoma City. It will probably arrive about Tuesday, be tested Wednesday, and certified Thursday.

Even now describing that awful moment recalls a sense of panic mixed with despair. What I am about to screw up is the rest of my life. Marie's mother had organized a major and formal wedding at St. Benedict's with the usual bride's attendant, maids of honor, flower girls, etc. Barney was lined up to be my best man, Dick Wharton and Charlie as my ushers. Invitations had been out for weeks, the church reserved, reception planned, etc. It was short of the preparations for D-Day but still a major logistic project and not something that can be casually postponed.

I race the eighty miles back to Borger. The only idea I can think of is getting Barney to pretend he's me and get his blood tested under my name. From Borger, I call Barney in Norman. Mama answers the phone. Barney is off somewhere, but she advises calm. With the aid of prayer, nothing is impossible. Have faith. She recommends I get home as soon as possible. I tell her I'm on my way.

But not quite. The time I had planned to use getting to the bank to withdraw traveling money, to borrow a suitcase, and pack had been used in the race to Guymon. Now the banks are closed and paying for the blood test had left me with about $3.00. Credit cards had not yet been invented. I race around Borger, borrowing money from my assorted coworkers, the sheriff, from cops on my beat, etc., five bucks here, ten there—handing out scribbled IOU notes where required and accumulating $61 and change. No time to pack. I grab my stuff and toss it into the backseat of my Ford and head through the twilight on a planned high-speed, nonstop race to Norman.

So much for plans. The first stop was abrupt, ending a slide off mud-slick U.S. 273 southeast of Pampa by crashing into the front of a car getting onto the highway off a section line road. Both vehicles left undrivable. I confess blame. His wife rigs up a handkerchief bandage over my bloody forehead bruise. He spots a car coming along lonely 273, races out, flags it down, and sends it on to Pampa to notify the sheriff and send a wrecker. We wait in our respective vehicles. The rain pours down. In about five minutes I realize I can't afford to wait without risking the loss of the girl of my dreams. I wad up my clothes, carry them up to the highway, and flag down a truck which deposits me, soaking wet, at the Pampa police station. There my plight provokes sympathy as well as amusement. The next bus for Oklahoma City is due about 5 A.M. I am offered a bunk in a cell adjoining the drunk tank. I wring out my wet wardrobe and sleep the sleep of exhaustion.

I can't remember the bus ride—only Barney awaiting me at the station to take me to St. Anthony's Hospital, where arrangements had been made to open the lab on Saturday to get the blood-work done and certified. All that remains now is getting the Pottawatomie County Clerk at Shawnee to rush out a marriage license before 9 A.M. Monday when the wedding is scheduled. That sounds impossible, but Charlie had been a tech sergeant in the Marines and half the folks in the county owed favors to either Charlie himself or my future father-in-law. Charlie says don't worry. I didn't need to.

A lovely wedding. I stand at the altar rail so blissful that I'm unaware the organist is playing that "Here Comes the Bride" theme over and over and over again. But Marie finally got there and, unlikely as it must seem after the foregoing, she married me, which means the next half century of this memoir is colored by my happiness.

Since my crippled Ford has been left in the Texas Panhandle mud at the mercy of some unidentified wrecker crew, Barney loaned us his car for our twenty-four-hour honeymoon and the drive back to Borger to our first home. That requires explanation. America of 1948 was suffering an awful housing shortage. This was complicated in boomtown Borger because nobody wanted to build in a town that wasn't there yesterday and might not be there tomorrow. I had found only two places affordable on a $55 a week salary. One was a lean-to built against the alley wall of a downtown office. The other was also reached by driving down an alley—a very small two-car garage, which had been partitioned into two spaces. One housed living room and kitchen, the other bedroom and bath. It was superior to the other (faint praise, indeed) but renting it required paying $600 for a small collection of ramshackle and worn-out furniture worth perhaps $50.

Years later when Marie and I (Santa Feans by then) were driving toward Amarillo we noticed the smoke smudging the northern horizon—Borger's carbon black trademark—and decided to make a nostalgic detour. Our newlywed home would be gone of course, and the bare dirt yards of the junior high where Marie taught would be covered with grass, etc., but the place would still be full of happy memories. The memories were there, and so was everything else. The school yard was still bare, trampled dirt innocent of any landscaping. And down the cluttered alley our happy home still stood. A clutter of trash blown against its only door just as we remembered but it was empty now. The lacy white curtains Marie had hung over the tiny kitchen window were gone and a leaky boat had been abandoned beside it but the air was full of fond recollections. Marie got out and took some pictures of the place to show to our skeptical children. I sat in the car, reliving the joy of parking there long ago, home tired from the newsroom, knowing Marie was in there waiting for me, ready to swap stories and turn the day's misadventures and disappointments into fun.

Marie got home first because she had landed a job as a teacher. Being at the bottom of the seniority list, Marie was given Seventh Grade-X. Seventh graders are notoriously preoccupied with puberty and virtually unteachable and her class's "X" designation meant her room was the habitat of the incorrigibles. "They're good kids," Marie would insist, who never saw one who wasn't. Borger, however, offered its share of surprises even in the gentle 1950s, and even in junior high. For example:

Good day today, she said. Seeing progress. Virtually no disruptions. Just one boy decided to be a smart aleck.

What did he do?

One of her little girls was missing. Marie asked the class if anyone knew why Alice was absent. The boy said Alice and her mother were in jail and of course everybody had to laugh. I had been in Borger long enough by then to know it might not be a joke. It wasn't. Alice and her mother were held on prostitution charges.

Fun though it was, Borger was not the place to advance journalistic ambitions. Tom, Brad, and Fred, one by one, found jobs elsewhere and fled, creating a vacuum that sucked me upward into the editor's job (no pay raise, of course), with night work added to the six-day-a-week routine. Winter came to the High Plains, with its famed Blue Northers sweeping down our alley and pushing soot-flavored dust through crevices around our window and piling such a mound of trash and tumbleweeds against the door that once Marie had to use a shovel to gain entrance. Even while I was calling on the good old boy network to rescue me from all this, I was learning from it.

For example:

A middle-aged cowboy comes in one such night, frostbitten and exhausted. He walks up the desk hat in hand, says he has a problem and asks if he can use the telephone. I say sure, hand it to him. He tells whoever he called that the current storm has driven a herd ofHerefords up against a fence and he needs help getting them toshelter. Upon which he thanks me and leaves, with me realizingabout then that he looked familiar because he owns the newspaper,plus the big paper in Amarillo, plus one of America's largestranches, plus one of the country's largest natural gas reserves.Where but on the windswept plains would one find a billionairemogul enduring frostbite to get his cows to safety?

The same storm taught me an indelible lesson about the natureof sports writers. Our basketball team, band, cheerleaders, etc.,had gone to White Deer for a game. They had been trappedovernight. All highways closed, all telephone and power linesdown. We were besieged by nervous parents wanting to know iftheir children had survived. Our efforts through state police, high-way maintenance folks, ham radio operators, everyone else we canthink of, had been fruitless. Then comes a Western Union messen-ger with a telegram. (Remember those?) Our sports reporter hadmade it to the railroad depot and persuaded the operator there tosend it. News at last? No. Our sports reporter has telegraphed usthe box score of the game.

The call that was to begin the second phase of our married lifecame from the *Lawton Morning Press*. The paper, apparently dyingfrom the inattention of its editor/publisher and fierce compe-tition from the strong *Lawton Constitution*, had been taken over by anewspaper chain and was being revived with an infusion of moneyand a new staff, hired mostly through the OU journalism depart-ment Class of 1948. Cousin Larry had been called in as SportsEditor, and he phoned me to take over the news desk. The pay was$60 for the standard six-day week. That sounded fine to Marie

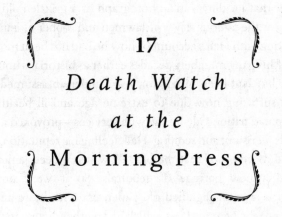

17
Death Watch
at the
Morning Press

O n e   s a w that the *Lawton Morning Press* might be seriously short of journalistic energy before walking through the front door. The paper's plant occupied space in a low-rent section of downtown. The building immediately across the street from it had been gutted by a fire so recently that the smell of cinders was still in the air. I had been reading back issues of both the *Press* and the *Constitution*—our afternoon competitor. The *Constitution* had a big front-page story on the fire, with dramatic photos. Incredible to any journalist, there was no mention of the fire in the *Press*.

But that was a few days in the past. Now a new regime occupied the newsroom—all fresh out of the OU journalism except Managing Editor Frank Hall and Malcolm, our farm editor, both of whom deserve some description.

Hall, a hard-bitten and very savvy newsman, had left his job as city editor of the *Constitution* in a sharp disagreement with its top management. Hall had proclaimed, in a banner headline:

JESSE JAMES ALIVE: IN LAWTON

Under that headline ran a photograph of a grizzled old fellow identified as the famous slayer of lawmen and robber of banks and trains, along with Hall's account of how he had not been murdered by one of his gang members decades earlier as historians uniformly believed, but had been hiding for years under an assumed name and was surfacing now due to extreme age and ill health. This story—spread nationwide by the wire services—provoked a storm of denials, derision, and scoffing. Hall, feeling his reputation soiled, presented more proof that the old fellow was indeed James. This provoked a new barrage of rebuttals. So it went until the *Constitution*, a most dignified old paper, cried no more and Hall went over to the *Morning Press*, which had neither dignity to protect nor reputation to lose.

Farm Editor Malcolm was a Manhattan native Ivy League graduate sent in from the home office of the newspaper chain that had bought the *Press*. Officially, his title was Farm Editor, but we presumed he was a company spy assigned to keep an eye on things. He was amiable, though, and smart, and we did what we could to help him overcome his absolute ignorance of all things agricultural. ("Holstein," Malcolm would shout: "Pig, chicken, horse, cow, what?" and someone would shout, "Cow," and Malcolm would resume typing.) While Malcolm wasn't one of the band of Boomer Sooner country boys he was one of our team and just as determined as the rest of us to beat the *Constitution*. He just had a different reason.

Meanwhile, Marie and I had found ourselves another garage. This one was in a residential backyard with a tiny apartment built on top of it. One climbed a steep steel stairway to its door and reached this stair by navigating a expanse of mud. Tiny as it was this apartment defied efforts to heat it. Unlike our cozy Borger home it was perpetually chilly. Marie rescued herself from this solitary confinement by finding a laboratory job at Fort Sill Indian Hospital, and we located a better home—a unit in a U-shaped six-plex.

While vastly better, it wasn't luxury. It had been built of plywood on a landfill between the highway to Texas and a set of tracks where the railroad parked its diesel engines between their assignments. When these diesels were left idling, they caused vibration in the shaky land under the unit's floor slab. First the pictures on the wall would shake, then dishes and pans would rattle, and soon the apartment would be filled with the sound of tinkling, clicking, and clacking.

The other problems were human. Three units held soldiers based at Fort Sill, the other three *Morning Press* staffers. The newsmen went to work about noon and returned about 1 A.M. to talk, dine, and tell jokes. The soldiers left for duty about 7 A.M. and returned late afternoon. We were getting reacquainted with our wives in the wee hours while the soldiers were trying to sleep. They were shooing their tricycling tots out into the courtyard about 9 A.M. when we were trying to sleep. How was the insulation? Through the thin sheet of plywood separating our bathrooms, I could hear the sound of my neighbor's razor blade scraping off his whiskers.

The above and the impending arrival of our daughter started us house hunting again. We lucked (our luck perhaps helped by buying an endowment policy from the landlord) on to a one-bedroom duplex, which Marie still remembers as "heavenly." Anne arrived, a lovely little girl afflicted with colic for what seemed like forever, and we were able to bring her home from the hospital into a house on a street with actual lawns (a first for us). Just about then the long hours, hard work of our rookie staff, and savvy editorial direction of Frank Hall began paying off. We were beating the staid *Constitution* on stories, our circulation was way up, the big advertisers were beginning to buy big advertising space. Being rookies in the newspaper game we thought this might produce pay raises. The following happened:

I was doing my late evening chores putting pages together when in walked Emmett Keough, the dreaded managing editor of the despised *Constitution*. He walked past me with a nod and disappeared into the office of Hall. The always noisy newsroom fell silent. This was as unthinkable as Yasser Arafat dropping in on a Jewish Anti-Defamation League banquet. There was no socializing between these two papers. We ate at different coffee shops, drank at different bars, ignored one another at news conferences. The rivalry was fierce and personal. After some nervous moments, the editor's door opens, both editors emerge, Keough departs and our editor hands me a page of typescript. "Run it on the front page," he says. "Put it below the fold with a two-column head."

He had already written the headline. It said:

CONSTITUTION-PRESS MERGE

Which the story under the headline repeated. In other words, we had been sold to the opposition. We had lost the battle. No. We had won. It finally seeped into our innocent skulls that we were the front-line troops in a fairly typical example of capitalism in action. Our goal was to cut the *Constitution*'s profits deeply enough to make buying us out cheaper than competing. Anyway, the war was over and who needs soldiers with no battle to fight? Termination pay? Not in 1950. Two weeks notice? Nope. As I remember, three of us were offered jobs on the morning edition of the merged paper and all three swallowed our tattered pride and accepted.

For me, it meant a raise up to $75 a week. More important, it moved me from a newspaper served by United Press on to an

Associated Press–member newspaper. United Press did not raid its clients' newsrooms when needing people. It raided AP papers. Thus after I worked a bit for the merged paper I got a call from Carter Bradley, the UP manager for Oklahoma, and became a member of "The Hold Down Club," a member of the American Newspaper Guild, and for the first (and last) time in my life I had a five-day, forty-hour work week, plus a two-week paid vacation.

Marie, baby Anne, and I moved to Oklahoma City and started house hunting again—for our fifth residence in two years of married life. We moved into an apartment just across the state's busiest highway from Tinker Air Force Base and soon learned those huge buildings across the base fence housed "run-up pens" where jet aircraft engine repairs were tested at night by gunning them to their screaming, screeching, top horsepower. It didn't matter as much as that suggests, however, because Anne's colic persisted and her stomachache howls drowned out the engine noise.

Now I had a job that might lead somewhere. I took a pay cut down to $62.50 a week to get it, but a raise was due in a month and future raises were automatic. We started looking for an actual house and found it, just finished in a new housing addition— genuine brick with the garage poked out toward the street so the kitchen could be built behind it. It had a combined living room-dining room, a bedroom, and a bath. A ceiling fan offset the lack of air conditioning and there was space in back for a garden. The price was $9,100—and we both can still recall our nervousness at that deep plunge into debt.

It was the summer of 1951. I had worked on three newspapers, reported everything—a cattle-killing blizzard, multideath traffic smash, oil workers' strike, murder trial, tornado, church fire, county commission meeting, election campaigns. I felt pretty good about my writing. But in the United Press Bureau in Oklahoma City I had dropped into a den of bona fide pros—a territory where the 11 A.M. deadline was replaced by the *"Deadline every minute"* rule of Hugh Bailey, the legendary whip-cracking czar of "Hold Down" country.

The few newsrooms I've been in since computers took over from teletype machines have seemed eerily quiet, more like a nest of accountants and lawyers than reporters. The newsrooms I remember from the fifties had been noisy, lots of yelling back and forth over the clacking of multiple teletypes, sounds of jubilation, despair, imprecations, jokes, camaraderie, and arguments. The song sung in the UP newsroom was dominated by the nervous chatter of teletypes as the dominant sound—the state wire, the trunk, the market wire, the sports wire, the radio wires. Each machine was delivering something that needed attention, was waiting in dreadful silence for you to feed it with something new, or was producing the *Ding, Ding,* which signaled the need was extremely urgent. No time for yelling, kidding around, assorted newsroom horseplay. The client in Tulsa wanted the story he'd requested and wanted it now. The division manager in Dallas needed an update on a sports story, and the time to file the noon newscasts was only seventeen seconds away. Now and then came a message from our nerve center, signed NX HB. NX was New York, and HB was Hugh Bailey himself. The Hank Browns, Hobson Belamies, and Horace Bungs of UP had to assign themselves other initials. HB meant *the boss* and we presumed he was the reason United Press had earned the title of Hold Down Club, since his proclamations tended to include an order to "hold down expenses."

But Hugh Bailey was invisible, half a continent away. In our bureau the boss was Carter Bradley, the most astute newsman I've ever known. He was also the least patient—as I started learning about five minutes into the job. I strode into the bureau and announced my arrival, expecting to be welcomed and introduced around as a new member of the team. Everybody was talking on the telephone, or rattling away at a teletype, or doing both. I stood waiting recognition. Another telephone rang. Bradley looked at me, frowned, nodded toward the phone. I picked it up and said "United Press."

"Stockers," the voice said. "Three hundred forty. Seventeen ten to eighteen. Bred heifers, too few to price . . ."

"Hold it," said I, grabbed a pencil and copy paper, and began jotting down the mid-morning cattle price quotations from the Oklahoma City stockyards. By now Bradley was off the phone, watching me, expression baleful. "Use your head," he said. "Type calls like that right into the teletype tape. Saves the time of doing it twice."

The basic and all-important skill of being a journalist (as opposed to being a writer) is information collection—and that was the area of Bradley's genius. It's not just a matter of knowing who has the information, it's knowing who will share it with you. For example, we hear on our police scanner a twin-engine plane has crashed in the mountains near the Arkansas border. Bradley puts me on it. I call the Oklahoma Highway Patrol, who have information but aren't in the mood to release it until the shift commander is ready to speak. I call the appropriate sheriff's office. Same story. I call the hospital at the nearest town. No luck. I tell Bradley whom I've called and that all I have is a general location back in the heavy timbered roadless high country and that rescuers have reached the scene. Bradley rewards me with a dour look, says, "Call the Forest Service." I do. The ranger has the same information as had the OHP, the sheriff's office, and the hospital. The difference is his work gives him scant chance to talk to the press and he's delighted to see himself quoted. Therefore while the competition is fruitlessly calling the obvious officials, we are filing a story reporting seven dead and no survivors in the crash of an Air Force "trainer" plane.

This story also demonstrated the drawback of this system. The Associated Press (code-named "Grandma" by the other wire services because of its policy of being slow but sure) subsequently announced six dead and we had to file a correction reporting one of the bodies we'd reported was that of the colonel's pet Doberman.

Bradley's acute sense of where to get information when the bureaucrats were declining to comment earned KO (the Oklahoma City bureau's code) a remarkable record on the monthly NX (New York) report card on "play" among the big-city papers, which had a choice between using UP, AP, or the International News Service. Bradley's policy was to get our story on the papers news desks first and with the best lead paragraph. When we didn't Bradley was not pleased. While Bradley was trying to teach me the skills of information retrieval, I was finding that I still had a lot to learn about writing from Phil Dessauer, the newswire editor, and Howard Wilson, our man at the state capital, was instructing me in the arcane science of reporting politics. Dessauer, a fine writer himself, went about his duties with tact, understanding the tender egos of learners. "Good piece here," Dessauer would say after I'd handed him a six-hundred worder on a kidnap-murder trial. "See if you can do it in two hundred and fifty." You'd find, of course, that you could cut out half of your prose, bad for the ego but good if you're trying to learn how to master the language. Wilson was a genius at finding leaks, at getting politicians and bureaucrats to talk when their best interest told them silence was wiser, and at learning what (and who) the special interest lobbyists had up their sleeves.

I was the second-stringer at the capital, covering the Senate when the legislature was in session (the important things happened in the House), and helping out when Wilson was assigned to special stuff. I had the good fortune to be spotted by Otis Sullivan, the long-time dean of the pressroom, as one of his kind—a farm boy. Sullivan ran coverage of politics for the *Daily Oklahoman*, wrote its stolidly right-wing capital commentary column, and had something to say about the paper's relentlessly regressive editorials. I remember Sullivan as a tall, skinny, unsmiling elderly fellow (when you're twenty-six those over forty seem antique) who sat at the very large desk under the only window that lit the long, narrow room, and who seemed to be engaged in a perpetual telephone conversation. His prestige and power were such that when he desired to interview someone he could simply call their office and summon them to the chair beside his typewriter to answer his questions.

I was summoned there on about the third day of my capital assignment. Otis grilled me about my job, where I'd worked, etc., then he said he'd heard I was a farm kid. From where? Had I ever chopped cotton? Picked boles? Castrated calves? Satisfied on all those scores, Sullivan wished me well. Months later he gave me a bit of advice I always remembered. I'd interviewed the Senate Majority Leader on one of the current controversies. The *Oklahoma City Times* ran my piece, Otis read it, called me to his desk, tapped a finger on my byline. The conversation went something like this:

"You write this thing?"

"Yes, sir."

Long, thoughtful pause. "Kid, you want to know how to tell when a politician is using you?"

"Sure."

"When you ask 'em a question, watch their face. When their lips start to move, they're lying."

Useful advice, because a few days later I'd be headed into a place where politics was king and the only industry. When I showed up to work the night shift, Bradley met me with a question. The Santa Fe Bureau manager had resigned. Did I want the job? Well, *yes!!* When Marie and I talked of goals and ambitions, mine had always been to edit a state capital newspaper. With a child to raise, we preferred a nonurban setting for this state capital—ideally in a non-California Western state, ideally in New Mexico, ideally in Santa Fe.

I remember asking Bradley something like when I'd have to

make this move and the answer—typical of the United Press—was they wanted me there tomorrow morning. I called Marie and we talked it over. Sure, she said. She'd stay behind to sell our house while I located a place for us. It was September 1952, and we were about make another move. This one a genuine life-changer.

18

Life in the
City Different

I've been away from Santa Fe for thirty-eight years now and I'm not sure if its occupants still call it "The City Different." Probably not. It still sits seven thousand feet above sea level on a mountain slope, has a lot of its original narrow streets, adobe walls, and Spanish/Indian ambiance, but it has been bloated with a yuppie population and owners of costly "second homes." Today its social structure is much like that in the upscale suburbs occupied by the toilers in Hollywood's sleaze mills. A few signs of this decay must have already been showing when I arrived in our old sedan in the autumn of 1952. The population was a bit more than twenty thousand—less than a third of the current number—but the Old Santa Fe hands were already mourning its loss.

The day I reported for duty, the man I was replacing as

New Mexico manager took me around to introduce me to potential news sources. One was the president of the Chamber of Commerce. I told him I was impressed by his city and got a different reaction than expected. "Oh, it's ruined now," he said. "Too damn big. People keep crowding in and no way to keep 'em out. You should have been here back in the thirties."

That night I went to a meeting of the Junior Chamber of Commerce, which represents in non-different cities the second level of boosterism. Pretty much the same attitude. The "Tejanos" were everywhere, the members complained. (*Tejano* being a pejorative term that covered Texans and all others with more money than manners.) The entertainment was what was called, in those innocent days, a "stag movie." Stag movies had no more artistic pretensions than did the venereal disease films the Army had shown us, were every bit as graphic, and were (as old-timers may remember) illegal. This didn't bother the judge or the undersheriff in the audience, but the district attorney, after taking a bit of kidding about it, put on his hat and left.

Santa Fe had other claims to being different—partly because of its Sangre de Cristo Mountains altitude and partly because it dates back to the start of the seventeenth century. The Spanish Conquistadores moved into an existing Indian settlement and let it grow. In 1610, Spain's reigning king named it the Royal City of the Holy Faith of St. Francis of Assisi and drew a square on his map to delineate its city limits. Appropriately, the square wasn't lined up by compass directions, so neither are Santa Fe streets. Urban planning was suspended for the next 350 years. Then, in the mid-1950s, a Historical Zone Ordinance was adopted, saving its narrow streets and adobe architecture and keeping Philistine developers from converting it into a mountain version of Lubbock. That saved the center of the city, which stands even now as a diamond mounted in a tasteless setting of the same strip-zoned highways that lead into all American cities.

Santa Fe sociology at that time was also different. The population was divided about equally between the Spanish and the Anglos—the first being the offspring of the pioneers who followed Coronado and Onate to the "Northern Frontier" long before the *Mayflower* landed at Plymouth Rock. When the Daughters of the Mayflower picked Santa Fe for a convention, the *New Mexican* headline read:

IMMIGRANT GROUP PLANS MEET HERE

The Hispanos, then, were the social cream. All others were Anglo, whether their origins were European, African, Asian, Samoan, or Turk. A popular *chiste* illustrated this peculiarity:

Hispano approaches African American at a Santa Fe polling place and asks the standard Election Day question:

"How much they paying for votes?"

"Don't know," says the African American, "they haven't gotten around to us Anglos yet."

The answer to that question in most precincts in 1952 seemed to be $2.00, but it might have been more. It was a vintage year for New Mexico politics with General Patrick Hurley trying to wrest a U.S. Senate seat from Dennis Chaves. Hurley, an ex-Oklahoma coal miner, had won a fortune in oil, uranium, and law. He was famed as the Secretary of War who sent young General Douglas MacArthur to rout the "Bonus Army" of World War I veterans from Washington during the Hoover Administration and burn their shantytown. More recently he'd been ambassador to Nationalist China and fervent supporter of Chiang Kai-shek. Chaves was the son of a distinguished *patrón* family and had, with many New Mexico Hispanics, shifted from Republican to Democrat during New Deal days. Campaigning was so fierce that the Santa Fe National Bank's supply of dollar bills was exhausted Election Day morning.

In Santa Fe the state capital, county, and city jobs were primarily Hispanic while the Anglos were heavily into the tourism and commercial end of the game. Cultural frosting was added by a lively art colony, which was reinforced by a delegation of "wannabe" painters, sculptors, etc., living off the largesse of wealthy kinfolks.

The most interesting members of any population, of course, are those marching to their own drummers—and old Santa Fe had those aplenty. I think first of "El Gigante," a distinctly Anglo New Englander who had been posted off to the inlands by her prominent family. As the nickname suggests, El Gigante was both tall and of sturdy build. She kept a spare house near her home, doors open and empty except for containers of paint. A sign outside invited children in to try their hand at doing murals on the walls. Needless to say, they did. Being Santa Feans, their parents seemed to consider this normal. Then there was Tommy Maciaoni, who had his name legally changed to "El Differente" when he ran for governor, who never met anything alive he didn't like, and turned out paintings for barter to feed impoverished folks and his vast collection of stray dogs. Another was Aristide Mian, the famed sculptor, who lent excitement to the neighborhood crusade against paving Camino de Monte Sol by using his pick at night to dig out curbs street crews put in by day.

There were other such aplenty, but the situation in the autumn of 1952 gave tyro political reporters such as myself scant time to enjoy them. New Mexico's Democratic Party, dominant since the rise of the New Deal, was in shambles. A Republican sat in the governor's office, a bunch of Young Turk idealists had ousted the good old boys from control of the legislature, an honest fellow had been put in charge of the state police, and grand juries were at work in a half-dozen counties. All this disorder had been triggered by what a lot of people believe was a sort of semiaccidental death.

The victim was Cricket Coogler, a pretty seventeen-year-old Las Cruces brunette, who worked as a waitress and liked to party.

Cricket disappeared one night. Time passed. Rumors reached across the Texas border to the *El Paso Herald Post*. It assigned a reporter to check. The sheriff announces foul play is feared and a suspect was being sought. Easter morning, boys hunting rabbits see Cricket Coogler's pale hand reaching out of the earth.

The covering of Cricket's body has been casual indeed—a bit of sand kicked over her corpse where she was dumped. But the cover-up of the crime was intense and so was the public reaction.

A half century of decaying American moral standards makes that reaction and its effect hard to believe today. Now the disappearance of a teenaged waitress wouldn't rate a mention. The discovery of the corpse might get three paragraphs on an inside page. Our insane "War on Drugs" has made murder a casual everyday affair. But even in those more civilized days the reaction to the death of Cricket Coogler was remarkable. I believe the careless discarding of the corpse touched a nerve—illustrated a sort of arrogance beyond human decency. The Beast was out of its cage in New Mexico. The common folk who had tolerated blatant violation of gambling and prostitution laws and open public corruption revolted. I don't remember the sequence, and doubt if it matters. (Who knows who initiated the mob that stormed the Bastille?) Rumors spread that a very prominent Democratic office holder was the killer and that the sheriff, who was also the county's political czar, had personally wiped out the tracks left by those who had discarded Cricket's body.

The *Herald Post* reporter, Walt Finlay, learned Cricket's body had been taken from its desert resting place to Las Cruces. There, after the sheriff's coroner declared she had been raped, the sheriff had her buried without funeral or autopsy. A clamor for a grand jury arose, was ignored by the district judge and the district attorney, but action was forced by the petition of citizens. The grand jurors decided the sheriff and the district attorney were stalling and made legal history by firing the DA and hiring their own counsel. They ordered the body exhumed for an autopsy, and discovered police had brought in bags of quick lime and buried Cricket in that, thus making the autopsy futile.

The heat increased. The state police chief came down from Santa Fe and took over the cover-up. Word leaks out that a Pittsburgh Steeler running back was locked away in jail as a suspect. The *Herald Post* reporter stalks into the jail, pretending to be an attorney, finds the halfback, and reports his alibi. He is released. A black U.S. Army artillery veteran, employed at a Las Cruces car wash, is then arrested as a replacement suspect. A social worker has reported that the sheriff has been checking young girls out of the state's orphanage to work in bars and for other less savory purposes. The new suspect has been taken to the place when Cricket's body was dumped by the state police chief, the sheriff, and other officers. A bicycle lock has been closed over his testicles and twisted while he is urged to confess. He refuses. Two of the state policeman balk at the torture and walk away. The suspect, badly swollen, is returned to his cell. The word of what has happened reaches the grand jury. Meanwhile a county constable makes a freelance raid on one of the more notorious gambling dens, the operator of which calls for help. Sheriff's deputies arrive, arrest the constable, replace the slot machines he has seized to their former positions, and haul the constable away with a warning. A grand jury indicts the sheriff for his alleged misusing of orphan girls. A friendly judge tosses out the indictment and reinstates him as sheriff. In Santa Fe the chief justice of the supreme court creates a precedent in U.S. legal jurisprudence with an order that, in effect, creates martial law in Dona Ana County. Another justice is sent to Las Cruces to oversee law enforcement. The sheriff, accompanied by a deputy, walks into Walt Finlay's room at the Amador Hotel (in tune with its name ["Lover"] the Amador substituted girls' names for room numbers and the doors were sans locks). The sheriff points his revolver at the reporter's head and says he has decided to kill him. The reporter tells the sheriff that would be a mistake, because he is just an inexperienced beginner and if he is killed the *Herald Post* will send up a team of experienced investigators. The sheriff sees the wisdom of this, agrees, reholsters his pistol, and walks out. Meanwhile, the grand jury decides to take the law into its own hands, summons suspected cops into the jury room, locks them in under guard, and makes the rounds shutting down various illegal operations. A federal grand jury is called and makes more history by indicting the sheriff, state police chief, and a DA's investigator for violating the civil rights of the black suspect. All three were convicted and sentenced to prison.

The center is no longer holding. Things are coming apart. Bugsy Siegel's agents are no longer making offers on Santa Fe real estate as casino sites. Two bag men, both policemen, making their collections at a gambling den, disagree over who gets what and one kills the other. When no charges are filed, the *New Mexican* discovers that the records show the shooter is serving a term in the state prison for a previous homicide. The warden had "given him a leave." The district attorney is asked why the policeman wasn't being tried for this new homicide. The DA says the case has been "settled out of court."

By the time I reached the scene all this was last year's news and I witness only the aftershocks of the earthquake.

For the first time in decades, overwhelmingly Democratic New Mexico had elected a Republican governor, who had campaigned promising to solve the Cricket Coogler murder case. He didn't, nor has anyone else, but the good old boys had lost control of the legislature as well as the state house. The revolution was over but lots of the old gang remained in state and county public offices and grand juries still labored here and there. For me, a young fellow who wanted to be a political reporter, it was the Promised Land.

As "New Mexico Manager" of United Press (with a staff of one man to manage), I was responsible for covering this scene. The one I managed was Jack Bacon, smart and fast but with only about six months of New Mexico experience and a few months newspapering elsewhere. Jack and I were competing against six Associated

Press reporters and, since the AP is a cooperative, the staffs of their member newspapers. How'd we do? Well, since I'm writing this, I'd say we did all right.

The situation in Oklahoma had been vastly different. There most of the newspapers and radio stations (TV was not yet a factor) were UP clients. The AP flagship, the *Daily Oklahoman*, was a sort of journalistic dinosaur—dedicated to keeping the state "dry" with its liquor prohibition law, killing off labor unions, and doing battle with what was left in the 1950s of the state's old tradition of political liberalism. Thus while AP and UP staffing was roughly equal, Carter Bradley was the Michael Jordan of Oklahoma and a lot of journalistic sentiment around the state leaned in our favor. On the other hand the UP was a newcomer in New Mexico, a weak underdog service providing news mostly to radio stations and a little chain of small-town papers put together by Lincoln O'Brien, a handsome and urbane New Englander.

Mr. O'Brien occupied a corner suite in what we called the Chief Wrong Font Buildings. Bacon and I, our three teletype machines, one desk, one typewriter, two chairs, and a filing cabinet were crowded into the tiny adjoining room with its never-washed window looking out at the statue of a huge Art-Deco Indian carving petroglyphs into a slab. (His Wrong Font name came from that most common of typographical errors in which, for example, a word printed in italic type is defaced by a letter from the wrong font, "*sUc*H *aS th*I*s*." The rest of our half of this Wrong Font building was occupied by radio station KTRC, an appropriately different voice for the City Different. The other building was filled by the *New Mexican*, a newspaper noted for the typographical errors that gave our Indian his name.

The contract our union had with United Press provided that Bacon worked a forty-hour week, with time-and-half for overtime. As management, I was paid about $10 a week over union scale, but sans overtime. Bacon opened the bureau about 6 A.M., phone-checked the state police dispatcher and other key sources for ongoing news, scanned the morning edition of the *Albuquerque Journal*, and punched the day's first radio news roundup into tele-type tape—sending it on its way into our radio client studios as he wrote. This system of writing allowed no errors (more accurately, no chance to correct them). One started a sentence knowing it must end properly. By the time you were punching the seventh word the third word was being typed into the radio station's broad-cast script. Our single typewriter collected dust—there rarely being time to actually write a story, read it for editing, etc. It was an unorthodox way to learn English composition, but it quickly con-ditioned the brain to manipulate the language and to zip through the stored vocabulary for those nouns and verbs that fit the need without a clutter of modifying adverbs and adjectives.

My day began about 10 A.M. making the rounds at state capital offices. A stop at the highway department to check the commission meeting agenda and troll for gossip and tips, duck into the State Corporation Commission for the same reasons, five minutes in the governor's office exchanging this and that with The Man or his press secretary (Republicans), and then down the hall to pick up political tips at the office of Secretary of State and Attorney General (all Democrats). So it went. If an office produced news you dialed the bureau number, organizing the information in your head while the telephone rang. Bacon answered with his headset on. I dictated my stories unwritten and unedited as he typed them into tape—sending the word out to the world as he typed.

Since our newspaper clients published for afternoon delivery and the big radio newscasts were at drive-time, the pace slowed after lunch. Time now to check tips. Why were repair crews replac-ing pavement on the Espanola Highway a month after the contrac-tor finished it? Barracks buildings at Camp Luna, closed down by the Army National Guard, were being hauled away by a private company. Had they been sold? Were bids taken? Where was the money going? (That one led to a grand jury indictment of a general.) Was it true that a shipment of 100,000 cigarette tax stamp stickers was missing? Why were $1,456 of State Racing Commission funds spent last year to pay florist shop bills? Has the Child Welfare Department solved its shortage of foster homes? And so forth. In one's notebook a dozen such tips and story ideas always waited time to check them. There was never enough time. Most of them died unchecked.

I'd reach the bureau about mid-afternoon, taking over from Bacon, who would be finishing his shift. Then I'd file the radio roundups for evening broadcasts, write the "overnight file" to be on the news desks of papers the following morning, take care of the paperwork, and head for home by about six-thirty. After sundown the friends one made at state police headquarters and other such news centers had your home number written on their desk pad to tip you in event of emergencies.

It wasn't a job that allowed time for relaxing but anyone who grew up as a daydreamer always finds time to let his imagination take him away. In my case to Stanleyville, the gem city of the Belgian Congo, which was going to be the setting of the great novel I was planning. Even the names are forgotten now, but at mid-century the city and the country were paying the awful price of generations of brutal Belgian colonial exploitation. The Belgians had walked away from the scene of their crimes and left a mix of tribal factions and commercial interests to fight it out. Every combat-trained psychopath who had developed a taste for killing in World War II had a well-paid job awaiting in the mercenary armies fighting for Congo Basin riches. The stately boulevards of Stanleyville were littered with the dead, a ghost city without power, food, or water. The only law, the gun. In other words, the ideal setting for a novel in which I would test the soul of my protagonist. But not now. No time now except to compose scenes in my mind as I trotted back to the bureau from the governor's office or drove home from work. I wrote one first chapter—my hero standing in the lobby of a posh Stanleyville hotel watching shooting and looting along the boulevard. That's as far as it went. Neither time nor skill to do it, but lots of talking about it, making Marie very aware that I yearned to be a novelist.

The 1950s had become the 1980s before that book was to be started. Belgian Congo had vanished from maps and from memories. But the urge to write the story remained and humanity never fails to provide killing fields. I moved the plot to Southeast Asia, named the hero Carl "Moon" Mathias, a much-admired rifle squad leader in Charley Company, and called it *Finding Moon*. It's the closest I have come to writing a book that satisfied me.

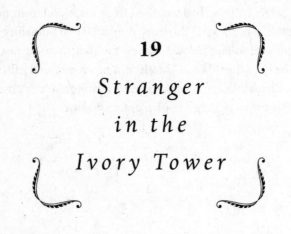

19

Stranger in the Ivory Tower

Bill Barkell, the artistic proofreader of the *New Mexican*, illustrated my decision to desert journalism for academia with one of his cartoons. I'm sitting in lonely isolation atop an ivory tower typing away. Workers are sawing the base of the tower with a foreman explaining the ivory will be made into piano keys. Barkell's wit cut close to the bone. The University of New Mexico was in political trouble. In the rhetoric of that Cold War year, it was a "nest of radical liberals and Soviet apologists." I've long suspected the trouble was why I got the job.

UNM President Tom Popejoy had worked his way through college and graduate school and became an administrator of one of Franklin D. Roosevelt's New Deal programs. Conservatives scorned him and when U.S. Senator Joseph McCarthy was climbing to power attacking the liberal left, like-minded folks in New Mexico joined him. Their targets were professors, not Tom himself, since Popejoy was one of ranch country's good old boys and as a student had kicked the UNM field goal to defeat Arizona. Nobody was going to believe he was a Stalinist.

I had seen this same paranoia in Oklahoma. There a new law required professors to sign a loyalty oath. While many faculty members, notably those just back from being shot at in Europe and Asia, had protested, academic administrators were as craven then as they are now. Two profs at A&M, the state's conservative school, resigned in protest. OU, haven of the liberals, lost only a noted botanist, who had to quit because he held a commission in the Royal Canadian Air Force. The RCAF wouldn't allow him to swear fealty to the United States.

Popejoy was a sort of old-fashioned constitutional patriot and not craven. He got himself invited to address the American Legion convention, a gaggle of right-wingers. He read them a stern lecture on the Bill of Rights and the purpose of the University and told them if they wanted to fire his faculty they would have to get him fired first. That drove the radical right back into its burrow for a bit. I wrote an editorial in the *New Mexican* hailing Popejoy's position and his courage. Years later I found out that he'd read it, learned that I had written it, and that the *New Mexican* was the only voice raised in his support.

I had parted company with the United Press in 1954 and walked across the parking lot behind Chief Wrong Font to become a general assignment and statehouse reporter for the *New Mexican*. And that requires what we fiction writers call "some flashbacking."

The UP had made the decision easy. Someone in authority had promised New Mexico clients to open a bureau in Albuquerque, by now the state's dominant population center. To do this we would operate with one hand (me) in Santa Fe, and one sixty-five miles south operating the Albuquerque office. The situation was impossible. I told my bosses it couldn't work. They said do it anyway. So I quit. By then Jack Bacon had left to join a Trappist monastery and determine if he was cut out to be a contemplative monk. He had been replaced by Jim Carberry, sent down from the Denver Bureau with a journalism degree, virtually no experience, and an uncanny knack for reporting. While we worked together only briefly, I must pause here to defend this claim with an example.

I had broken Carberry in on our routine, showed him around a bit, arranged for a relief man to be sent down from Denver to lend a hand, and took a long-delayed vacation. We were five hundred miles away when maximum-security convicts revolted and took control of the prison in Santa Fe. The governor, the warden, and the state police imposed a total news blackout. All the press knew was that hostages had been taken and the rebels controlled the prison hospital. Carberry, a greenhorn stranger in town, was competing with the mobilized forces of the Associated Press, plus reporters of the *Albuquerque Journal* and the *New Mexican*—AP member papers. Here's what he did.

He read through the back files on past prison unrest and noted two troublemaking lifers (call them Dent and Jackson) as likely riot leaders. He found himself an unwatched internal communication telephone, ordered the switchboard to connect him to the prison hospital, told whoever answered to get Dent or Jackson. Jackson came. Carberry identified himself, told Jackson this was his chance to speak to the public. Jackson gave him a rundown on complaints, hostages, number injured, and demands for amnesty and escape vehicles, deadlines, and death threats. Lesser fellows might have been satisfied with this total scoop (a word current then) but not Carberry. After he called it in he tipped off the authorities that someone had been using the internal phone without clearance— thereby assuring the competition couldn't match his story.

I can take no credit for that coup but retelling it reminds me of how bad it feels to be the victim instead of the victor. In this case the scooper was Mary Goddard, a charming little lady with the *Daily Oklahoman*. Two children of a prominent couple had been savagely murdered in the small Oklahoma town of Pauls Valley. The police were silent. Those of us covering had only a rumor that a woman was being held in the tiny county jail. While the rest of us were trying to worm information out of cops and jailers, Mary entered a bar, drenched herself with beer, and became disorderly enough to be arrested and tucked into the lockup's only cell for women. She bonded out with an exclusive interview —the family's baby-sitter described the gruesome affair while they were cell-mates. (The *Daily Oklahoman*, true to its prohibitionist leanings, refused to pay for the beer listed on her expense account.)

The gruesomeness of that crime reminds me of another coup—a mid-century torso murder case in Oklahoma City in which a tip from a cop provided a break on the victim's identity. The body had been known by the media only as a teenaged female with "RAT" carved into her bosom—the killer having disposed of her arms, legs, and head. (I digress here to illustrate the difference between the UP [Untidy Press] and the AP [Grandma] in those days. My story had said: " 'RAT' was cut in the girl's bosom." The AP story said: "The initials 'r.a.t.' had been cut in the victim's chest." Conclude from that what you will.) Days later came another tip. A driver saw a head floating under a bridge. A quick call to a friendly fellow in the coroner's office and we were out with a bulletin. Our teenaged victim became a middle-aged woman and we were way ahead of AP with the story.

There's a footnote to that. Weeks later another head turned up—this one of a teenaged female. By then it didn't matter. I had been transferred to New Mexico. Let Bradley deal with it.

In Santa Fe my yen to become a novelist grew stronger. The UP Bureau was just up the street from where Territorial Governor Lew Wallace had written *Ben Hur*. Across the parking lot in the newsroom of the *New Mexican*, Oliver LaFarge, whose *Laughing Boy* had won the Pulitzer Prize, was a columnist. The book review editor's *Scrimshaw* had won the National Book Award for poetry. A reporter who regularly sold his short stories to *The New Yorker* had just left, and people who lived by literature could be seen on the plaza, at the grocery, even in the jail drunk tank. All things seemed possible. I started writing short stories, collecting those painful rejection slips, and dreaming about writing the Great American Novel. But on the family front good (albeit distracting) things were happening.

20

Janet, Tony, Monica, Steve, and, Finally, Dan

When destiny ruled that Anne was the only offspring nature would provide us, Marie and I decided to finish building our family by adoption. We were healthy homeowners without criminal records who drew no gender or racial lines. Since official sources announced a surplus of kids and a shortage of would-be adoptive parents, it sounded easy.

It wasn't. Being a political reporter when we started this exhausting process, I guessed it was an attitude problem. Social workers were looking upon themselves as shepherds, the kids in their custody as sheep, and would-be parents the ravening wolves circling their flock trying to snatch away their lambs.

We first applied in Oklahoma City. There Marie's kindly notion that adoption agencies would look upon us as allies was shorn away. We left for New Mexico and filed a new set of applications in Santa Fe. Maybe things would be better there. They were, but not right away.

I was covering the State Capitol and made it a point to focus on the Department of Public Health, custodian of child welfare services. Since the Pill was not yet in universal use and practice of bumping off unwanted sons and daughters pre-birth had not yet been legalized, there was a good supply of kids and a serious need for parents. But the supply of babies was dropping by then and the social workers seemed to see themselves as car dealers with the United Auto Workers on strike and the show rooms being emptied. If they surrendered the kids in their custody to parents, with no new supply coming, they'd put themselves out of work.

Marie still thought my theory too cynical, presuming the adoption bureaucrats were trying to protect the kids from pedophiles and neurotics who thought adoptions would save a shaky marriage. Maybe she was right. Because after months of braving hostile suspicion and smiling our way through various interviews, reference checks, and home inspections, the call finally came.

We rushed down to Albuquerque and met Janet, a petite dark-haired girl of nine months, and were allowed to take her home. Janet wailed relentlessly for three days and three nights before she decided to accept her fate, and then settled happily into a role as baby sister. Meanwhile, Marie, Anne, and I worried about whether they would let us keep her? They would.

With our credentials now established (and a kinder-gentler bureaucrat in power) things got much easier. We managed to add another daughter and two sons to our flock in four years. The first of these was a plump blue-eyed, bald-headed boy whom Marie described as "bewitching." He became Anthony Grove Hillerman, Junior. Tony came with a full and active set of allergies, including aversions to such common stuff as dairy products, wheat products, cats and dogs, etc. Despite that, he was sort of a stoic—smiling through sniffles, rarely crying, happy to entertain himself if any-thing was in reach that he could pretend had a motor in it, and cheerfully accepting supervision by Anne and Janet.

Next came Steve. He was even skinnier than Janet had been and it was easy to see why. Steve was an infantile model of perpetual motion and a baby insomniac. Even now, half a lifetime later, with a tour on a U.S. Navy frigate behind him, I doubt if he's ever missed seeing a sunrise.

Monica was already her own woman when we landed her, a sturdy three-year-old when the welfare people surrendered her to our custody. She had beautiful brown eyes, a charming smile, a four-inch lift built under one shoe, a complicated leg brace, and came with a dire warning. The medical prognosis we received explained that the bones of Monica's short leg lacked a fibula and the usual growth centers. Thus as the good leg grew the shoe lift would have to be repeatedly increased to compensate—eventually to be replaced by crutches and then by a wheelchair.

Along with this disability, the Good Lord had given Monica a remarkably efficient immune system, unusual tolerance of pain and an independent spirit—a product perhaps of being moved from one foster home to another since birth, with long periods spent in hospitals. Hospitals, in fact, seemed to be her favorite resi-dence, and homes merely places she stopped off between them. It took a year or so for Monica to conclude that we were her perma-nent Mom and Dad and maybe she should settle in.

With Monica we closed the books on adoption. Three daugh-ters and two sons seemed about right. A bit later I quit the *New Mexican* and was making the sixty-mile commute down to the UNM campus in Albuquerque while Marie scouted for houses there large enough for seven of us, and near enough for Monica to walk to school until wheelchair time arrived. We found a "fixer-upper" across a vacant lot from a grade school with a full basement adaptable for kids. We moved down from Santa Fe to Albuquerque, from 7,200 foot altitude to 5,200 feet and 65 miles closer to the Carrie Tingley Crippled Children's Hospital. That was significant. We'd discovered that researchers had developed a way to stretch leg bones that refuse to grow and a young doctor practicing at the C.T.C.C.H. had learned the process.

The C.T.C.C.H. then was located in Truth or Consequences which, despite our move, was still a weary 160 miles down the Rio Grande—a drive we had memorized before this treatment was finished and Monica was home again to stay. It began with careful measure of bone lengths and some scientific guesswork at Monica's eventual natural height. When the optimum natural bone length was reached in the good leg, the surgeon stopped its growth. The short leg was fastened into a rack and meticulously broken to avoid damage to the sheath of tissue which covers it. Pins were put through the bone above and below the break and attached to a turnscrew. When the break had almost healed, the screw was turned, the break was widened and left to heal again. It sounds like torture technique from the Tower of London but it worked. She gets around fine with a hardly noticeable special shoe.

We thought we'd moved to Albuquerque with the family complete but it was not to be. The social workers couldn't seem to get Monica's records right. That led to a trip to their downtown office to make sure corrections were made. There we met Daniel Bernard Hillerman. Those who don't believe in Divine Providence, as do Marie and I, would call it an accident.

The office manager was making a pitch to recruit us as a temporary foster home. To illustrate the acute shortage she described one the agency was closing because the woman operating it was neurotic. Only two little boys were left there now. Arrangements were made for one and the other was in limbo because of an undiagnosed health problem. Would we like to meet him?

We would. He clung fearfully to the leg of the woman who brought him in for the introduction, a handsome toddler who, once we had seen him, had no chance of escape. A second visit was arranged and we took him home.

A sympathetic caseworker on a home visit suggested the undiagnosed illness which had kept Danny off "ready for adoption" list was caused by neglect. She said he'd lived his two years in the solitary confinement of a playpen, with no one talking to him, holding him, or playing with him. Do I exaggerate? Our lawn was the first grass he'd ever walked on (scary at first), and the world outdoors in general was new and awesome. A few weeks later we rented a fold-out trailer and took the kids for a mountain campout. It rained, of course, and the night was cold enough to motivate Daniel to speak his first words to us. "More bankey," said young Dan, and was rewarded with an extra blanket.

Danny rewarded us in return by being incredibly reliable. For example he had to wear an eyepatch to correct cross-eyes. Having worn one myself for many an unpleasant month while my injured left eye healed I couldn't believe a three-year-old would wear one. Danny did, and without complaint until the problem was cured. But this reliability led me into the most terrifying evening of my life. When he was thirteen I took him (by then a fervent fisherman) and his friend, Steve Langdon, to the Chama. While I was rigging up my flyrod, untangling the line, etc., the boys rushed off to the river and waded across to Danny's favorite spot. When I got to the bank I was aghast. Spring runoff had started early. The Chama was high and rising. By shouting back and forth over the roaring torrent, they told me they had barely made it without being swept away. I told them to stay put. I'd find a safe way to retrieve them. The nearest bridge upstream was miles up the Chama canyon. Downstream was the Heron dam, which a local fisherman said would require only a two-mile walk down the river. I told the boys to walk down to the dam while I drove back to the bridge and then circled back to pick them up. I was a little uneasy about it, but Danny would use his head and do nothing dumb. It was a long circular drive to Heron and I expected the boys to be at the dam waiting when I got there. They weren't. I climbed down to the stream and began working my way up to it. The river was higher now—a roaring torrent—going was hard, my bad leg was showing the strain, and it was getting dark. Maybe I had missed them somehow. I climbed back to the rim, found another local citizen and told him my problem. He told me the walk from where they'd started to the Heron Dam was about ten miles, not two, and probably impassable with the river this high. He used his CB radio to call the Game Department for a search party. I climbed back down the dam fence, made another effort to get upstream, found it impossible in the dark, and climbed out. It was totally black now. I was exhausted. My newfound friend's radio was dead but he'd wait here in case the boys showed up. I sped off, fueled by dread and fighting off panic, seeking a house connected to a telephone pole. I finally found one. The owner let me use it to call Marie while he got the Game people on his own CB radio to arrange the search party. I'd tell her I had lost the boys in the Chama canyon, ask her to call Steve's parents (probably wondering why their boy was late) and assure them that there was no need to worry. While this was Steve's first fishing trip, Danny was an old hand at river canyons. He'd find them a safe place to spend the night, build a fire, etc.

I dialed. Marie would be cool, I knew, all the way through this. The search for the drowned boys, the finding the bodies, the whole horrible affair. The telephone rang, Marie's voice saying "Hello."

"Marie, I have some—"

"Tony, I've been trying to find you," said she. "Danny just called and—"

DANNY JUST CALLED!! Imagine if you can an instant transition from the black despair to total joy. Danny and Steve had hit a place where downstream movement was impossible and were looking for a place to spend the night. A fisherman on the opposite bank saw them, directed them to a Ponderosa which had fallen partly across the river and then waded far enough out to get them across. He asked where they were to meet me. At the dam, they told him. He took them to El Vado dam, miles away. From there Danny called Marie.

Danny was the last addition. He's a pharmacist now, the doting dad of his own son and daughter, and still a fisherman. Monica, her leg stretched to full utility, provided us with four granddaughters, Steve did a Navy stint in the Pacific, drove 18-wheelers, worked in cable TV, is now fathoming computer programming, remains a bachelor, and stalks the streams and lakes of New Mexico in search of the wily trout. Tony, Jr., maintained his childhood focus on things mechanical and is a technician with American Airlines, proof that genetic blessings aren't erased by conditioning.

Tony had an incredible ability to understand how things work and to fix them. By junior high, my contribution to home maintenance was restricted to showing him the problem, fetching the tools. For example, I lost a section of *The Blessing Way* in the bowels of my new Radio Shack computer. Company technicians weren't able to help. Tony, 15 at the time, volunteered to try. That was a generation before kids cut their teeth on computers and Tony had never been around one. He nagged me into remembering every key I had struck before the disaster, considered this, and devised a complex reverse formula which forced the TRS 80 to print out the missing prose. He and his lovely wife, Lori, have a cat, dog and two horses.

Anne has added a grandson to the family, did tours with the UPI and two newspapers, and now does technical writing, has three non-fiction books to her credit, and helps her husband run a public relations operation. Janet and her husband contributed two grandsons and a granddaughter. She cut off a career in art to concentrate on perfecting them—although I did get her to illustrate my only children's book.

Before we leave this subject and move into the odd world of academia, Marie and I hereby submit our answer to the universal question of those considering adoption. The question concerns parental love for kids you haven't produced yourselves. The answer is don't worry about it. As veterans of raising both kinds we can testify that all of them provoke affection, irritation, worry, joy, dismay, care, pride, anger and, most of all, love. Each and every one of them is our child. Don't try to tell us they had another set of parents. Nor need you worry about adding adoptees into an existing family. Each of our five was greeted with excitement and enthusiasm and had to tolerate being mothered and big-brothered by the siblings they'd joined.

To pursue this sales pitch further, I will report that Barney and his wife Irene had a similar experience. They adopted Carl, Eric and Lucy who formed a happy functional gang, won various kinds of college scholarships and now operate successful families of their own. The same kind of business went on in Marie's side of the family. Happy adoptions everywhere you look, with the latest being Margaret Teresa, collected by out niece Susan McDermott and husband Pat.

For another viewpoint on these issues, I will borrow the article which follows, written by Anne for the *Albuquerque Journal*.

THE SUNDAY JOURNAL

Adopted family very real

■ *Suddenly, there were six stockings to fill, not just one.*

BY ANNE HILLERMAN
For the Journal

Holidays mean family, at least to most people. If we're not celebrating with our parents, children, or siblings, we're remembering when we did.

Because there were six children in my family, the

holidays always brought joyful chaos to our house. Or maybe they just amplified the chaos that was already there.

Realizing that there wasn't much difference between us and our friends' families—at Thanksgiving, Christmas, or any other time of year—we Hillerman kids made it a point to let people know that everyone but me was adopted.

As my parents' first child and the initial grandchild, I spent my earliest years in Oklahoma surrounded by adults who considered me an angel sent to Earth for the sole purpose of receiving their undivided attention. I'm sorry I was too young to recall my first Christmases; life must have been sweet.

Then, when I was about three, we moved to Santa Fe. Shortly thereafter, the adoption of my first sister, Jan, displaced me as the family princess.

My parents said, "Congratulations. You're a big sister." Tony, Monica, Steve and Dan followed and before long there were six Christmas stockings—all the same size— under the tree on Christmas Eve.

My parents stressed to Jan, Tony, Monica, Steve, and Dan that their adoption made them special, much loved, chosen children. They continually reminded me that, as biggest sister, I had to set a good example for this crew. Until I got to be twelve or so, I liked the big-sister business. We had fun. We had fights. We made each other presents and took them back. We loved each other to pieces and got so mad we could hardly stand it.

Then, swept away by the hormonal hurricane of adolescence, I decided I would have been happier as an only child. I could have had a pony for Christmas, I fantasized, if my parents hadn't had so many other gifts to buy. In fact, I would have gotten all the presents, and, even better, all the attention. I pictured my young self as a pirate standing over a chest of golden love tokens, the family treasure, gloating, "All mine. All mine."

During this teen angst period, my family moved to Albuquerque. My classmates at Our Lady of the Annunciation hadn't heard the story of my adopted family so, even though it wasn't as cool as being an only child, I used this legend to win points.

"Don't you have any real sisters?" my new best friend asked. (We didn't care about brothers.)

"Nope," I said smugly. "All adopted." But her contrast wormed its insidious way into my brain's back country. It waited uneasily in the underbrush, stuck on the thorny difference between "real" and "adopted." Then, over the holidays about ten years ago, the thorns turned to roses.

The weekend before Thanksgiving, I was listening to some acquaintances complain about the weirdness of their families and how they struggled through the holidays with their imposed togetherness.

One woman said, "One Thanksgiving morning as a kid—I still remember it—I woke up and I thought: 'This can't be my real family. There must be some mistake here.' But I went downstairs and there they were. As real as it gets."

Her words struck with such resonance that I didn't know whether to laugh or cry. Nothing in my life was more real than my adopted family. What could have been more real than watching Tony on his second birthday, which fell on Thanksgiving Day that year, sitting in his high chair banging a turkey leg against a metal tray, driving us bonkers? What could have been more real than Jan surreptitiously eating cookies in the double bed we shared, then falling asleep on my side, leaving me with the scratchy crumbs? What could have been more real than the six of us, hot and grumpy, squabbling in our station wagon during our annual summer vacation? What could have been more real, or more perfect, than waking up on Christmas morning to a roomful of presents, more than enough for all six of us, under the Christmas tree?

Families have more to do with common memories than common genes. They're more about sharing experiences than sharing blue eyes or curly hair.

When I open my metaphorical treasure chest these days, I realize my parents' investment in love paid dividends that any princess would cherish. Growing up in a big family taught me about differences and commonalties, about compassion and fairness, about the purpose of tears and the healing power of humor.

When I sit down for Christmas dinner, joined by my five adopted siblings, our parents, and our own children, I'm thankful that I wasn't an only child. I intend to celebrate the holidays this year with my real family. I hope you're able to do the same.

Anne Hillerman is a freelance writer living in Santa Fe

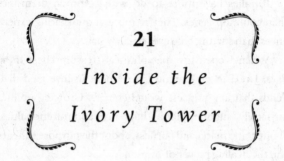

21

Inside the
Ivory Tower

Skip to the winter of 1963, to the office of the acting
chairman of the Department of English at the University of New
Mexico, to yours truly, aged thirty-eight, applying for admission as
a graduate student. The acting chairman was unimpressed by the
credits I had accumulated from my two tours at Oklahoma A&M
or with my University of Oklahoma grades, and even less with my
fifteen years as a journalist. The fact the appointment had been
made for me by the President's Office added the negative of a possible political connection. The acting chairman set aside my paperwork and looked me over.

What had I been reading? I listed *Lee's Lieutenants,* Winston
Churchill's autobiography, *All the King's Men, Profiles in Courage,*

and added William Carlos Williams and a couple of other contemporary poets I thought might make the proper impression. How about the English poets? I admitted that the only ones I enjoyed in that category were Keats and Yeats.

"Here," he said, with a smirk, "we pronounce that Yeah-ts."

I exited his office carrying a list of undergraduate courses I'd have to pass before I could be a full-fledged graduate student and an enduring psychic glitch (Is it Kates and Yeats, or Yeah-ts and Keats?). I left behind the notion of my own importance as an ex-newspaper editor, ex-wire service state manager, and a reporter who had wrenched an angry "no comment" from General Dwight D. Eisenhower and had been effective enough in the most recent Democratic presidential nomination campaign to be called a "dirty son-of-a-bitch" by Pierre Salinger (Senator John F. Kennedy's spinmeister) and a "miserable son-of-a-bitch" by Senator Lyndon Johnson himself. The acting chairman of English had clarified my status. I was now a student. In 1963 neither civil rights laws nor Lincoln's Emancipation Proclamation covered that bottom of the barrel category of citizenship.

The high points of that return to scholarship persuaded me that education is indeed wasted on the young. One was Professor Catherine Simon, who got me so absorbed in Shakespeare that I actually believed I'd found a new understanding of his techniques in *Hamlet*, that most thoroughly plowed of literary fields. But best of all, Dr. Morris Friedman.

Friedman taught a writing course that focused on the essay. He was himself an author, which impressed me, and he saw promise in my work—which impressed me even more. Early in this course he asked me why I never wrote in the first person. I told him journalists are conditioned to be invisible, to be what Walter Lippmann called "the fly on the wall," seeing everything and feeling nothing. (Alas, less in fashion today than in 1964.) Try it, he said. Do me a memoir bit. I proposed a thousand words on something that had happened last month. No, he said. Memories age well. Time turns slag metal into gold. Skip way back.

I did. I found the capital I on the typewriter and described my father's dying day as an account of myself watching this happen. It opened a new field for me. Friedman gave me an A on that paper and I was eager to know why.

For example, Friedman said, "You show us not just his books on the shelves, but the glass which preserves them."

I said, "Yes, he loved his books."

"From the titles you mention, I'd say they were politically inflammatory for the times. So, as your reader," said Friedman, "I think that glass protects both his books from the dust, and his children from the books."

Exactly!

Thus, Morris Friedman caused me to begin thinking of what can be done with those significant little details, and the value of the sort of ambiguity from which readers form their own conclusions.

My second debt to Professor Friedman came when he chaired my master's thesis committee. Friedman knew the seven Hillermans were living on savings, a part-time salary, and my freelance writing efforts. For my thesis he suggested I do a series of essays about places, people, or situations I wished to describe and that they should be aimed at a popular audience. Doing these well enough to reach the target audience by magazine publication would weigh favorably on the academic scale. (Those essays were subsequently published as *The Great Taos Bank Robbery and Other Legends of Indian Country.*)

Dr. Friedman also helped the cause by endorsing me to his agent, Ann Elmo, and telling her to expect some of my articles.

With a toe in the door of the New York publishing world, I put a bunch of my stuff in a briefcase and flew off to get acquainted with my agent. I expected a leisurely lunch to talk about prospects and I'd tell her about the novel I intended to write. I arrived exactly at the 11 A.M. appointment time, introduced myself to a fellow in the outer office, and was waved in. Ms. Elmo, a small lady, was barely visible in her chair behind a tumbling wall of what I presumed were manuscripts. I introduced myself. She looked puzzled. I mentioned the letter Friedman had sent. Oh yes, she said. Morris said you might send me something. Did you bring it instead? I said I had. How long would I be in New York? Until tomorrow evening. Leave your stuff with the secretary, Ms. Elmo said, and give him your hotel number. I'll call you.

On the way out I noticed that it was now four minutes after eleven—about an hour and 56 minutes less of her time than I had expected.

Her telephone call was equally brisk and efficient. She believed she could sell two of the items, perhaps three. Would I accept commissions for other story ideas if she could find them? Yes, I certainly would. Have a safe trip home.

Ann promptly sold the two for more money than I'd expected and sent back the third with suggestions for a different approach for another mag. For several years she sold my stuff and lined up assignments until I escaped from freelancing into fiction. Then came a problem, but this isn't the place to deal with it. I must get back to my part-time job with the office of UNM President Tom Popejoy.

22
Doer of Undignified Deeds

Journalism is a small world where word spreads fast in the network. Keen Rafferty, the chairman and founder of the University of New Mexico Department of Journalism, contacted me. He was getting old, he told me, and wanted to retire in two or three years. Professor Bud Germain, his right-hand man, didn't want the chairman job. How about getting a master's degree at the U and taking a shot at it. I said how about making a living in the meantime? Well, he said, after President Popejoy's speech warning the American Legion they'd have to get him fired if they wanted to abolish academic freedom, Popejoy had asked him how many newspaper editors had backed him and you were it. Rafferty said he would see if Popejoy needed a graduate student assistant.

Guess what. He did. Some days later the call came. Would I

drop down to Albuquerque and talk to Popejoy. It became one of those days Marie and I vividly remember.

The job interview involved Popejoy, Dr. Sherman Smith, who was a noted professor of chemistry, and John Perovich, who was the university's comptroller—the trio whom I knew as the U's lobbying team during legislative sessions. We chatted about the most recent session for a bit. Smith left to attend a meeting. A little later, a call came for Perovich and he departed. Shortly thereafter, Popejoy's secretary reminded him he had an appointment. He got up to leave, shook my hand, gave me an envelope. It's a contract proposal, he told me. Think it over and let me know what you think.

Thus ended the job interview. Not a word had been spoken about what I would be doing. The hours, the pay, duties, or responsibilities were never mentioned. The contract was a little more specific, but not much. If I signed it, I would begin "part-time" employment on January 1, 1963, at a pay somewhat higher than Marie and I had decided we had to have. Jubilation!

This undefined and untitled job began with settling into a very small office in the administration building, getting enrolled in classes, meeting people, doing a little work in the Public Information Office, guest lecturing to a couple of journalism classes and learning to live outside the pressure cooker of fierce competition and relentless deadlines. After a bit Popejoy would suggest I attend this committee meeting, or that hearing. Then I was added to those planning a celebration of the school's Seventy-fifth Anniversary, which finally involved some writing. But now I was out of the real world and into the society of intellect, where one was expected to think about it first.

For example, departments interested in botany, hydraulics, herpetology, geology, mineralogy, insects, and all things natural were lusting for a few thousand acres of the Maria Elena Gallegos Land Grant, which extended miles from the Rio Grande to the crest of the Sandia Mountains and separated Albuquerque from the reservation of the Sandia Pueblo. One Thursday I was handed a bundle of documents prepared by the various departments explaining why this land offered unique research possibilities. My assignment was to write a statement summarizing all this for the edification of the owner and those advising him.

It produced the familiar nostalgic feeling of pressure. It's Thursday, I thought. I'll read through the stuff tonight, get on the writing Friday morning. I should have it wrapped up by midafternoon. I asked Popejoy how soon he needed it. Popejoy directed the question to Sherman Smith, who was ramrodding the project. Smith said he was meeting the important people on the seventeenth. He'd like to see it by the fifteenth. Odd. Today was the nineteenth. My puzzlement must have showed. Smith asked if that would give me enough time. When I asked him, incredulous, if he meant the fifteenth of next month, he said: "If you can have it finished by then."

Looking back on that happy period of working for Popejoy and his little unofficial cabinet, I can't claim many accomplishments. I would like to claim credit for the establishment of the University of New Mexico School of Medicine, which quickly spawned a massive hospital, cancer research center, noted burn and trauma operation, and one of New Mexico's largest payrolls. But that claim would have to be based on the same theory that credited losing a kingdom to losing a horseshoe nail.

My role involved burned mattresses.

You're going to get a call from the Sandoval County sheriff, Popejoy told me. He had a fire in his jail. See what you can do for him.

Fresh from handling political news in Santa Fe, I didn't need to be told the name of the sheriff nor of his kinship with a member of the State Senate. The sheriff called. His prisoners had acted up, started a fire in the cell block and burned eleven mattress. He had no budget to replace them and he didn't want to alert the press to this affair. Could he get some from the university? I told him I'd call him back.

While the dorms had none to spare, we had recently completed an "Outward Bound" program for the Peace Corps. Abandonded corps mattresses were filling storage space under the football stadium. I told the sheriff where to pick them up. He did. Case closed. But that's not the way politics works.

Months later in the Senate hallway, where I was working as a sort of "gofer" on Popejoy's lobbying crew, I was accosted by the sheriff's senatorial brother, whom I will call Eloy. Hillerman, he says, you're holding my IOU. I don't like unpaid debts. What do you need?

I told Eloy our top priority was to get the med school authorization out of the Senate Finance Committee. We were one vote short. Eloy examined my list of Ayes and Nays and tapped the name of a Nay Senator from an eastern county. Change him from No to Yes, he said. I explained that this Eastsider was leading the opposition. That's all right, said Eloy. He owes me one.

Thus evildoers in the Sandoval jail got mattresses and New Mexico got an incredibly expensive medical school and I am one of a multitude of folks who can claim a bit of credit.

My job with Popejoy bore neither title nor authority, but university people began referring to me as the president's assistant and I began referring to myself as assistant to the president. As the foregoing suggests this might have been "Doer of Undignified Deeds." Here's another example.

Popejoy called. Go down to Ecuador and inspect our little campus in Quito, he said, and give me a report. I think, "Why me?" The campus was devoted to cosmic ray research in the high Andes, to linguists studying the languages of Andean populations, and so forth. Not my fields and I speak only Border Spanish, and don't even have faculty status. I point this out to the president. Well, says Popejoy, I also want you to take some money and contact a lawyer whose name I'm going to give you, because we're trying to get three students out of jail.

Naturally I want to know the charges. Popejoy seems to have only vague and secondhand information: a young fellow killed, dope dealing possibly involved, our students innocent victims of a misunderstanding, and a Quito lawyer taking steps to have them freed. Popejoy suggests that the less said about the contents of the briefcase I'll be carrying the better and that Marie should go with me.

So Marie and I arranged for someone to oversee our young-sters and made round-trip arrangements on Air Ecuador's old turboprop—the only carrier then making daily Miami to Quito flights. We also started greeting at our door the parents of Quito campus students bringing envelopes and packages for delivery— some gifts and some of what we were thinking of as bail money. The mission was accomplished. The three students came home and the university avoided bad publicity and I accumulated a new bunch of characters, situations, and scenes for whenever I got around to writing an action-adventure novel. That book has never been written but the material awaiting it still rattles around in my shopping cart. To wit:

(1) A socially prominent U.S. ambassador who knows neither the language nor the history of the nation in which he is stationed; (2) A real estate ad in the Quito paper offering for sale a huge ranch, with home, barns, stables, eighteen horses with equipment, approximately a thousand head of cattle and eleven families of workers; (3) Three middle-aged Ecuadorian men walking slowly down the cobblestones bent under their burdens—great sheets of plywood; (4) The tux-and-diamonds crowd in the downtown Quito casino, playing mostly roulette, watched by the silent hard-eyed men who looked exactly like the same fellows watching the black-jack tables at Binions in Las Vegas, the Moulon in Manila, the Seasons in Ankara, Club Bien Suerte in Mexico City, Trump's place in Atlantic City, and the paddle-wheel gambling joint in New

Orleans; (5) A middle-aged American carrying a Well-Tab briefcase on the airliner who, when I tell him that Barney had logged wells for Well-Tab, tells about me the recording tapes he's carrying back to the home base labs from the wildcat wells being drilled at Ecuador's contested border with Colombia—a laconic recitation of intrigue, jungles, Army conspiracy, danger, and immense amounts of money. Enough stuff for a dozen novels; (6) Ecuadorian Air Force officers lounging around the Quito airport after seizing the national airline on our departure day; (7) The lawyer who'd accepted the envelopes from our briefcase doing his magic with the local Braniff Airlines *jefe*, causing him to accept our now worthless tickets and giving Marie and me seats on Braniff's once-a-week flight back to Florida.

Mix those and others with a plethora of images of barren Andean peaks and vast empty landscapes and all you need is a sensible plot and a central character. But that year I was added to the journalism faculty as its third man. Thus began my teaching career. Heavy-duty writing had to wait because I couldn't escape the lure of campus politics.

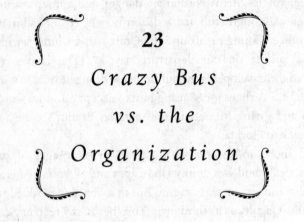

23

Crazy Bus
vs. the
Organization

In those olden days degrees were granted and academic policies decided (so we were supposed to believe) at meetings of the entire faculty. At these we debated whether to abolish the F, eliminate "well-rounded education" requirements, exhort the city council of Lovington to recognize a garbage workers' union, insist on our right to pick our own "faculty representative" for the National Collegiate Athletic Association, require football players to actually attend classes, and so forth. Since I was suffering withdrawal symptoms after long immersion in real world politics, I found academia's version of the game fascinating. Before long I became identified with a faction called "the Organization," composed mostly of high-tech types, those from the hard sciences, and some from the more traditional fields, such as history. At the other end of the spectrum stood the "Crazy Bus," driven mostly by professors in the Department of Sociology, the College of Education, School of Law, younger anthropologists and philosophers. Crazy Bus philosophy was a mix of 1930 Marxism, Nihilism, Hedonism, and disgruntlement. Ours was basic pragmatism with an overlay of Harvard Envy and survivalism.

That survivalism isn't as exaggerated as it sounds. The usual uproar over whether the U should shift from being an educational institution and become a instrument of social reform had been drowned out by a fuss over a poem. This poem, aptly entitled "Love Lust Poem," was more lust than love. It had been included in a stack of poems a teaching assistant had copied and put out for his freshmen to select from for the basis of a required critical paper. Think of "Love Lust Poem" as the flint.

Now think of the tinder as a legislator who yearned to be a congressman but had no name recognition.

Think of the person who pulled the trigger, striking flint to steel and igniting the tinder of ambition as an African American housewife and mother who had enrolled in this course to advance her education. She and another older student were offended by this piece being used among the kids in freshman English. They objected up the administrative channels all the way to the president and past him to the regents and hence to the legislature. At the capital, the Xerox machines went into overtime action, making "Love Lust" a contender as the most widely distributed, read, and discussed poem in the twentieth century and the keystone in the congressional election campaign of State Representative Harold "Mud" Runnels.

• The candidate was known as Mud Runnels, mostly because his business was selling oil well drilling mud I'm sure, but his repertory of jokes and anecdotes were not the sort one heard at church picnics. While the poem was a remarkably specific and earthy description of a multitude of ways to produce sexual gratification, I doubt if it included language Runnels hadn't used in his stories. However, the desire to become a congressman had improved his standards. Copies of the poem went to legislators, civic clubs, church groups, veterans' organizations, etc., with demands that the offending teacher be fired, the dean dumped, the English Department chairman replaced, the university president ousted. At Runnel's urging, the House Appropriations Committee voted overwhelmingly to cut the appropriation of the university to one dollar for the next fiscal year.

Expressions of outrage came from all parts of New Mexico. For example, the Silver City Council suggested the university be shut down. (The councilmen considered the "Love Lust Poem" serious enough to take time off from their own problem. The madam of their main street whorehouse had been sending her protection money to the FBI Academy in Washington for delivery to the Silver City lawman taking a refresher course there. Something had gone wrong with the delivery of the money. Arrests were made which aroused the fury of the lady operating the whorehouse.)

This poem uproar was wonderful grist for the faculty mill. The Crazy Bus folks invited the governor down to a rally on the mall, where one of the academics read the poem to him over the public address system, with heavy emphasis on the four-letter words and to the cheers of students. The chairman of the English Department (who had previously accepted a job offer in New England) invited local TV newsmen to attend a freshman English class and brought in gay and lesbian folks to explain to the youngsters the sexual mechanics of their life style. On the other side of the spectrum, The Organization was more quietly engaged in discussing how some semblance of academic freedom and paychecks might be salvaged from this mess. They were, but no thanks to us.

The university president then was Dr. Ferrell Heady, an all-around admirable man. He kept his cool and his sanity and refused to fire anyone. The teaching assistant was shifted to a more mature section, and Mud Runnels became our new Democratic Party congressman. Bedlam at faculty meetings shifted back to whether

we should declare the campus a Safe Haven for Vietnam draft resis-
tors, eliminate all grading and entrance requirements, prohibit the
National Guard from entering university property, etc.

The anti-guard sentiment grew out of a protest of the bombing
of Cambodia. Students declared a sit-in of the Student Union
building and sat. I sent some of my reporting students over to show
me how they could handle the event. Campus police showed up,
got the students to separate themselves into those who wanted to
be arrested and those who didn't, and brought in a bus to haul the
arrestees (including my students) off to be booked into jail. All very
civilized.

But the governor somehow came to believe that he had been
asked for help. He called out the National Guard. The National
Guard brass sent in several truckloads of guardsmen—mostly
teenagers and some still high school students. The guard officers
seem to have told these kids that the sit-inners were Communists
and were probably armed with machine guns, etc. So the kids
climbed off their trucks preterrified by their officers—helmets on
and bayonets fixed.

The first casualty of this was a guardsman bayoneted accidentally while getting off the truck. As the fiasco wore on the toll
climbed to eight. The other victims included a TV cameraman (the
guard spokesman insisted he had been stabbed by a rosebush),
assorted folks who had gone down to see what was going on, an
injured athlete passing by on crutches on his way to class, and two
fellows carrying an early victim to an ambulance on their stretcher.
Since the sit-in folks had all ridden away on the jailhouse bus they
missed the excitement.

When Dr. Heady tired of the foolishness and retired, the
regents looked at William E. "Bud" Davis, president of Idaho
State U, to replace him. Since Davis was a blue-collar fellow
untainted by Ivy League elitist pretensions and could cite success in
nagging the Idaho legislature for funding, he looked good to me.
On the dark side, he was a former coach and had once even

coached the Colorado U footballers. True, he had been drafted into the job after the regular coach and much of the team had been fired for NCAA violations and, true, he had been replaced after a single disastrous season. But none of us in the Organization wanted to be presided over by a coach—even a losing one.

Davis apparently sensed this opposition, apparently wasn't aware that no regent even knew we existed, and asked to be invited over to my office to field our questions. In about thirty minutes he had converted us. When he got the job he came by my office again and asked me if I'd be his administrative assistant. I said I wanted to continue teaching. He said how about trying it for a year until he learned the ropes, meanwhile still teaching one course. Pay raise? Such philistine matters are not discussed in the lofty world of academia, but the answer is no. The recompense was a second office and the added status of having fellow faculty members believe you knew what was going on.

My new office in the administration building was larger and its broad oft-washed windows looked out on the grassy mall surrounding the duck pond. The grimy window in my faculty office looked down on Yale Park, the staging area for student protests and the launching point for the demonstration-of-the-month. City crews had removed river stones from the landscaping in the divider on adjoining Central Avenue depriving the Doves of their ammunition, but the lawn still often carried the aroma of fresh tear gas and it was a view I hated to trade for the dead calm outside my new window and the more intellectual excitement at the seat of power.

The intellectual excitement was quick to come. Davis, who had been splitting his time between winding up affairs at Idaho State and lining up financial support in the New Mexico legislature, arrived Saturday to take over full time. He was awakened Sunday morning by a call from the chairman of the Senate Appropriations Committee. Had Davis seen the front-page headline in the *Albuquerque Journal*? No. What did it say? It said that a modern dance troupe from New York scheduled to perform in Popejoy Hall would doff its tutus and do its thing with genitalia adangle, in the name of high art and improving the culture of the outback. The Senator had been one of the U's supporters in the antiwar riots and the "Love Lust" affair. He said he didn't think he could deal with this in his committee. If the dancers' skivvies went down, the U's budget would inevitably follow.

Davis called a meeting of those he could reach on Sunday morning and asked our opinion. He doubted naked dancing on the university stage would have raised eyebrows in Idaho. How about New Mexico? I pause here to put this in context. This was about thirty years ago when some semblance of public modesty still survived. Davis was a certified Democrat and had been the Idaho party's nominee for U.S. Senate. Members of the group he'd managed to assemble were also of the Democratic persuasion—but mostly of my own fuddy-duddy blue-collar John L. Lewis, Harry Truman type—not the modern, politically correct demos of today. Our preliminary suggestion was to declare that we needed money for faculty pay raises and new hires more than we needed liberation from our vagina/penis inhibitions. He should tell the dancers to keep their tutus on.

"First day on the job," says Davis, "and you want me to establish myself as the only Philistine among the Greeks." How about some better ideas? Being the gofer, I located the manager of Popejoy Hall. What's his opinion? He doesn't care. Does the contract provide for a naked dance? It doesn't. This is a new one they've been practicing and want to add, sort of to see how it flies in Toonerville. Maybe I should just tell them to stick to the original program, he says. Good idea, I say. Davis agrees.

In an odd way, typical of academia, it was. Here's how it worked. The dancers decide their artistic integrity is being stained. They bitch to friends in the Department of Dance, who spread the word that our new president has laid the heavy hand of censorship on art. The cry of censorship reaches the media. The president's office, where I now have a chair, gets calls from the outraged.

Reporters arrive and are told the president has been made aware of
the situation and is looking into it. More calls. President informs
those interested that he understands the dancers are going to
dance just as their contract provided. The university is making no
modifications in the original contract. (How's that for creative
ambiguity?)

The dancers, of course, defiantly doff their tutus and do their
thing au naturel.

I am not a fan of modern dance, didn't go and wasn't aware
until weeks later that what was then called "indecent exposure"
had been committed in Popejoy Hall. The press saw no need to
cover a dance without the controversial full-frontal nudity and
apparently didn't attend either. Those who had so fiercely opposed
naked dancing on the taxpayers' stage stayed home happy in the
mistaken belief they had won. The thousand or so in the audience
were apparently unimpressed. (A student of mine who went said
he'd seen better every morning in the latrine of his Army barracks.) And the legislature gave the U its best appropriation in
years.

Alas, Davis was not always so lucky. The very worst of it hit him
just after he emerged from a flight at the Albuquerque airport. I
emerged from another flight and ran into him in the lobby of
Albuquerque International Airport just as the bad news arrived. A
reporter who had been awaiting the president's return rushed over
and asked Davis what he had to say about the Federal Bureau of
Investigation raiding the Pit.

A jaw-dropping question. The Pit is UNM's eighteen-thousand-
seat basketball arena, New Mexico's version of Madison Square
Garden and the home of the U's athletic money machine—its basketball team. The FBI, Davis and I were told, had paid its visit hunting evidence of illegal interstate gambling. Rumors of point spread
fixing, etc., added frosting to the cake. In New Mexico basketball
is king. Even with dismal losing teams, the beloved Lobos were
outdrawing UCLA during John Wooden's string of championship

seasons. Today sports scandals are too common to draw much attention. But that was back in the age of relative innocence. In New Mexico, this was a disaster akin to being annexed to Texas.

The FBI's gambling raid produced more smoke than fire but investigators of the NCAA were more successful. Most of the team turned out to be ineligible, coaches were jettisoned, sports writers found it hard to believe that Davis, a former coach himself, didn't know what was going on. More painful for me, they found it hard to believe that I, Davis's gofer and an experienced investigative reporter, was as ignorant of all this as I insisted.

That experience may have improved my journalism teaching. Having written many a caption under photos of embarrassed politicians trying to explain things, I now learned how it felt to be the face staring sheepishly into the camera above those captions. It teaches compassion.

Looking back on my two sessions as presidential gofer I can think of only one improvement for which I can take total credit. The medical school surely would have been established even if I had not found those eleven mattresses for the sheriff's jail but I alone improved the scenery beside the Administration Building. The landscaper had carefully measured off the space between my office and the duck pond, and carefully placed trees rooted in tubs exactly where he wanted them to be planted the next day. One of them blocked the view from my office window. When the workday had ended I went out and moved the tree about fifteen feet to the north. There it still stands—the only monument to my gofer career.

I had hoped I had produced a permanent solution to another university problem—elimination of a chronic exam-day bomb threat—but I doubt if the cure lasted. The solution was to ask the president's secretary to divert the bomb threat calls to me. These came early on mornings when important tests were scheduled and the procedure had been to immediately notify campus police. They would go to the threatened building, search for the bomb, and inform all instructors they could either move the class outside to the lawn or reschedule it later. My policy was simpler. I thanked the caller for his courtesy, hung up, told the secretary it was just a joke, and forgot it. This produced "deniability" in case the word got out that we were ignoring bomb threats. But what bomb threater is going to publicly complain? Classes were held as usual and after five or six such episodes the fraternity boys who were getting F's on the exams they hadn't showed up to take discontinued the practice. I don't know if the bomb threat tradition has been restored. One day after delivering a lecture so bad even I knew it was boring, I decided to quit academia and return to the real world.

For about fifteen years teaching had been fun. Now what I enjoyed doing was writing. I quit academia, knowing I wouldn't miss the administrative chores of the Ivory Tower; thinking I would miss teaching even though I had lost the edge. Miss it I did but not for long.

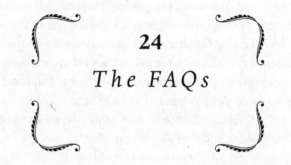

24

The FAQs

If my experience is typical the Frequently Asked Questions faced by writers at book signings are "Where do you get the ideas?" and "When do you write?" In my case, the first question is often how did a white man such as myself get acquainted with the Navajos and their traditional culture. Answering that requires a brief biographical recap, eight grades in an Indian school, Indian playmates, growing up knowing that the us of the us-and-them formula put us hardscrabble rural folks, Indians and whites, in the same category—contrasted with urban folks who had money, or so it seemed to us. In other words, I had no trouble at all feeling at home with Navajos. They were the folks I grew up with. To experience exotica, I attended a College of Arts and Sciences faculty meeting. Navajos like Alex Etcitty, Austin Sam, James Peshlakai,

and a good many others, seemed to sense this, and that I was seriously interested in their culture. They helped. For example, when I
told Peshlakai I intended to have Jim Chee take the woman he was
wooing to witness a traditional wedding, Peshlakai sent me a
videotape of his daughter's wedding. When I was working on a
subplot involving friction on the Navajo/Hopi border, he took me
to meet some of those most bitterly involved. When I was having
trouble with *Talking God* because I had never seen the Yeibichai
curing ceremony which was crucial to the plot, Austin Sam found
one and took me to it. From the time Alex Etcitty thumbed a ride
with me on the road to White Horse Lake until his death he was a
hugely helpful bridge between the scholarly dissertations on
Navajo mythology and the Way of the Dineh I was reading, and
the current world of sheep camps, bootleggers, and the shaky
assimilation of teenagers. Etcitty was born to the Taadii Dineh, the
clan of his mother, was elderly when I met him, and never failed to
field my questions. He helped me understand the Dineh values,
which make having more than you need a sure symptom of evil,
which make beauty in sky or landscape valuable enough to stop the
car and watch the cloud shadows move across the valley, which
make adding your prayers to an aunt's curing ceremonial far more
important than keeping your job.

There were many others who helped me. A teacher of English
at Shiprock who had his students consider a subplot I was planning
to see if it would work. It wouldn't. I had to junk it. A young man at
Tuba City explained to me how an eagle is caught when an eagle is
needed for a ceremony. A Marine Corps veteran—one of the
famous code talkers of the Pacific war—described his journeys to
the Four Sacred Mountains to collect the elements required for his
medicine bundle.

Even with this kind of help, even with the knowledge that
myth, ceremonials, and taboos vary among the multitude of
Navajo clans, I was nervous about my role as a white man describing Navajo ways. That problem was eased at the 1987 Navajo Tribal

Fair. When Marie and I showed up at Window Rock to attend the event I was told I was supposed to ride in the fair parade. After I asked for an older and fatter horse than the one offered, I was relegated to a convertible and traveled down the highway one car behind the Navajo tribal princess through rows of highway-side spectators greeting me with shouts of "Who the hell are you?" The tribe more than made up for that put-down by presenting me with a plaque declaring me

SPECIAL FRIEND OF THE DINEH

"As an expression of appreciation and friendship for authentically portraying the strength and dignity of traditional Navajo culture."

The answer to the "Where do you get the ideas" question is that writers' minds are a jumbled, chaotic attic cluttered with plot notions, useful characters, settings for events, bits and pieces of information, overheard remarks, ironies, cloud formations, bumper sticker slogans, unresolved problems, bon mots, tragedies, heroics, etc. One's memory contains enough stuff to produce three or four longer versions of *War and Peace* if only one could sort it out and form it into a coherent fable.

That leads to the next FAQ. "When do you write?" One writes while peeling potatoes, driving to work, standing in line, suffering through a boring movie, eating oatmeal, digging out dandelions, trying to drift off into naptime sleep. Finally when the sorting is mostly completed and the next scene is set in the imagination, one goes to the computer and types it onto the screen.

I liken the writer to the bag lady pushing her stolen shopping cart through life collecting throwaway stuff, which, who knows, might be useful some way some day. It's an apt analogy and I can't imagine a better profession for such scavenging than journalism, where "If it ain't interesting it ain't news." The dinky little state capital at Santa Fe, with its mixture of artists, Indian cultures, nuclear scientists, ski bums, refugees from embarrassed kinfolks, hippies drifting down from their big communes around Taos, etc., was a fruitful place for a wannabe novelist to load his shopping cart.

That's true wherever a reporter works. Borger gave me the wise, amiable, and honorable sheriff who, with some Navajo culture added, became Lieutenant Joe Leaphorn.

So what memories come to mind after forty years?

I see a well-dressed young matron happily shopping in an upscale department store in Oklahoma City—a woman I'd watched a month earlier as murder trial defendant facing a charge she had killed her sleeping husband and their baby. At the same time I was covering another trial—an orphanage runaway who had abducted a vacationing family of four and killed them for their money and their car. Both defendants pleaded insanity. She was represented by the best legal team her wealthy family could hire. He was represented by a court-appointed lawyer. She was committed to a mental hospital until cured. He was sentenced to life in prison. There should be at least a short story in how quickly a rich girl's insanity is cured and a poor boy's overlooked.

A teenage boy sitting nervously on a bench in the police station—the only survivor of a fire that killed his mother and two younger sisters. Why was he sitting there? I don't know. Neither, I suspect, did he. Probably because firemen found him crying and distraught outside the flaming building and didn't know what to do with him. While awaiting whatever happens next he seems to have indicted himself for negligent homicide. He chooses me, waiting down the bench to talk to the captain, as his jury. He explains why only he is alive—persuading me, but not himself. Another short story waiting to be written.

General Dwight Eisenhower, newly retired, at a press conference. His aide, a newly retired colonel, has sternly instructed the half-dozen reporters present in his hotel suite that the general will talk only about the nonprofit association he now heads. No political questions will be allowed. The general talks. He asks if we have questions. "General," says a retired one-stripe private, "it's said you're willing to accept the Republican nomination for President. Is that true?" The ex-five-star general glowers at the ex-one-stripe private, snaps out a "no comment," and thus completes for me a glorious moment of civilian status fully savored.

Johnson Murray, son of former governor "Alfalfa Bill" Murray, has been elected to the post his father held. I am sent to interview the old man. His home is a second-floor room of a down-and-outer hotel on Fourth Street. We had met briefly a year before. He'd come into the Oklahoma State Senate chamber with a book sack filled with copies of *The History of Oklahoma*. He'd written it and while he was governor the state Board of Education had adopted it as the text required in all schools. Now he was going up and down the aisle, a skinny, bent, and bearded old man, offering copies for sale to the Senators and stopping to chat with us at the press table.

He opened his hotel room door to my knock and stood in his socks, inviting me in, holding the shoes he'd been polishing in his hands. "Another chance to sell you my Oklahoma history," he said, "but you want to talk about Johnson."

I did, but he didn't. He wanted to talk about Alfalfa Bill, of how he had wrestled control of the Democratic Party from the oil exploiters, of deeds he'd done for the poor, of sending the Oklahoma National Guard to seize control of the Red River highway bridges when Texas tried to put in tollbooths, and so forth. For me that was old news, and back at the UP Bureau Carter Bradley was waiting for what Alfalfa Bill had to say about his son's election. I maneuvered him back to that.

"He's not all that bright," said Alfalfa Bill. "Not as smart as you'd hope. But then, the people of Oklahoma weren't voting for my boy. They were remembering Alfalfa Bill." Which is the way I wrote it. Bradley tossed it back to me. "Just you and the old man in the room," he said. "Use your head. This gets printed. Tomorrow we're running his denial. Never said a word of that. Never even talked to you. Which is what our retraction has to say."

So my revised story reported that former governor Alfalfa Bill Murray says he thinks the election of his son reflects good memories folks have of him, recalls some of his exploits as Oklahoma's first Indian governor, and provides enough details of the poverty in which he is living to put a little dent in the generalization about political corruption. I'm left with one of those intensely graphic memories of a proud old man in a dingy room who shares a bathroom down a long hallway with the same poor folks he tried to help. I haven't found a use for it in fiction yet, but I can't get it out of the shopping cart.

Another incident I've never forgotten was directly useful in a novel and had a lot to do with making me dead serious about trying to become a novelist. It happened at Santa Fe.

The call from the deputy warden was directly to the point. Robert Smallwood, scheduled to die that evening for a cold-blooded double murder, had asked to talk to me. If I wanted to see him, be at the prison main entrance at 2 P.M. "Just me?" I asked. "You and John Curtis," he said. "Curtis said he'd come."

Curtis was manager of the Santa Fe bureau of the Associated Press but we were friends as well as competitors and made the fifteen-mile drive from Santa Fe to what was then the "new prison" in his car. Smallwood was the news story of the day. At midnight he would become the first person executed in New Mexico's shiny new gas chamber. He had been condemned for murdering a newlywed couple who had stopped to help him with a stalled (and stolen) car and he was a suspect in a list of other unsolved homicides. Such a death row visit was not new to me, and certainly not to Curtis, who was years my senior in the reporting business. We didn't expect much. Smallwood would reassert his innocence, or (better for our purposes) he'd admit the deed, proclaim his sorrow, and ask us to plead with the governor for a stay of execution. Or he would promise to reveal the identity of the actual killer. Who could guess? Neither of us expected a big story and we didn't get one.

Instead, I got a notion implanted in my brain; a sort of life-changing weirdness that never went away. It was the thought that fiction can sometimes tell the truth better than facts. After listening to what Smallwood had to say I tried to write a short story, and kept trying until I finally got one written. It was bad. I didn't try to get it published. But I kept it and Smallwood remained in my memory until, years later, I needed him. Then he became Colton Wolf in *People of Darkness*. Those who have read that book already know what Curtis and I heard on death row of Cell Block 3 that afternoon.

Death Row included five cells, their barred doors facing a row of high windows through which sunlight streamed that afternoon. We were ushered into the sunny corridor, and a guard provided us folding chairs. Four of the cells were empty. Smallwood was awaiting us, standing at the door of his. We introduced ourselves, getting through the formal courtesy required on meeting a human who has nine hours left to live.

Smallwood was embarrassed, hesitant, but finally he got to the reason he had invited us there.

Would we be writing about what was happening to him tonight?

We would be.

Would the stories go around the country, where a lot of people would see them?

Well, yes. At least they would be sent out to newspapers and radio stations.

Good, Smallwood said.

"Good? Why?" I asked.

"Maybe my mother will see it," he said. "If she knows about it, I think she'll come and get my body."

"Give us her name and address," John said. "We'll make sure she knows."

Smallwood stood at the door, his hands gripping the bars, eyes down, preparing himself to tell two strangers of the humiliation that had ruled his life, giving me a visual memory that can no more be erased than that of the helmet filled with part of its owner's skull—another tattoo on my brain. I still see, for example, the smooth stub of the finger from which he'd lost the last two joints, see that stub move as he loosened, and tightened, and loosened, his hold on the bars.

Smallwood didn't know his mother's address. He didn't know her name. He doubted his name was Smallwood. It was the name of the man she'd been with the last time he'd seen her.

"And when was that?"

He remembered the date exactly. His twelfth birthday. He'd been chased away by the man his mother was living with, had been living in a school friend's garage, had come back to his mother's trailer and found the space vacant. The trailer court manager had no idea where they had gone. Smallwood had been hunting her ever since, around the country and down through the years, accumulating a criminal record on the way, looting America for whatever it had taken to keep the chase going and his hope alive. First car theft as a juvenile, shoplifting, more car theft, burglary, and finally worse. He thought his mother might have gone to California. He thought his mother had come from somewhere in the midwest, remembering talk of big shade trees over the street.

John and I asked the routine questions. How about the murders for which he was about to die? He just shook his head. What had he ordered for the traditional last meal? He wasn't hungry and hadn't decided. What did he think about dying? The prison padre had taught him about Jesus and he didn't think Father Theodore had any reason to lie to him. He'd be going to a better life and they said dying didn't hurt much. He produced a shy smile when he said that, and said he wondered how they learned that without trying it. Then he'd pointed to scar tissue on the side of his neck. He said: "I can stand pain pretty well," and produced another shy, deprecatory smile. But he'd like to go home, just once. It would be good, he said "to be buried with my family."

Smallwood walked into the execution room about ten minutes before midnight with the chaplain beside him, the warden walking in front and two guards behind, and John and I watching from the witness gallery. The chaplain answered some final question, patted his arm. They embraced. The guard held open the door of the chamber. Smallwood, a tall man, bumped his head on the metal threshold, grimaced at the pain of that, and eased back into the chair to make it easier for the guard to fasten the straps. The door was closed. The warden looked at his watch, signaled. Somewhere someone closed an electrical circuit causing cyanide pellets to drop into a container of acid beneath Smallwood's chair. We could see a faint mist of fumes rising. Smallwood glanced out at us, an expression I interpreted as a mixture of embarrassment and fright. Then he inhaled.

I wrote my report for the next day's edition that night, of the details of the execution going smoothly, of Smallwood's demeanor, of the crime he died for, something of the young Good Samaritans he had murdered, and of the other crimes for which other states had warrants issued for him. I think I gave his hunt for his mother a paragraph and I know I mentioned his hope that she would come for him and take him home for burial. I didn't think she would and she didn't.

I was left wondering if Smallwood's mother had any better luck forgetting him than I did. I was left thinking the bare bones story I'd done left too much unsaid. Here was the Mid-Century Tragedy of American culture. If I was going to be a writer, I should be able to do something with it. I wrote a sort of minimalist short story, in which the reader sees the reporter just back from the execution in the empty, predawn wire service bureau, putting his yarn together, working against the electric clock behind him and the three-hundred-word space allotted it on the trunk wire, sorting out what he has seen and his memories of his interview with the man about to die. I left it totally devoid of emotion or opinion—trying to cause the reader to see and hear precisely what the reporter had seen. As the above might suggest, it wasn't much of a short story. I stuck it in my Unfinished Business box and there it sat, refusing to be forgotten. Smallwood didn't fit in a short story. He needed to be a character in a novel. Years later, he came alive again as Colton Wolf in *People of Darkness*, and more years later, the old story came out of the drawer, underwent another rewrite, and was published as "First Lead Gasser."

That incident kept alive my yearning to become a fiction writer—kept it alive until one evening in 1961 Marie suggested I drop out of the news business and *"Just do it."*

The ad agency that designed the "Just do it" slogan for the Nike Shoe folks, the "anthem for the totally irresponsible," did it to encourage the young to pay a hundred and fifty bucks for $15 sneakers. It worked for Nike, but it didn't seem to fit our situation as it stood in 1961.

Things had changed since we'd moved to Santa Fe. Most notably, we now had five children. If Marie was dismayed by this economic problem she didn't show it. Her position was based on one hard fact and a double presumption. The fact was that the six-day-week, long-hours schedule I was working allowed neither time nor energy for anything creative. The presumption was that we could support our gang of seven until I became a successful author and that I would be good enough at yarn spinning to actually get a book published. Marie had more confidence in my writing than I did.

There's an odd side to this that will be hard to understand by those not blessed by having a spouse who really loves them. Marie personally shuns celebrity, is embarrassed by it. She believed for years that giving talks, doing book signings, having fans confront me for autographs was onerous to me, a cross that I bravely bore because the author role required it. Usually she reads me like a book but she had trouble believing that I enjoy this. Thus came our leap into the dark—from newspaper editor to a part-time university job and the immersion as graduate student into the world of classic literature, which I'd missed studying journalism. I wondered for a while how I had been reckless enough to do it, but there's no real mystery there. It was because Marie (Oh, woman of infinite faith) got me to believing I was as talented, competent, etc., as she believed I was.

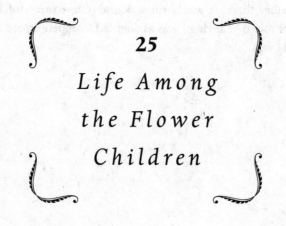

25

Life Among the Flower Children

The middle sixties were the ideal time to start if one was fated to spend almost twenty years teaching journalism at a university. Student lethargy still ruled as late as 1963, providing a taste of lecturing to a disinterested audience. But even then the long, loud, and lusty revolution was moving in. Before I could conclude that a professor's life tended to be boring, the late sixties were upon us and students were showing up full of fire, demanding to be taught something relevant, protesting war, the establishment, parking tickets, poorly prepared lectures, prejudices against pot smoking, unisex rest rooms, police brutality, and so forth.

Odd as this may sound, it was a wonderful time to be teaching. Students were interested, grade mania and the resulting grade inflation had barely emerged, the curse of political correctness had not yet paralyzed deans and department chairmen and corrupted the faculty. Teaching a roomful of bright young folks who yearned to learn and were willing to argue forced you to defend your position. Sometimes you couldn't. You were learning as much as they were, and it was fun. It wasn't until the early eighties that lethargy restored itself. The numbing dogma of PC hung over the campus, tolerating no opinions except the anointed ones. With free speech and free thought ruled out by inquisitors running Women's Studies and the various minorities studies, the joy of learning had seeped out of students. With it went joy of teaching. Time to quit.

Keen Rafferty retired as Journalism Department chairman after breaking me in and I was moved by default into the job no one wanted. At first I taught Introduction to News Writing, the News Writing Laboratory, Advanced Reporting and History of Journalism. As enrollment, and our faculty grew, making such things possible, I developed two courses of my own. One we named Social Effects of Mass Communications, which gave me a chance to reteach what H. H. Herbert had taught me at Oklahoma and grind my own accumulated axes. However the course I dearly loved, of which I boast when the opportunity arises, was Persuasive Writing.

By the 1960s almost everyone (the exceptions being editorial writers) understood that editorials are not persuasive. They simply report the position of the newspapers' owners. Actual persuasion is accomplished on the news pages. I had always suspected this, but the Borger *News-Herald* provided an opportunity to test it. The titular editor, who represented the owner's position, wrote essay after essay on the editorial page endorsing the incumbent congressman as a true-blue archconservative and attacking his Young Lawyer challenger on grounds that the fervency of his anti-communism and therefore his patriotism was doubtful. However, we in the newsroom liked Young Lawyer. We found an excuse to do a human interest article about him. We found a way to work his photo into a thing we did on father-son relationships. The Sunday before the election, there he was on the front page helping set up tables at a church picnic while the paper's official opinion on the editorial page rated him a possible communist sympathizer. Guess who won? Young Lawyer by a bunch.

I had attended an informal one-student seminar on that subject while covering the state capital in Santa Fe. It was taught by Mike Gallegos, an elderly Guadalupe County rancher, political philosopher, and longtime activist in Democratic Party affairs. As had Otis Sullivan of the *Daily Oklahoman*, Gallegos spotted me as a fellow country boy and decided I might be enlightened on how politics operated. I learned from Mike, for example, the formula for public works budgets.

Mike's formula: "A job requiring ten citizen workdays, requires twenty merit system [state] workdays, or forty civil service [federal] workdays." He had held both merit system and civil service jobs himself and insisted that was pretty close to the accepted budgeting formula.

On political patronage: "When candidates quit giving jobs to kinfolks of those who help their campaigns then Southern Union Gas Company, the telephone people, the railroads, and the insurance companies move in and do the work for them. And corporations expect a lot bigger pay than kinfolks."

Mike rated editorial influence as trivial in races for highly visible offices such as governor, Congress, mayor, sheriff, etc. But voters didn't have a clue about the county treasurer, clerk, assessor, or the other mostly invisible offices. In those, the paper could be dominant. We tested Mike's theory in a race for county school superintendent, which involved a situation so convoluted that even diligent voters couldn't be expected to understand it. A group of parents of kids attending the schools at Pojoaque had sued to separate from the county district, thereby running their own schools. If they won, the office of the county superintendent, then Henry Trujillo, the incumbent, would see his job abolished. Henry opposed this plan.

Pojoaque is an old valley village, once Indian and Hispanic but now a bedroom community for high-tech newcomers building the nuclear bombs at Los Alamos whose children attend Pojoaque schools. These claimed the district judge, a friend and political ally of Henry, was stalling the case until after the election. They demanded that the newspaper expose this conspiracy and do something about it. That seemed like a good idea. I wrote an editorial arguing for splitting off Pojoaque and exhorting the judge to act on the case. Nothing happened. The Pojoaque PTA returned, angrier than ever. I wrote another editorial, demanding that the judge explain what he's waiting for, hinting that he was stalling so that Henry can stay on the payroll another two years. This irks the judge. He tells me I'm guilty of a blatant attempt to influence a pending civil judicial proceeding. If I continue he will cite me for contempt and lodge me in the county jail.

While I ponder this, the Pojoaque folks arrive again—demanding action. I explain the problem and propose a solution. If they pick one of their own as a candidate against Henry in the Democratic primary, the *New Mexican* will endorse this person and provide full and accurate coverage of the campaign. If the Mike Gallegos theory is correct, maybe we can beat Henry at the polls. But the only hope lies in a simple campaign run on a single issue.

Most of the votes are cast in urban Santa Fe, folks totally disinterested in Pojoaque schools, but who approve of such notions as home rule, freedom, apple pie, and parents running their schools. So the single issue must be: *Let Pojoaque Parents Control Their Own Schools*. No name calling. No comparing credentials. They agree and pick their candidate.

Sounds like a sure winner. Right?

The Pojoaque group picks as their candidate a woman from

a well-known Santa Fe County Hispanic family. Great, because Henry is also old-family Hispanic. After that, it doesn't look so good. Our choice is from a family that has been ardently Republican. Our choice is a bartender. Our choice's education credentials stop with high school. Henry worked his way through college, then went back and worked his way through to a master's in Education, has taught school, has administrative experience and a fine reputation. More important in the Santa Fe County Democratic primary, his family has been Democrat forever.

The political grapevine, which covers Santa Fe as kudzu covers Georgia, had told Henry what was afoot. He comes in to ask me what we're up to. I tell him we want Pojoaque split off into a separate district and the only way we can get it done is to beat him in the primary since he has been winning by such margins that the Republicans no longer oppose him in the general election. He says he'll bet me $5.00 he'll win. We shake hands on that, with me thinking by then that I'm probably just making a donation.

The campaign is quiet. When we hear our Pojoaque bunch is violating our single-issue policy and slamming Henry we stop that with a couple of telephone threats. On election eve the Pojoaqueans follow my suggestion and picket noisily on the Santa Fe plaza, asking city folks to give them control of their schools. We run a front-page photo of that, and our endorsement editorials repeat the plea. We describe Henry as a fine fellow but a roadblock to parental control.

The polls close. Henry drops in again and we go down to a typical city voting precinct to see who is winning our bet. The poll clerk gives us a reading—with Henry losing by a ratio of about four to six. Which means Henry has lost the urban vote, which means he lost it all. Henry hands me $5.00. When the polls closed, the stinger comes. While the disinterested urban voters had defeated Henry, the voters of Pojoaque (for whom I had thought I was speaking) picked him two to one over our candidate.

One of the participants in a poker group I joined in 1965 wears a shirt emblazoned with the question: *"Why are you telling me this?"* I suspect many readers are asking the same question. It's because for years I described that incident to students in my Social Effects class. In the middle sixties years of lethargy they listened without questions. I was simply illustrating how a newspaper could influence public action if the issue was simple. When the Vietnam protests hit campus, things changed. Hands went up. Wasn't it my responsibility to know that the PTA group did not represent majority opinion? Should I have defied the judge and exposed his politically motivated delay? Such questions cause the professor to admit that he didn't want to go to jail, and that he was totally conned by the PTA, and that his ignorance cost Henry his job.

In that course my premise was that power to persuade lies in the ability to make people see—sometimes literally—the situation as the writer sees it. Instead of telling readers the city should improve its maintenance programs, walk them down the street with you and show them those same details that drew you to that conclusion—the roaches around the drains, the trash collecting on the fences, and so forth. Based on that argument, I'd send them forth. They either come up with their own ideas, or choose from my list. For example:

Go to the airport and the bus station, watch people waiting at both places, isolate the details that led to conclusions about them. If you think they represent different socio-economic classes, let me see enough to lead me to the same conclusion. And keep it in eight hundred words.

Go to a gay bar and a country-western bar. What do you see that identifies them?

Go to a trial. Watch the jury. Don't tell me that certain jurists look bored, and certain jurists looked interested. Show me what you saw to cause you to think that.

And so forth.

The next step requires marking up the resulting papers, finding a crucial paragraph in each, typing all of these paragraphs off along with suggested modifications, handing them out at the next class meeting, and trying to teach something by dealing with the resulting arguments.

"You say 'obviously drunk,' " I say, "What made it obvious?"

Everyone knew what a drunk looked like, they told me. Why waste any of those eight hundred words you allow? We finally settled on showing our citizen leaning against a Coke machine, missing the slot with his coins, giving up, etc., with the class and I agreeing that readers would be more willing to accept an undescribed drunk in the bus station than at the airport. Then it was on to the next paragraph where we reversed a sentence to change the emphasis, and dumped "walked slowly" in favor of "strolled," after deciding "ambled" didn't fit the scene. By the end of the semester, students were rarely modifying verbs or nouns.

While this was going on I was slaving episodically away on the book that became *The Blessing Way*—trying to impose the same standards on my own prose.

I was writing episodically because this short book stretched about three years from 1967 into 1970 from first paragraph to final revision—with progress frequently interrupted by periods of sanity—probably induced by fatigue and sleepiness. Most of my efforts at fiction were done after dinner when the kids were abed, papers were graded, and the telephone wasn't ringing. Sometimes in those dark hours I would realize that the scene I had finished was bad, the story wasn't moving, the book would never be published, and I couldn't afford wasting time I could be using to write nonfiction people would buy. Then I would pull the paper from the typewriter (remember those?), put the manuscript back in the box, and the box on the shelf to sit for days, or sometimes weeks, until job stress eased and the urge to tell the story returned.

I had approached this first book with a plan. It wouldn't be the Great American Novel. It would be a trial run to determine if a sprinter, conditioned to sum up disaster, triumph, tragedy, and love in five hundred words, could complete the marathon of a full-sized book. But before doing the marathon, I would try a mile. Not the five hundred thousand words that even a short version of *War and Peace* would require, but maybe eighty thousand or so of the suspense/mystery yarns Eric Ambler and Raymond Chandler had been writing. I read a lot of the books I intended to emulate in this first effort. I read the essays George Plimpton had done for *Paris Review* about how Hemingway and other great ones got their paragraphs hung together, and I tried to diagnose my own talents, and lack of them. I decided I was adept at description, good at moving narrative along, and dialogue was no problem. I had no idea whether I could develop a plot or how I could shape characters. Given the above conclusions, I would write a story in which the stage setting was more important than the play. If the actors and the story line were weak, maybe I could make the stage scenery so interesting it would carry the book.

I come up with a plot about an emotionally challenged anthropology professor at work on Navajo culture, a woman hunting for her electrical engineer husband last seen on the Navajo Reservation, and an espionage scheme. The bad guys had hired the engineer to record the behavior of the missiles fired from the Tonapaw base in Utah across the reservation to the Army missile test site at White Sands Proving Grounds. The only important Navajo character in this plan was a "city Navajo," a professional criminal raised in Chicago (where hundreds of Navajo families were relocated during the 1930s) with no knowledge of his tribe beyond what he'd collected from books just to prepare himself for this job. Specifically his job was to scare away the few Navajos who lived in the empty country where the engineer was setting up his monitoring devices.

You'd meet lots of local Navajos in the book, in trading posts, at curing ceremonials, during visits to hogans, etc., but they would be minor characters. That was my plan. That wasn't the way it worked out.

Early in the book my fictional professor needed information

from a friend, a Navajo policeman. I named him Joe Leaphorn, a totally un-Navajo name suggested to me by Mary Renault's book on ancient Cretan culture *(The Bull from the Sea)* in which Cretan cowboys leaped over the horns of bulls. It was a mistake that I have never repeated. But Leaphorn proved a more serious problem. Making him seem genuine forced me to admit I didn't know nearly as much as I should about the Dineh.

I talked to Navajo friends, discovered I didn't even know enough to ask intelligent questions, and began endless hours of reading. Reading everything: various versions of the creation myth, of curing ceremonials, of witchcraft beliefs, clan structures, sand painting, social life, sexual beliefs, taboos, puberty ceremonials, place names, hogan building, etc. I read Ph.D. dissertations, proceedings of dignified and scholarly societies, collected papers of the Peabody Museum, the autobiography of Son of Old Man Hat, the accounts of River Junction Charley, and on and on and on. Now I was ready to interrogate Navajos. And the Navajos I asked were ready to recognize that I was motivated by something more than idle curiosity.

The last chapter of what was to become *The Blessing Way* was one of the very few that I have signed off on knowing it was a bad one. It was late in 1969. I had been working on the book off and on for about thirty months. Some parts of it were good. One part, a scene in which my hero escapes Big Navajo in the darkness of Many Ruins Canyon, is as good as anything I've written. Other parts badly needed improvement. In sum, the book wasn't nearly as good as I'd intended. I was disappointed but I wanted to be done with it and it needed a terminal wrap-up chapter. I'd written two of these, both unsatisfactory, started a third one, which was going nowhere. To hell with it. I took the better of the bad ones, spruced it up a bit, printed the whole book out on my Radio Shack "Trash 80" computer, and sent it off to my agent.

Ann Elmo, may she rest in peace, didn't want me to write fiction. She said I was competent at nonfiction, a rare quality, and probably would get better. She could sell that for me. Why waste my time trying to be another wannabe novelist with which the world was already infested? I told her my scheme. She was not impressed. If I did it, she'd read it, and if it was any good she'd try to sell it somewhere. Now she had it and I waited for a response. After three weeks of silence I called her.

What did she think? Could she sell it?

No.

Why not?

Because it's a bad book.

Bad? How?

It's neither a mainstream novel nor a mystery. Reviewers won't know what to say about it. Booksellers won't know which shelf it goes on. Publishers won't know where to list it in their catalogs.

Did she think I could fix it? She didn't recommend the attempt. Well, I said, just send it back to me then. I think I'll rewrite it. Did she have any advice about that? She recommended "getting rid of the Indian stuff."

Today that sounds like bad advice. In 1969 it's about what every competent literary agent would have said. Aside from textbooks and anthropology journals nobody was publishing material about our tribes. In the field of fiction Indians existed only as the enemy of the cavalry in westerns. If I had been paying any attention to the market, I'd have noticed that.

But it seemed to me that the only worthwhile part of my manuscript was the Navajo Nation and its culture. I didn't try a rewrite. I let it sit. Providence steps in—an article in *Writer* by Joan Kahn, the famed editor of mysteries at Harper & Row. Ms. Kahn liked mysteries less involved with plots and puzzles and more involved with character and culture. So did I. I wrote her that evening, telling her I had written a mystery set on the Navajo Reservation, that my agent and I disagreed over whether I should rewrite it, and asking her if she would read it and give me her opinion.

Back came a typical publishing house response.

Dear Mr. Hillerman:
   In re your inquiry of Monday. Yes. Send it in.
                                    Joan Kahn.

A few days later some sort of Journalism Department accreditation meeting took me to New York and I stretched the trip to visit daughter Anne, who was doing a semester exchange student tour at the University of Massachusetts. Changing planes at Kennedy I called Ms. Kahn to see if she'd had time to read my manuscript.

The resulting conversation is inscribed in my brain.

"Yes. Haven't you got my letter?"

"No. I've been away."

"Well, we want to publish it if you can write a better last chapter."

"I can," I said.

Jubilation is a wonderful word but not strong enough here.

Ms. Kahn's letter was not as terse as her telephone conversation. It was a three-page list of flaws and shortcomings of the book with no words wasted on praise. Had I not made the call I would have seen it as a detailed explanation of rejection.

One's attitude toward a manuscript changes when one learns it's likely to be published. I worked night after night clicking off the improvements Ms. Kahn wanted, coming up with a more satisfying finale, and inserting a bunch of new stuff to better develop Leaphorn's character and expand his role. This drew another Kahn letter, suggesting a few more modifications and asking me to send her a list of "possible titles." The name of the book, *The Enemy Way*, was already typed on the title page of the manuscript and on all other pages, but who was I to argue? I sent her eight possible names, leading with *The Enemy Way* and listing *The Blessing Way*, which has nothing to do with the plot but is the most important of the Navajo ceremonials, as choice number seven. Ms. Kahn chose number seven. I still wonder why but it didn't seem to matter. The only complaint I received was an indignant letter from a woman who had her bookstore send one to her elderly mother thinking it was a religious work.

I used the word "jubilation" a moment ago and I will use it again when the Harper & Row business rep came through Albuquerque with a copy of *The Blessing Way* dust jacket in his briefcase and a third time when I opened a package Joan Kahn sent me and pulled out a copy of the actual book. After writing for more than a quarter century I was now, formally, officially, and incontestably an author. Does it bother me that the Mohawk Indian whose profile forms the cover looks no more Navajo than does Bill Clinton? Hardly at all.

Time here for an explanatory digression. A few years later Harper & Row published my one and only venture into children's books, a simplification of an ancient Zuni account of how one of the tribe's religious societies was founded. A Czech artist was chosen to illustrate it and his Indians had a distinctly Central European appearance. Having recovered from the "first baby" mental block by now, I felt that was a cultural slight. When a new edition was published the illustrations were done by my daughter Janet, who had a Zuni boyfriend at the time. This leads into another digression—the foolishness of calling Indians "indigenous people."

I have occasionally used the Native American term. I was cured of that failing when the Smithsonian formally established its division for artifacts from tribal history and named an Indian as its director. He came to Santa Fe, a panel was assembled to discuss affairs of this new division, and I was invited to sit on it. There were nine of us, I believe, representing Hopi, Navajo, Mescalero Apache, Taos, Cherokee, Choctaw, Modoc, and a couple from the Eastern tribes that had somehow escaped the total extermination policy of our British ancestors. I sat as Mongrel-American. One of the first questions from the audience was which title the panelists prefered.

The first respondent asked for a show of hands of those in the audience who hadn't been born in the United States. Two hands appeared. Then all the rest of us here are Native Americans, said the Indian. We are all the offspring of immigrants. He said his people preferred to be identified as Modocs, but if you don't know our tribe, call us Indians. So it went down the row, each respondent preferring his tribal name, saying that Indians call each other Indians if they don't know the tribe. The verdict was unanimous, with the Apache adding they were only thankful that Columbus was looking for India and not Turkey. The Cherokee noted that the real insult was to be called indigenous people. Since the Western Hemisphere had no native primates from which humanity descended, that suggested they had evolved from something else—perhaps coyotes—and were not really human. The Navajo concluded this discussion by proposing that all be happy Columbus hadn't thought he'd landed on the Virgin Islands—a sample of the sense of humor that makes the Dineh my favorite folks.

But now it was time to part from these favorite folks. *The Blessing Way* was out. The time had come to quit stalling and actually write *The Great American Novel*, which would concern journalists and politicians and have nothing to do with Indians. I was going to call it *The Fly on the Wall*, Walter Lippman's metaphor for the ideal reporter who saw and reported everything but kept his opinion to himself. But putting *The Blessing Way* behind me wasn't as easy as it sounds. I had a bad feeling I hadn't done it very well. My goal of denting the ignorance of Americans about Navajo culture hadn't been reached. When I finished *The Fly* I would have to go back and try again.

Besides, that first book had taken on a sort of life of its own. In 1970, the nomination committee of the Mystery Writers of America put it on their short list for Best First Novel along with Dick Francis's first book. Those who have read both won't be surprised to hear that Francis won the Edgar Allan Poe Award and I got the Honorable Mention. Even so it caught the eye of Eleanor Timmerman, who ran the Warner Brothers scouting office in New York. She decided Warners should option it for a movie.

I was in the big city again on university business and had taken our daughter Janet along to see the sights. Timmerman wanted to talk to me. I was taking Janet for a ride on the Staten Island Ferry (10-cent fare in those bygone days, and right past the Statue of Liberty) and we stopped at Timmerman's office en route. It was a short and amiable conversation with no assurance that any movie would ever be made. Ms. Timmerman said she was having lunch with Dustin Hoffman and invited us to join them. I said we wouldn't want to intrude. She said it was just a social lunch and they'd be happy to have us. I said thanks but no thanks, citing the promised ferry ride.

This must be put in perspective. Janet, in her early teens, was a movie buff typical of her age. Dustin Hoffman's star was at its zenith that season. I was not then, am not now, and will never be, interested in actors. I hadn't a notion that Hoffman was a superstar and didn't recognize him when the elevator door opened and he stepped out to let us step in. Janet did, of course, and made the ride down in a sort of stunned silence digesting the fact that her brain-dead, fuddy-duddy dad has denied her the thrill of a lifetime.

In addition to adding to my admiration of Janet (who never complained) this affair with Warner Brothers it caused Avon to add a "Soon to be a major motion picture" legend to the cover of its paperback and provided me with my first close view of the movie industry. The caller identified himself as Arthur Rowe, a writer for Warners. He had been assigned to script *The Blessing Way*. How about coming down to his hotel, having a drink, and talking about locations?

Rowe proved to be a true professional writer. He told me he had been sent because he had a little time left on a multiyear contract with Warners and the company didn't want him to waste it. He said he doubted a movie would come of this but the company would have a script on file. Maybe they'd sell it somewhere. His first suggestion was changing the Land Rover I had Big Navajo driving to a Ford or General Motors product. Why? Because Land Rover didn't give freebies for using its cars in films. U.S. makers did. When I suggested places on the Navajo Reservation for various scenes, Rowe said he wanted to take a look at an Indian pueblo. I said the book involved sheep camp Navajos, who live scattered around the landscape in hogans. They don't live in pueblos.

"You know that," Rowe said. "Now I know it. Nobody else knows it. This is for a movie. We're not in the educational business." So we visited Isleta Pueblo. But then Rowe chartered a little single-engine Cessna and we flew to the Big Reservation, landed on a dirt strip to take a look at Chinle and Many Farms and then flew up narrow Canyon de Muerto, often in so low we looked up to see the rim of the cliffs on both sides of the aircraft. I didn't appreciate that at the time, but twenty-eight years later it was useful when I had Jim Chee doing the same thing in *Hunting Badger.* Writers do not waste useful memories.

Now it was time to tap a fifteen-year accumulation of journalistic memories to write the important book. It would concern a hard-bitten political reporter who followed Walter Lippmann's dictum, proudly serving as "the fly on the wall," reporting all with total objectivity. I would confront this fellow with an awful choice. Should he expose corruption in the state highway department even though his story would destroy a good man and save an evil one? The setting would be the State Capitol Building in Oklahoma City. It offered an ideal site for a fatal push (a four-story drop from a balcony to a marble floor), slow and creaky elevators, and spooky echoing silence after working hours. You can invent such details but why make your imagination work when you can remember them?

I didn't name the state and disguised the city a bit so my old

Oklahoma newsroom friends wouldn't be finding themselves among the characters. I based the plot on the way "bid rigging" used to be worked in New Mexico road contracting.

I lucked into a six-month sabbatical at the University. Instituto Allende offered me free lodgings and other perks in return for teaching a writing course at San Miguel Allende, Mexico. Anne stayed behind in her own courses at the U. Tony, Jr. had lined up a mechanic's job in the garage down the street he didn't want to quit and Tony was one of those mature teenagers parents can leave in charge of things (including themselves) with absolute confidence.

So we piled the four younger kids into our old station wagon, paid the customary bribe to the Mexican immigration cop at Juarez and headed south.

San Miguel Allende in 1971 was a small, cool, lovely, and historic town infested with hard-drinking middle-aged Americans blowing their inheritances where things were cheap. The *instituto* as far as I could tell was run as a place for the affluent to send troublesome college-age offspring and for older folks to amuse themselves. The students to whom I lectured about writing showed no particular interest and the stuff they turned in tended toward romance and fantasy. Thus no challenge, minimal work, time to write *Fly*, and to get acquainted with a most unusual place.

For example, the small cathedral on the plaza bore an uncanny resemblance to Chartres in France. Someone had sent the Mexican architect a picture postcard of that famous place and he had recreated one here at about one tenth the size. It was a beautiful job, made slightly lopsided by the explosion of fireworks being arranged on the facade for a patriotic celebration. The blast had eliminated both the arranger and some of the French Gothic features. The town bandsmen who serenaded the plaza in the evenings wore Austrian-looking uniforms, the musical menu was Central European, and the sound was brass—tubas, french horns, etc. The joyful sound of the mariachi orchestras was not to be heard. Only the bullfights in the little arena, the language, the *pul-querias*, *farmacias*, and—most of all—the market reminded you that you were in the very patriotic heart of the Republic of Mexico.

The town's patriotism had been celebrated fairly recently with the government giving San Miguel Allende a great bronze statue of its namesake in Mexico's war to evict its French emperor. The city fathers had declared their own artistic independence by having the bronze preserved under a seal coat of neon green paint. That offended the intellectual aesthetes in Mexico City, but the locals were fond of it. It gave their statue the special San Miguel touch, just as the fireworks explosion had fixed their cathedral.

When I poke about among my memories of that summer in Mexico I come up with a lot of happy stuff. The little house we rented was built on a hillside. You stepped from the cobble-stone street through your gate into an entry court dominated by bougainvillea. Steve and Dan occupied a bedroom below, their doorway guarded by a mud nest of young swallows who stuck their heads out and solicited food when one passed. After a hit-and-run bus driver sideswiped our station wagon a passing mechanic saw it parked by our wall, offered to fix it for about 20 percent of what an Albuquerque body shop would charge, and drove it off with none of the exchange of references, etc., needed in the U.S.A. He kept it an extra day to take his family on a picnic (observed by Steve, who misses nothing) but brought it back good as new. The remarkably ugly dog that emerged from under a table at the town market and bit Marie proved to be non-rabid. The rusty ice pick that Dan and pal were using to perforate a jar top for their insect collection, and which stuck through Dan's hand, proved free of tetanus. When the license plate disappeared from our vehicle in Guanajuato, Steve advised me to check with the police station. A cop handed it back to me after I handed him the fee for illegal park-ing. Things went well.

Janet, ready to enroll in college come autumn, had been a reluc-tant participant. But she found an interesting sculpturing course in the *instituto*, and among the fellow students was an interesting young man with whom friendship formed. Monica was sort of taken over (or, remembering Monica at fourteen, took over) by a neighboring family with kids her age. Danny found a soul mate his size and rich territory for collecting unusual stuff, and Steve got acquainted with a family who made coffins and fireworks for the town folks.

The book got written, and San Miguel was a wonderful source of memories. But too many of those were the sort that make the "truth is stranger than fiction" aphorism true itself. The fresh beef one found in the market after bullfights, for example. For another, the morning a writer (I'll call him Davis) making the town his permanent home went to the local utility company office to deliver an ultimatum to Mrs. Sandoval, the manager. He would not make the payments due on his electric and telephone bills until she corrected consistent billing errors. Then, said Mrs. Sandoval, we will discontinue your service. Davis told me he was unconcerned by this threat because the company was notoriously slow about everything. For example, his telephone was still listed under Alanzo Garcia, who had lived there many years and many occupants in the past. No hurry, said Davis. No rush. But when he got home a flatbed truck was parked by his wall. A utility man standing on it (wearing rubber boots and rubber gloves) was using a gardener's limb lopper to quite literally cut off his power and phone service. Marie and I had no telephone and used the one at the post office now and then to see how Tony and Anne were faring. And week after week of never hearing a telephone ring—the delight of that, the joy of being free from that at last — crops up when I think back to that Mexican summer. After years of living on the end of a chain, the shackle was finally off. No more slavery. Free at last. Then I think of a night at La Casa del Inquistador. It was raining that night, and when it rained in San Miguel the power failed in celebration. Thus no one except Marie and me had come to the old, old House of the Inquisitor for dinner. The only illumination was candlelight and the musicians had no one to sing for but us. I had them sing *"La Paloma Blanca,"* the romantic song of the white dove, and Marie—whose Spanish was fine now—got them to sing the sad, sad songs of the Mexican Revolution. How good it is to be with the woman you love on such a rainy night.

The author looking
guilty while trying to
explain to reporters why
he was ignorant of any
funny business in the
university basketball
scandal.

Deer season in the Brazos
high country. The author
never actually shot at a deer,
but the rifle gave him an
excuse to be out there after
fishing season ended.

With Barney and Cousin Joe Grove, who kept the Hillerman horses for them in World War II.

The author showing grandson Brandon Strel the art of holding a fish closer to the camera to augment its size.

The author, center as usual, with Scott Turow and Studs Terkel, laughing at their own witticisms at a library fund-raising event.

Tony Hillerman (as prison warden) and Lou Diamond Phillips (as Jim Chee) during the filming of *The Dark Wind*. The facial expressions of both men are explained by Hillerman's forgetting his lines for the third time. The author's role ended up on the "cutting-room floor."

The Dick Pfaff Card Club at its Memorial Game for Jesse Price (*front, center*) who had just been told by his cancer specialist that he had only one more game to live. The other participants are (*back row, left to right*) John Whiteside, Jim Belshaw, Pfaff himself, Bill Degenhart, and Jim Stapp. *Front row:* Bill Buchanan, Price, and Hillerman. Participants in this forty-year-old poker game have some forty books to their credit, ranging from essay collections to fiction, art history, physics, and scholarly works on reptiles. (*Photograph by Michael Mouchette*)

Tony amid students at a seminar for English teachers in California.

Hillerman on the TV show *Politically Incorrect* with, from left, Al Franken, Bill Maher, Graham Nash, and Betsy Hart.

Marie and Tony with Carl "Moon" Mathias, Betty Mathias, and Mickie Brock, with
Tom Brock, another C Company survivor, as photographer.
Yes, Mathias is the Moon of the novel.

"If Ya Kain't Run With the Big Dogs, Stay on the Poarch!" Tony and
the Shiprock "Dog Pack" of the Navajo Tribal Police in 1994.

Hillerman country. Photo by Marie, who understands
the hamburger's attraction to the author.

The Navajo Tribal Police headquarters at Window Rock,
where Joe Leaphorn and Jim Chee have offices in more recent books.

Some of the secondhand buildings of St. Bonaventure School,
scene of a fictional murder in *Sacred Clowns*.

Tony and Marie at the 2000 Mystery Writers of America convention. Hillerman was the presenter of the Grand Master of Mystery award to his old friend Mary Higgins Clark. Hillerman suffered a "senior moment" at the microphone, forgot Mrs. Clark's name, and floundered around until she rushed up and rescued him.

The world's greatest editor, Larry Ashmead, with two of his beloved authors—Tony Hillerman and Susan Isaacs. (*Photograph courtesy of Larry Ashmead*)

Actually catching one in the San Juan river.

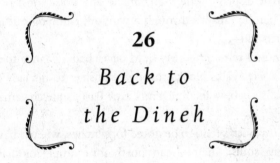

26
Back to the Dineh

While finishing The Fly on the Wall I had come to a couple of conclusions. It was pretty good, including two or three top-notch scenes, but it wasn't likely to be heralded as the Big Book I'd intended. Second, the urge to go back to Officer Joe Leaphorn and the Dineh and do that right had persisted.

Joan Kahn's demands for improvement of *Fly* were more modest than they had been for *Blessing*—mostly involving revision of the first chapter in which my hero was writing a political column crammed with names. She also wanted light cast into a couple of foggy corners and better motivation a time or two. But somehow this queen of mystery editors missed an awful boo-boo, and so did I, and so did the copy editor, and the book reviewers. Then one day with the book already out in paperback I ran into an old reporter friend from my Oklahoma City days whom I had used, thinly disguised, in the plot. Had he read it? Yep. What did he think of it? Okay, he said, but why did you have the hero going barefoot through those last chapters? What did he mean? Remember, he says, you have him remove his shoes and leave them atop that game department display so he won't make any noise? Yes, I remembered. Then he escapes through a window, climbing out into the sleet storm and—

And now I remember. My hero never had a chance to recover the shoes. He walks blocks through the sleet to his lady friend's house, calls a cab, visits the Democratic Party state chairman, etc., all in sock feet.

Alas, my books tend to be noted for glitches, where I have characters drive south when I meant north, for example, or change the name of characters in the middle of a chapter, etc. However, the only one I can think of that matches the barefoot-in-the-sleet business happened when one of the two Navajo police I use was interviewing a Vietnamese woman in Albuquerque. Other duties interrupted me. When I returned to the scene, I switched policemen right in the middle of the conversation. No one in the editing sequence noticed it but judging from the letters I've received, it confused a lot of readers.

Fly got generally good reviews, although one editor-reviewer noted that a reporter suffering all those bleeding-heart doubts my hero endured should "quit the newspaper business and become a college professor." (Exactly what I had done.) No movie options this time, but Harper & Row upped the advance from the $3,500 paid for *The Blessing Way* to $4,000. If you've worked for United Press, small newspapers and a university, that's a handsome raise.

Long before the above was happening I had *Dance Hall of the Dead* well launched. This one was going to be my apology to the generic American Indian for the mistakes I'd made in *The Blessing Way*. As far as tribal culture was concerned, this one was going to be just right.

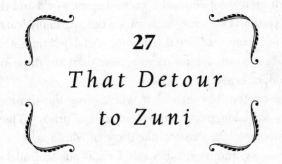

27

*That Detour
to Zuni*

I've been asked (obviously by those who hadn't read the book) how I came up with that *Dance Hall of the Dead* title. I found it somewhere in the thousands of pages of books, articles, and scholarly reports I'd read to carry out this project. One of these scholars had thus translated the Zuni words for the place where the good souls arrive in their afterlife and do their celebratory dancing. Since my plot concerned a neurotic Navajo boy who wanted to become a Zuni and go to their heaven it was a natural for the book. But why do all this research in re Zunis when I was already sort of semi-informed about the Navajo? Why not stick to them? Because one of the galling examples of the American ignorance of tribal cultures is the notion (pervading movies, television, and the media in general) that all Indians are alike. I set about to dent this ignorance by moving Leaphorn a hundred miles south to the Zuni Reservation. There he'd be hunting a Navajo youngster suspected of killing the Zuni boy, who was to be the personifier of the Little Fire God in the tribe's most important religious ceremonial. I would force anyone trying to follow the plot to learn along with Leaphorn quite a bit about the kachina spirit world and the Zuni cultural system. One thing such folks would certainly learn is that Navajo and Zuni traditional religions, social/political structures, and values systems are no more similar than are those of traditional Buddhists and Presbyterians.

However, the difference that worried me the most was the matter of intruding into a very sacred zone of privacy. The Navajo relationship with the Creator, like those of Muslims, Jews, my fellow Christians, and most other religions, is public. But the Zunis and most of the so-called "kachina" religions of the pueblo tribes of New Mexico and Arizona operate on a philosophy that knowledge of religious rites by unbelievers dilutes their effectiveness. I am vastly oversimplifying this belief, and it varies among the pueblo tribes. In some, for example, brothers initiated into different groups responsible for the conduct of different ceremonials could not ethically exchange information. In some, having one's photograph taken would weaken one's religious power. In many, a polite person doesn't ask questions relating to religious affairs.

To make this a bit more difficult for Leaphorn, there's a long history of animosity between the tribes. (In the old days Zunis seeking initiation into the elite Bow Society were required to submit a Navajo scalp.) Since Leaphorn was investigating the murder of a key personifier in the Zuni Shalako Ceremonial, his position was touchy and he didn't have any more knowledge of the Zunis than was available to interested outsiders. In other words, no more than I did.

Considering the problems, I think it came off well. The book was judged the best mystery novel of 1973 by the Mystery Writers of America and I broke my pledge never to wear a tuxedo by wearing one to the MWA Edgar Award banquet. Another movie option followed and the kids at Zuni High School voted to ask me to be their commencement speaker.

But nothing in Zuni is as simple as it seems. When I showed up at the auditorium, the man who greeted me told me the "tribal historian" would like to talk to me after the ceremony. Not the sort of message you like to receive when you already have pre-speech nerves. When I was escorted into the principal's office the "tribal historian" proved to be seven or eight elderly men—the spokesman for whom held a copy of the book. The questioning, formal and courteous, had a single focus. The elders asked where I had derived specific bits of information about religious matters. I cited my sources, most of them from scholarly publications, some from attending various ceremonial dances, from watching the personifiers of the Council of the Gods coming down Greasy Hill to enter the village, from chatting with those feasting on the goodies provided for visitors in the Shalako House. All true, and also correct, since none suggested the member of any of the kiva organizations had been revealing sensitive stuff to an outsider.

Somewhat later I had a call from a tribal official. The *Albuquerque Journal* and the *Tribune* were printing an advertisement for a city bar that featured a drawing of one of the kachina spirits as a waiter serving drinks. Did I know how this sacrilege could be stopped? I said I would call the publishing company's advertising manager. I did. He stopped the ads.

The *Dance Hall* movie option was with a production company that I will call BB Films, which specialized in doing programs for television. I was hired to write the script. That sent me to the library to check out a collection of award-winning screen plays, and to actually see a movie, which I believe was *The Thomas Crown Affair*. Not a word was spoken for the first eight minutes, which made it look easy. It was, requiring about three weeks of evenings. The producer declared it fine and dandy and paid me my fee, which I later learned was about half the Screen Writers Guild's minimum rate. But the check didn't bounce—which as everyone in show biz knows is the important part of the story.

The option was renewed a couple of times and then dropped. Shortly thereafter my agent called. BB Films company wanted to renew the expired option. Okay? I said sure! A costly mistake. No movie was made, of course, but had I read the original contract I would have known that with that final renewal check the producer had bought television rights to Joe Leaphorn. Years later when Robert Redford decided to option the Navajo police books, I found my lieutenant was held hostage. Ransoming this figment of my imagination cost me twenty thousand dollars and earned me a place in Guinness Book of Records if it ever lists classic stupidities.

However, the circumstances behind this surprise option renewal provided me with another adventure in tinsel town. Someone at BB, or perhaps at Warners, had spotted a possibility at NBC-TV. Would I come out to Beverly Hills and talk? I came. We talked about whether I could come up with an outline for a one-hour pilot film that would use Joe Leaphorn as the central character and would lead into a series of brief TV episodes. Sort of like "Hawaii Five-O" except mountains and desert instead of ocean. Could I do that? I said sure. (And who among those reading this couldn't?) They would have more meetings and let me know. I went home, turned in my expense account, and promptly received a check.

Weeks pass. Another call. We have an appointment with the NBC-TV mogul for program acquisition. On the first trip I had been housed in nice little hotel up Rodeo Drive. On this one the reservation is in the Beverly Wilshire, which in the seventies was very posh indeed. The scent of money must have been detected.

The Mercedes convertible of the BB Films owner (hereafter referred to as Owner) has just been stolen from the parking garage so we arrive at the très chic luncheon place in his Mercedes sedan. The haughty parking lot attendant sneers at it and hides it at the bottom of the lot, behind a screen of Ferraris, custom-built beauties, Jaguars, Lolas, etc. Inside we find two young men awaiting us, a representative of Warners and someone who must have been an agent. Warners does the talking. First, the mandatory words of high praise for *Dance Hall of the Dead*. Second, the sad fact that it must be modified for the pilot film. Then the news that this modification must be outlined in "five hundred words or so" to be presented to the new vice president for Program Acquisition at NBC-TV at a meeting we have with him at 10 A.M. tomorrow. Okay?

Being a veteran of the "deadline every minute" regime of United Press it sounded okay to me if he could provide a typewriter and a place to write. Owner volunteers both.

Now phase two begins, with the usual preamble of praise.

"I loved that ending," says Warners, "but you understand you can't kill that boy. You need an upbeat ending."

That boy being George Bowlegs, a desperately unhappy Navajo kid seeking admission to the Zuni heaven, which ends with the villain killing him. Since I believe in life after death and a God who loves us I consider it a happy ending. I say the kid wanted to go to heaven. He goes to heaven. Upbeat ending.

"Not in the movies it's not," says Warner. "Takes too long to explain."

We agree that I can think of an alternate, which takes us to the next revision. "Leaphorn's a great character," says Warners, "but he can't be a Navajo tribal policeman."

To put it mildly I am *taken aback*. "Why not!"

"Just think about it," says Warners. "You'll have to come up with about fifteen episodes, maybe more. You have fifteen Navajo police ideas?"

At that moment I can think of maybe two. I suggest we could have Leaphorn transfer to the Bureau of Indian Affairs Law and Order Division.

"Same problem," says Warners and he asks me if I know what department the *Hawaii Five-O* cops belong to. I admit I don't. "Exactly," says Warners. "Neither does anyone else."

With that settled, Leaphorn being licensed by some ambiguous agency, we move on to the next subject. Warners points out that Leaphorn is the only "continuing character" in the book. The girl in it is a hippie, with cigarette burns on her hands and hard life behind her. Not the heroine a TV series needs.

I can see that. I will provide another heroine. Easy enough to write in the shapely blue-eyed blonde Hollywood prefers. And now Warners tells me we'll also need a comic relief. "Somebody like Gabby Hayes?" I ask. Exactly, says Warners, who is immune to sarcasm.

By then *Listening Woman* had been published and Warners had noticed in it a cranky trading post operator named McGinnis. He suggests we use this guy in the pilot. Easy enough. Once one abandons any notions of artistic integrity, professional skills, etc., one sees no problems in any of this. And if you are honest with yourself you admit you left all that behind when you booked the flight to tinsel town. Piece of cake. No problem.

Then Warners says: "It will have to have an urban setting."

Urban setting? I presume that anyone who has gotten this deeply into this memoir knows that my Navajo tribal police stories are not urban. The great, beautiful, high, dry country of the Colorado Plateau is the setting. I had decided early in this conversation that I was writing a pilot for a "Hawaii Five-O" type series, with deserts replacing the Pacific Ocean. Now I am lost and Warners sees it.

"It has to appeal to the young urban audience," says he, and explains the demographics, which buyers of TV advertising measure. A handful of city yuppies are worth half the elderly farmers in Iowa to the marketing people. It sounded a lot like a page from one of my Social Effects of Mass Communications lectures. "But," Warners continued, "you could do it by putting Leaphorn's office in the city. Have the episodes start there so the city audience feels comfortable with it."

"It wouldn't have to be a big city," says Owner, who has been mostly quietly taking notes and who has an offspring living in Santa Fe. "Why not use Santa Fe?"

And so we decide that Leaphorn will have a Santa Fe office next door to a shop specializing in Southwest Indian art. This will be run by pretty blue-eyed Jane with the help of grouchy, comic relief Gabby Hayes. Maybe I will consider adding a very traditional, unwise-in-white-ways assistant for Leaphorn, whom the audience and I will think of as Tonto.

The waiter brings the dessert menu. Time is short and the waiter suggests a new specialty the très chic café is introducing. It will be complimentary. He hurries away and returns with four frozen Mars bars, each encased in its original, but now frosty, package paper. When Owner got me to a typewriter back in his suite of offices on Rodeo Drive it was still too hard to bite.

Warners drove us out to the NBC-TV offices the next morning in his convertible Rolls-Royce, the only one of these beasts I have ever seen. We were ushered into the new VP's office right on time. He was a handsome young African American. A copy of the pilot treatment was already on his desk, so I presume he had read it. I also presumed that his race caused my companions to believe he might be an easy sale for a minority film. Whatever the reason he listened patiently to the pitch Warners and Owner jointly made. (I had been told to respond only to questions and none were asked.) After maybe fifteen minutes the VP said he would think about it and let us know his decision. Out we went.

Back in Albuquerque, I typed up my expense statement, sent it in, and waited. I have never been told the decision of NBC-TV but when years have passed with no check arriving to refund one's expenses one presumes the response to one's work was negative.

I've had a few other encounters with the film industry. A New Mexico–born movie actor of considerable repute dropped by the

house one day and said if I would give him a free six month's
option on an article I'd written on a screwball bank robbery
attempt in Taos (*The Great Taos Bank Robbery*) he would raise production money. A film would be made in which he would perform
and we would both profit handsomely. I told him he could have it
for $100. We typed up the document, signed it, and I still have it.
The $100 is long since spent.

Another approach came from a fellow who identified himself as
a producer who had come to Albuquerque to negotiate an option
on *Listening Woman*. I invited him to the house. He didn't have
transportation. Could I come to see him? He named a Motel Six
beside Interstate 25. I pleaded a tight schedule and suggested he
take a cab. Well, he was a bit short of cash. How had he reached
Albuquerque? By bus. Nothing came of that offer.

The film deal that brought me prestige among moviegoers, the
friends of my teen-aged daughters, the daughters themselves, and
about half of the members of the poker club to which I have been
contributing for almost forty years, came from Robert Redford.
Mr. Redford has a longstanding interest in the Mountain West and
its tribes, and has many friends among them. His idea was to produce a series of three films using the Navajo tribal police characters, the maximum of Indian actors practical, and to do as much as
the form will allow to provide an accurate view of tribal culture.
We negotiated a renewable option with the understanding that I
would clear up Leaphorn's hostage situation. That cost the $20,000
previously mentioned.

My improved standing with my fellow gamblers came because
Redford called one Tuesday before any deal was made and suggested we get together for dinner that evening and discuss it. Since
1965 Tuesday night has been poker night. I told Redford I'd be tied
up. He said how about tomorrow at lunch. I said fine. I mentioned
the above at the game and it produced a wonderful example of
generational differences. The old duffers understood perfectly (as
did Mr. Redford) with no explanation needed that no decent person

would break a social engagement to talk business. The younger players were amazed. I am sorry to report that I am still frequently asked (always by people under sixty) if this really happened. When I explain that Redford would not have expected me to forgo the poker game they look at me as if I am either a liar or an idiot.

As this is written one film was produced as a result of that option (*The Dark Wind*), the contract remains in effect and a report has reached me in Albuquerque that Redford's company may make *Skinwalkers* and *A Thief of Time* into TV-format films.

Producers of films tend to involve writers of books in the moviemaking process as little as possible, for the sensible reason that it's hard enough to make a film without having an interested amateur meddling in the process. The scriptwriter for *The Dark Wind* sought my advice a couple of times. I told him I thought the plot of the novel was far too complicated, twisted, and convoluted for a movie and he cut some of it. But not enough.

Redford, in Cuba making *Havana*, had hired a noted maker of documentaries as director. When he returned, he asked me to take a look at the "rough cut" and to let him know if I wanted my name taken off the credits—giving me the impression that he wasn't happy with the product. Lots of beautiful scenes but I (who had written the book) found it hard to follow the story line. It wasn't released in the United States but was shown in France and England with fairly good reviews and finally turned up in the video rental stores.

On the positive side, this affair put a dent in one of my most cherished prejudices—a disdain for show biz in general and the acting profession in particular. I was written into the script as the state penitentiary warden. I take Jim Chee (played by Lou Diamond Phillips) into the clerk's office, introduce him, and tell the clerk to show Chee the records. After blowing the lines three times, my part was cut to two lines and in the final version I was left (as we actors say) on the cutting room floor. I was also left with some respect for those who can act.

Later, this movie produced an incident so bizarre that I have trouble believing it happened. I was on a book-signing tour in France and on this miserable rainy day Rivages (my French publisher) had sent me to Toulouse, escorted by Pierre Bondil, the translator of all my books. I presumed this would involve sitting behind a table in a bookstore, signing French editions and pretending to understand my French readers speaking their version of English. (The French have no better luck speaking intelligible English than Americans do pronouncing French.) My presumption proved wrong. Pierre, who had become a friend as well as my interpreter, had also been ill-informed. Now he learns I am to make a speech in the downtown Toulouse movie theater. I am rushed in, the film is interrupted, the manager and Pierre herd me onto the stage, where I stumble through a few words about the Navajo culture, with Pierre repeating it (and I hope improving it) in French. That done, we leave the startled audience, the movie resumes, and I am rushed off to a news conference.

The sponsors of this affair had set up a free bar, which attracts reporters as well in Toulouse as it does in Chicago or Albuquerque. I say a few words about Navajo taboos, etc., with Pierre translating. Then it is question time. Two or three easy ones, adroitly handled, then a burly middle-aged reporter (henceforth called Burly) asks Pierre a question that sounds sort of hostile. Instead of passing it along to me translated, Pierre responds himself. This provokes another question—this one sounding puzzled. Pierre responds. Another question, clearly angry. Pierre deals with it, and gets another from the same fellow. Other reporters in the audience now join in the affray, yelling at Burly, booing, whistling, etc. I sit there clueless. As the other reporters subdue Burly, Pierre explains. Burly has seen *The Dark Wind* movie with French subtitles. He thinks Pierre is Lou Diamond Phillips and refused to believe otherwise. He is angry because the Jim Chee role should have been played by a Navajo. Pierre clearly is not a Navajo. It is equally clear to anyone not lubricated with five or six bourbons that he is not Lou Diamond Phillips. You'd be as likely to mistake Woody Allen for Clark Gable.

Ah, well. No damage was done. We move through the rainy day to our next stop and I am left with the memory of my oddest book tour experience.

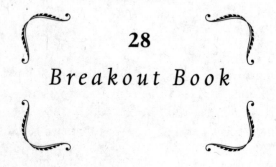

28

Breakout Book

I was introduced to the notion of "breakout book" at a lunch with Perry Knowlton, operator of Curtis Brown Ltd., and Larry Ashmead, senior editor of what was then still Harper & Row. They agreed I should write one. I said I didn't know how. They didn't know how to explain it, beyond suggesting I read novels at the top of the *New York Times* best-seller list. Easy enough. I stopped at a bookstore on the way back to the hotel, picked the latest Ludlum off the bestseller rack, and read the first chapter. We're on a merchant ship being buffeted by a terrible storm in the English Channel. The hero is struggling with two men. He is stabbed. He is shot. He makes it to the heaving deck, is swept overboard, and vanishes beneath the waves. Then the ship explodes. Good chapter, I think. Efficiently written. Nary a word wasted. But where did it lead? All the characters established have been thoroughly killed. Even the evidence of the crime wiped away. I turn quickly to Chapter 2. A hospital room, a terribly injured man in bed. Who could it be? I read on. Light dawns. The fellow I'd seen fatally stabbed, shot to death, drowned and detonated is here before me, recovering. I put the book back where I found it. Clearly my creative imagination is too feeble for a breakout book. But I tell Ashmead and Knowlton I'll see what I can do. I'll try harder. Maybe reading tastes will change.

I must pause here and explain why Knowlton is now my agent instead of Ann Elmo, and Ashmead my editor instead of Joan Kahn. Ms. Kahn had disagreed with Harper & Row management, resigned, and began editing for another publisher. Ashmead, who had joined Harper & Row (now HarperCollins), inherited some of her writers, including me.

Previously, after the business of buying back TV rights to Leaphorn, I had decided to handle the contract for *Listening Woman* with Joan Kahn myself. I asked her the names of agents she liked. She mentioned several. I called the top fellow on the list from my hotel. He suggested I send him a book. I did. He took a look at it and said he'd represent me. Good. When I get my next book written I'd have him handle it for me. A few weeks later I get a terse letter from him firing me. I had caused embarrassment to him and his foreign rights people in Europe. They had started peddling a book agented earlier by Ann Elmo. Elmo had already sold the German rights.

Oh well. Agentless again. But not for long. I went to the University of California at La Jolla to lecture at a writers' seminar and met Perry Knowlton. At a lunch a California boat owner and Knowlton discussed the joys of sailing. I learn that Knowlton's sailboat is twenty-eight feet long. Even a landlubber knows that's a lot of boat. And writers who have yet to write that breakout book want to have agents who can afford such luxuries. Besides, he has already told me he likes the way I write. He asks me if I have an agent. I ask him if he'll represent me. I've been with his Curtis Brown Ltd. ever since.

Satisfaction of the Knowlton/Ashmead desire that I produce the breakout book remained far in the future. First I had to create Jim Chee, a second Navajo police officer, and then be inspired to work him in tandem with Leaphorn—as sort of an uneasy team. I have been known to claim that Chee was the product of an artistic need, and that is partly true. But since I have promised nothing but the truth in these recollections I will admit to you my fondness for Joe Leaphorn was undermined by the knowledge that I only owned part of him, having signed away TV rights. This new book, *The People of Darkness,* would be set on the so-called Checkerboard Reservation on the eastern margin of the Big Reservation. It appealed to me story-wise because there the nineteenth-century railroad moguls had been given blocks of reservation land as a reward for laying transcontinental track, and more of the Navajo country had been divided off into alternate square miles of public land ownership. Not surprisingly, this had odd sociological effects—a mixture of Navajo with every type of unhyphenated American and a dazzling variety of religious missions—from the two versions of the Native American Church, through Catholic, Mormon, Presbyterian, Mennonite, Southern Baptist, and a galaxy of fundamentalist Evangelical churches.

I had started this book with Leaphorn as the central character, but by now my vision of him was firm and fixed. Leaphorn, with his master's degree in anthropology, was much too sophisticated to show the interest I wanted him to show in all this. The idea wasn't working. This is the artistic motive. Behind that was disgruntlement. If any of my books ever did make it into the movies, why share the loot needlessly? Add greed to art and the motivation is complete.

Thus I produce Jim Chee, younger, much less assimilated, more traditional, just the man I needed. I modeled him after nobody in particular—a sort of composite of ten or twelve of those idealistic students of the late l960s.

Chee was easy but the book wasn't. The two key ideas that melded to form the center of the plot came from (1) visiting Barney while he was logging an oil well in Texas, and (2) writing a biography of a banker who had been blinded by a premature explosion of the nitroglycerine used to "shoot" such a well. My villain would be a geologist logging a wildcat well near Ambrosia Lake. Checking a very shallow section of core he notices the bit has drilled through a thick deposit of uranium-rich pitchblende. He doesn't log this treasure, sabotages the well, picks up the lease when it expires, and when the book opens has become immensely wealthy through the Ambrosia Lake uranium boom.

Happily, this book led Barney and me into our first joint venture since the pasture-fencing and creek-taming projects of our late teen years. While he analyzed core samples under the floor of a drilling rig in Texas and I watched, looking for plot ideas, we had the conversation that led to *Hillerman Country*. Barney, an Army Reserve map reproduction officer, had had his career as geologist interrupted by a summons to serve in the Korean War, and was still a bachelor. He was thinking of making his photography hobby a career and thus switching from a nomadic life of chasing wildcat oil wells to a permanent residence. Mama was well into her seventies by then and the memory loss that took the fun out of her final years was beginning to show. He decided he'd build a house for them both, with studio-darkroom attached. If he did, we would try to capture the Four Corners country we both loved in words and pictures.

Barney built a house/studio in Oklahoma City. Years later, after he had met and married Irene and they had adopted two sons and a daughter, we found time for the book. The experience taught me that, published author or not, one's role as Little Brother lasts as long as life. *Hillerman Country* was published by HarperCollins in

1991. Before he had a chance to notice that the reviewers were more impressed with his landscapes than with my text, he had a sudden and fatal heart attack while shooting another assignment.

Since *People of Darkness* needed a crime worse than cheating I have our villain fear that his Navajo friends on the drilling crew might know what he'd done. I'd heard of a Brazilian musician who'd stolen a radioactive device pipeline crews use to check welds. He'd left it in a coat pocket in the family closet, causing him and several siblings to die of bone cancer. This took me to the University Cancer Research Center, which maintains a "tumor registry." There I dreamed up a way (approved by the cancer specialists) to do mass murder slowly but surely with radioactive fetishes. Sounds good, but Chee had to track down all these victims. It proved terribly tough to keep this from being as boring to read as it was to write.

This crazy plot gave me the opportunity to try my hand at what the bona fide masters of suspense were doing. First I had to have a professional hit man—a species I have never believed in. Then, to make the book work, I had to make him a sympathetic human. Here my memory of the death row interview of Smallwood came to the rescue. I gave my asocial killer a modified version of the story Smallwood had told me of coming from school to find Mom had abandoned him and, thereupon, spending his life hunting her. Smallwood's terrible fate proved to be good fortune for me. Getting a publishable book written requires a lot of luck.

Luck, for example, caused me to put Chee and Leaphorn in the same book. I was on a book tour promoting the third of the books in which Jim works alone. A lady I'm signing a book for thanks me and says:

"Why did you change Leaphorn's name to Chee?"

It took a split second for the significance to sink in. A dagger to the heart. I stutter. Search around for an answer, and finally just say they're totally different characters. "Oh," says she, "I can't tell them apart."

I am sure there are writers self-confident enough to forget this. What does this old babe know? But that was not to be for me. Like what St. Paul called his "thorn in the flesh," it wouldn't go away. I decided to put both characters in the same book to settle the issue for myself. I tried it in *Skinwalkers*. It worked so well I tried it again in *A Thief of Time*. Hurrah! It was the breakout book!

I learned about it on a book tour in California. I was with Gabe Barillas, Harper & Row's sales representative in Southern California. I had been signing *TOT* at bookstore A and we were en route to bookstore B. As usual on tours, no time for lunch. We stopped at a grocery and went in to buy a loaf of bread and baloney while Gabe checked in with New York. It was the day when publishers' spies get their advance tips on which books have made the *New York Times* bestseller list. Gabe calls me over to the telephone, hands it to me. I say, "Hello," and hear shouts, yells, a horn blowing. Someone congratulates me. *TOT* is on the list.

Back in the car, inching our way through Los Angeles traffic, Gabe is almost too ecstatic to eat his baloney sandwich. I ask why is this such a big deal. The books have been creeping up the sales charts, making bestseller lists in Boston, the *Los Angeles Times*, the *San Francisco Chronicle*, *Miami Herald*, etc. Why the excitement now?

Gabe explains it. All bookstore managers check that *Times* list to make sure they have copies of the bestsellers in stock. My efforts to date had been in a small minority of such stores. Soon they would be in almost all of them. *And* they'll be up front on the shelves reserved for best-sellers. Plus, in a day or two they'll be in thousands of airport bookstores—key purchasing places for those seeking to stave off the boredom of flying.

Sales of my books had been moving up, slowly but steadily, in a puzzling pattern. Arizona, New Mexico, and Utah bought some, as I'd expected since they're the scene of the action. Except for Florida, the Confederate States of America were a virtual blank and so was Oklahoma. But sales were heavy (by my standards) around San Francisco and Oakland, in Southern California, and along the Northeastern seaboard—most notably Boston and New York. I saw no sense in that pattern until I began doing book signing tours.

For some reason a lot of the people who read me wanted to explain why. They'd tell me they once lived in Window Rock, or had visited friends in Burnt Water, or had taught school at Teec Nez Pos, etc., or loved to vacation in the high dry empty part of the world, and my books reminded them of good times. That didn't surprise me. However, a lot more people began the autographing chat with a disclaimer. They'd assure me they were not mystery readers. They read my books because of the tribal cultural material intermixed with the plot line. They wanted to learn a bit about American Indians. It occurred to me that I had tapped into a mass of American readers who suffer from the same workaholic problem that besets me. Reading for idle amusement left them feeling guilty. My books, like a sausage sandwich spiced with antiacid tables, give absolution along with the sin.

I must admit that these chats at the book-tour tables have affected the attitude of Leaphorn—and particularly Chee—toward the FBI and the Drug Enforcement Agency. My goal was to make my policemen as real I could—based on cops I'd known covering law enforcement and the courts. At signings, I routinely asked policemen who were buying a book of mine if I was being too critical of federal cops. That provoked so many time-consuming anecdotal accounts of FBI and Drug Enforcement Agency blunders and ineptitude that if the line was long, I stopped asking. If the U.S. Attorney General happens to read this, and wants to share wisdom derived from anecdotes collected from a remarkable number and variety of state, city, and county police, I will here summarize the conclusions. Perhaps they will counterbalance the half-century of abject hero worship for G-men that the movies (and now TV) have piled upon the taxpayers.

On the good side, the real street cops report that FBI agents tend to be honest, intelligent, and diligent. They rate the Bureau as usually efficient in the technical areas—tracing credit cards, telephone usage, forensic evidence, etc. On the bad side, they find them (with some exceptions) clueless when it comes to the sorts of crimes real cops deal with daily. Cops find the agents they work with are handicapped by a huge, overstaffed and mindless "by the books" bureaucracy that injects Washington politics into law enforcement. This shows up in cases that attract television coverage, causing the Bureau to take over and bungle investigations not out of bad intentions but due to ignorance of both the territory, the community, reliability of tipsters, etc. Still on the bad side, handicapping their work is what one veteran detective captain told me is "federal arrogance." He said that when he was studying at the FBI Academy his fellow students out of non-federal police agencies called it "Arrogance 231." Add to the downside complaints a feeling that the Bureau is so overstaffed that some of this troublesome interference is the product of boredom. (The last official figures I've seen showed some eleven thousand people on the Bureau's payroll. Since they police only federal laws, how many federal laws does it take to keep that many agents at work? Couple this with their background as lawyers, accountants, and technicians, and it's no surprise they fumble when injected into the sorts of crimes state/county/city cops deal with every day.)

We had an example of this in New Mexico recently when a fellow picked up a woman in Albuquerque's seamy section, drove her down to a lake resort area, and, according to her complaint, tortured her and made porno videos. She escaped and complained to the sheriff. An investigation began. TV was attracted by the sordid sex angle. TV attracts the FBI, which decided this was a kidnapping and therefore federal. Reporters who covered the resulting circus reported from twenty-one to thirty federal agents swarmed to the scene looking for buried bodies and other evidence. They dug up numerous chicken bones and barbecued ribs buried by tidy picnickers but no bodies. The accused perp was finally charged with improper conduct far short of murder and the jury couldn't agree. It required a retrial to get a conviction.

In writing *Hunting Badger* I took advantage of this FBI tendency to charge in and take over where it knows not what it's doing. While I based it on an imaginary robbery of the Ute Mountain gambling casino and the subsequent search of the Four Corners canyon country for the bandits I had my fictional Navajo police remembering, with a mixture of amusement and dread, a real manhunt of the previous year. They recall how the federals had swarmed in literally by the hundreds when three local tough guys stole a water truck, murdered Dale Claxton, the local officer who tried to arrest them, and then disappeared into the Four Corners emptiness. The federals set up a hunt headquarters into which information from citizens and local cops was funneled—but from which information was slow to escape out to the crews searching the mesas and canyons. Thus Search Team A would find itself following Search Team B, etc., tracks found in the dust would be fanned away by federal helicopters coming in to take a look, and so forth. One of the old pros in the Navajo tribal police told me that his search team was informed early that the FBI has taken command, that this pretty well eliminated any hope of an early capture, but since the FBI would need a scapegoat for the failure, they should be careful not to make any mistakes.

And so it went that long summer. The federals ordered the evacuation of Bluff. Locals found the body of one of the suspects and the feds declared him a suicide. After months of floundering around, the feds faded away and went back to whatever they do. A Navajo found the body of another suspect, with no fed available to proclaim the suicide. The third killer, as far as anyone knows, is still out there somewhere. Net result of this epic fiasco is the unavenged murder of a highly regarded policeman, the wipeout of tourist season revenues for the folks of Montezuma Creek, Bluff, Mexican Hat, etc., and the depletion of overtime budgets of every police agency in the Four Corners country.

The only good that came of it is my plot idea and a rich deposit of anecdotes to enliven conversations for years. Marie and I drove over into the war zone because I could not bring myself to believe press reports that (1) the federals had ordered the evacuation of Bluff or that (2) the good people of Bluff would respect such a silly order. Most of them had, it seemed. The first fellow I asked described the incident thus:

"This FBI man pounded on the door and said I had thirty minutes to pack up the family and leave. My first impulse was to grab him by his necktie, lead him back out to the road, and tell him not to come on my property without a court order. But then I thought I had kids to get through college and I'd be spending all my savings hiring lawyers. So we went."

A Bluff matron awaiting a chance to return home parked at a lookout point and watched the circus. "You'd see a dozen or so cars with their sirens going racing down the highway from Montezuma Creek toward Mexican Hat. Then you'd see another bunch of cars—different paint jobs—racing up from the other direction, and then after a while here'd come some more from this direction and that."

If that sounds remarkable, remember the FBI was choreographing the performance of at least twenty different sets of federal cops, ranging from U.S. Park Service to the Immigration and Naturalization Service and U.S. Treasury Department. Other highlights of the event including setting fires that burned out the woodland along the San Juan and tales of near-misses in which one band of man-hunters would discover it was being hunted by another band of man-hunters before an interagency shootout ensued. A quarter-million-dollar reward advertised by the FBI for capture of the killers added an exotic flavor to the chaos—attracting bounty hunters carrying rifles with telescopic sights, big binoculars, and the paraphernalia collected by readers of *Soldier of Fortune* magazine. One of these fellows, who tried to rent a canoe from a friend of mine, explained that he would paddle down the canyon and detect the culprits by their psychic vibrations. After a week or so, the Bureau issued another directive telling the bounty hunters to go home. Some did.

If the previous paragraphs sound disgruntled, it's because I watched this Keystone Copish squandering of our tax dollars aware of the poverty of the local police—too short of money to buy modern equipment, so understaffed they patrol alone and face death with no hope of backup support. That is exactly what Officer Claxton did when he stopped the stolen water truck and was riddled with bullets. Perhaps the local officers wouldn't have nailed the killers even without the federal meddling. Those canyons are a wonderful place to hide.

I had my first close look at the San Juan River's draining system when I was trying to find a setting for *A Thief of Time*—which turned out to be that elusive breakout book. Specifically, I needed an isolated Anasazi ruin where my characters could do their illicit artifact digging unobserved and where I intended to have one of them murder the other one. I mentioned this to Dan Murphy, a naturalist with the National Park Service. Murphy knew of a place that met my needs, reachable down the San Juan River from Bluff. Better still, Murphy knew of a generous fellow with a deep interest in archaeology who had been helping finance some research on the Navajo Reservation. He was taking friends on a float trip into Anasazi country and Murphy was going along as the flora-fauna authority. If I'd tell campfire tales of mythology and culture he could get me a free ride to the places I should see.

Journalists are not inclined to turn down freebies; such perks compensating for the poverty-line pay scales newspapers paid. And I was bogged down in the first chapter of *ATOT* because I couldn't visualize the places where a lot of it would happen. I have always needed to lean back in my chair and pull up a memory of the sites I am writing about to feel comfortable with the description.

The place Dan Murphy knew I needed was in the wall of a mesa overlooking Chinle Wash—a few miles up from where the wash dumps runoff water into the San Juan and a couple of hundred meandering miles from the place it emerges from Canyon de Chelly. Back in 1988 when my memory of this was fresh and green, I wrote a piece published in the July 1989 edition of *Audubon* magazine. I have just reread it and found that I wrote as well then as I do now—alas, perhaps better. Therefore, I will plagiarize myself and take you to our campfire at the juncture of Chinle Wash and the San Juan.

"I begin collecting the kinds of impressions my victim would make as she arrived at this place. She would make the trip secretly and at night, since the dig would be illegal. She would be burdened with the sort of nervousness law-abiding people feel when they are breaking the rules. Still, she would be stirred by the evening as I am stirred. Violet-green swallows are out patrolling for insects. A beaver, looking old and tired, swims wearily up river, keeping out of the current and paying no more attention to me than he would to a cow.

"The song of frogs comes from somewhere up the wash. The rising moon lights the top of the cliff and a coyote and his partner began exchanging conversation far above on the Nokaito Bench. The nighthawks and swallows retire for the night and are replaced by squadrons of little bats. They flash through the firelight, making their high pitched little calls. I filed all of this in my memory."

When I am back at my computer my soon-to-be murdered anthropologist will be experiencing all this, saving wear on my imagination.

The next morning Murphy took me up Chinle Wash. We passed a Navajo pictograph—a man shooting a bow at a black-hatted horseman who was firing a pistol at the Navajo. Nearby is

an elaborate larger-than-life Anasazi pictograph of a figure standing behind a huge reddish shield that looked so much like the chest
protector of an umpire that the river people called this fellow
"Baseball Man." About here the climb began—first from the floor
of the wash to a flat expanse some thirty feet higher, and then
another, steeper climb to an even flatter expanse of exposed sand-
stone. This spread away to the cliff walls of which support the vast
igneous roof of Nokaito Bench.

Murphy pointed, said, "Over there," and added that he wanted
me aware of how these people hid themselves in this empty world.
We moved along the cliff, and past another gallery of pictographs,
one of which depicted Kokopela, resting on his humped back playing his flute between his raised legs. Anthropologists believe he is a
fertility figure a lot like the Greek Pan and the hump he carries represents a sack of seeds. Whoever he is, he stimulated my imagination. I began thinking how spooky it would be if my foredoomed
anthropologist, already frightened, began hearing the sound of
flute music approaching in the darkness. With the problem of
working flute music into the plot still on my mind we turned a little corner and we were there. In the towering wall of the mesa
nature had formed a cavernous amphitheater in the cliff, some fifty
feet deep, a bit wider, and maybe seventy feet from floor to ceiling.
A live seep high up the cliff supplied enough water to grow a lush
(by desert standards) assortment of ferns and moss here and to
feed a shallow basin perhaps twelve feet across and eight inches
deep on the stone alcove floor. Tiny frogs are all around it. On a
ledge a few feet above this pool the Anasazi family had built its
house—its roof gone but the walls, protected here from wind and
weather, almost intact. At the mouth of the alcove footholds had
been cut into the cliff leading upward to a higher shelf where an
even smaller stone structure stood. A lookout point, Murphy
guessed, or a last-chance stronghold if danger trapped them.

While we rested in the cool shade, I dumped the already written first chapter of A Thief of Time. A quite different book was

taking shape out of what I'd seen on this raft trip. And here's the way I thought the new first chapter would go:

By now the victim has definitely become female. She has reached this proscribed ruins just as Murphy and I did, but at twilight. She has seen Kokopela's pictograph, the ruins, the pond, and the little frogs around it. She has decided she will sleep and start her dig with daylight. She notices the frogs seem to jump toward the water but never reach it, investigates, finds that scores of them have been tethered with yucca strings to twigs stuck into the ground. This seems cruel, sadistic and totally insane to her and since the frogs are still healthy, done recently. The mad perpetrator must be near. Then she hears the sound of a flute. Thinks of Kokopela. Listens. Recognizes the melody of "Hey, Jude." Then sees figure walking into the darkness toward her. End of first chapter.

From whence the craziness? We had paused at a ruins beside the San Juan. A raft crewman told me it had been vandalized by a Navajo boy reputed to be schizophrenic. How will I use him? I won't. I will transfer the craziness to the fictional son of an area rancher. The boy has murdered his mother and siblings years ago. His father, filled with love and pity, is secretly slipping him supplies in the wilderness.

Why do I need such a character anyway?

Because (1) I need some chilling suspense in Chapter 1 and (2) I have seen that my murder victim must survive, therefore must have someone to care for her until Joe Leaphorn arrives to rescue her.

Why survive?

Because I must have a way to motivate Leaphorn to involve himself in a none-of-his-business case and take three or four days to float down the river and crash around in the canyons. That had been one of my two major plotting problems when I climbed aboard the raft at Sand Island to begin this trip. The other problem was also motivational. I needed a believable motive for an anthropology professor—even more amiable and nonaggressive than the average professor—to slaughter a fellow prof. I had planned to use mere scholarly ambition—the desire to uncover a major Anasazi cultural discovery before a rival did it. I had already used that motive in *DHOTD*. Here somehow it didn't seem quite good enough.

Providence, which looks after well-intentioned mystery writers, handed me the notion for motivating Leaphorn the first twilight of the trip. A snowy egret flushed from a sandbar we were approaching and flew downstream, a graceful white shape outlined against the dark cliff ahead. I recall the form of an egret (this one with human feet) carved amid a mural of other spirit forms we'd noticed on a cliff earlier that day. But what was this bird doing here, solitary, without another of his species near? Were egrets, like some other species, monogamous? Had his mate died and left him here to live out his life alone? That reminded me (God alone understands how a writer's mind works!) that I had almost made a widower out of Leaphorn in the previous book—saving Emma only with a last-minute decision to have her recovering from a successful brain tumor extraction. I also remembered how Leaphorn had discussed his cases with his spouse and was influenced by her advice. Inspiration strikes. Emma will have died after all (post-surgery staph infection). Leaphorn, in mourning, will know that Emma would have wanted him to find this missing woman. Out of his jurisdiction or not this effort will be his farewell gift to her.

I thought of the solution to the other motivation problem because of my self-made-man syndrome. I like them. Admire them. Know a bunch of them. On university search committees, given candidates with approximately equal attainments, I favor them—downgrading those with prep school and Ivy League credentials on grounds that while they were now on the same lap of the race with the graduate of North Dakota State, the Ivy Leaguer had been given, through family, money, the good-old-boy networks plus the inherent snobbishness of academia, a huge head start.

I was reminded of my prejudice on the trip while boasting to one of the other riders that one of our Navajo boatmen was a genuine self-made man. Born on the reservation to a family too poor to raise him, he'd been farmed out to a grandmother across the river (and the line) in Utah. Left thus with no birth certificate in either state, he couldn't qualify for any tribal job because he couldn't prove he was a Navajo. Starting from ground zero, he now owned a four-wheel-drive truck equipped with towing, battery-charging, and tire-inflating gear. In the winter he prowled the snowbound reservation serving stuck customers and built his estate in the summer working the rafts.

"How's that," I boasted, "for being self-made?"

The recipient of this boast countered by telling me our generous host also qualified as self-made. He'd begun his career as a lowly runner and gofer for brokers at one of the stock exchanges. From that very bottom of the rung he had worked himself up to wealth, fame, good name, and financial prominence.

All day I enjoyed the thought of being on the same raft with two self-made persons. Then evening came and our host emerged from his tent. He was wearing a boating cap emblazoned with the name of one of the planet's most expensive, most exclusive, most oldrich boy prep schools. I am seriously taken aback. And that evening, while enjoying this fellow's largesse at dinner, I began examining my changed attitude. He is still genial, witty, friendly, etc., but now he is one of *them* and not one of *us*. Why? Because despite what Papa tried to teach about the foolish evil of stereotyping people, I nurse a mindless grudge against those fed from the silver spoon.

Since I'm a Roman Catholic, this should have suggested I do some act of contrition and resolve to improve myself. Instead I immediately see how I can transfer my own bigotry to Maxie Davis, bright and beautiful anthropologist and love interest in my yarn, and make Randall Elliot, the handsome anthropologist who loves her, the victim of my personality flaw, which I have passed along to Maxie. Motivation problem solved.

I give Elliot (note my bad guys tend to have famous old Anglo family names) a haughty prep school and Ivy League background, an admiral uncle, Navy Air Force commission, and the appropriate medals for Vietnam service. I make Maxie the product of a poor dirt farm who worked her way through a little land grant college with a doctorate from a state university, and a brother who served in Nam as a grunt and won the decoration grunts tend to receive—the posthumous Purple Heart mailed to next of kin. Thus Maxie thinks Elliot is a nice boy and maybe someday he'll be a man but all he's done so far is accept what's handed him because of his social position. Thus our villain, desperate to impress his chosen woman, cheats to prove his scientific theory, is caught at it, etc. I am happy with this solution. Bigotry can be useful.

A Thief of Time made the *New York Times* list of notable books of the year, climbed up the paper's bestseller list, and has made it into print in seventeen languages—a record for me. It also held top place on my own list of favorites—and stayed there until I finally got my original dream book written about Joe Pilgrim finding himself in the lawless chaos of the Belgian Congo.

That brings us to *Finding Moon*, about as far from Africa's Congo Basin as you can get. And to another trip full of memories for me.

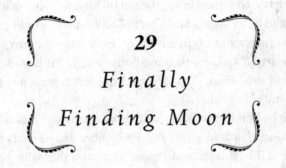

29

Finally
Finding Moon

Marie had been hearing me talking about writing my Belgian Congo novel for approximately thirty-five years when, in 1985, we watched a television documentary marking the tenth anniversary of the fall of Saigon. Scenes of civilians struggling at the gates of our embassy reminded me of the chaos I had intended to depict in Stanleyville. With the Congo bloodbath long forgotten by the world, I decided to move the story to Southeast Asia. I talked to my agent and editor about it and detected no enthusiasm. The two things you want to avoid on the cover of a book are the picture of a spider or anything about Vietnam, which we were trying to forget. My own common sense told me they were right. It would be stupid to stop writing Navajo tribal police mysteries, sales of which were soaring, to turn out a book nobody wants. But the idea was fully revived now.

I talked about it to Marie. Marie, as always, advised me to trust my own judgment. If I saw a good book, write it. I began day-dreaming my way into a plot. It would take place in the few days leading up to, and away from, the fall of Saigon. Some of the set-tings would be in Manila and a lot in Cambodia. It would concern an older brother whom circumstances force to go into my version of the heart of darkness to bring home a child his now-deceased sibling had sired there. That settled, I needed to get a feel for the settings and visual material.

It was bad timing for visas. Neither Vietnam nor Cambodia was giving them. I would go to the Philippines and see where that would lead. Here, once again those years as a journalist paid off. Press credentials can make getting into interesting places a lot easier. I connected with a travel writers' organization and joined a junket sponsored by the Philippine government to promote tourism. This netted me a business-class ticket on the Philippine national airline, plus a room in a new hotel built by Imelda Marcos, wife of the president and the promoter of this push for tourism.

Two problems developed immediately. First, as we prepare to land at Manila I notice I had picked up the wrong passport. The one I hold in my sweaty palm as we roll down the runway has CAN-CELED stamped across my photograph. It expired in 1974. My new one is on my desk in Albuquerque. Again Providence saved me. The supporters of Cory Aquino have just overthrown the Marcos government, Ferdinand and Imelda had fled to Hawaii, a general strike is on, and the preoccupied customs agent simply stamps my arrival date on the back page and waves me past.

The bum passport, however, blights my hope to get across the South China Sea to Nam or Cambodia. My plan to talk my way into a visit of Manila's vast Bilibad prison was thwarted because Cory's government is busy releasing more than five hundred politi-cal prisoners. Instead I get permission to visit the nonpolitical maximum-security gaol on Palawan Island. While I head south Marie sends my good passport to Imelda's Manila hotel to be held for me there until I pass through again en route home.

On the plane I sit next to a dealer in "ethnic items" to be sold in places like Melbourne, Hong Kong, and Tokyo. He had boarded the plane at Zamboanga, where he had made a deal for some artifacts, and was headed for Puerto Princesa, to demand better quality control from his blowgun supplier. From his bag he took a hollow bamboo tube and a sack containing four pointed sticks split from the same plant. "Shameful," he said, displaying them to me. "Not even a tourist would believe it would work."

Before I could ask him what sort of work it did, he was pointing out the window at Mount Mantalingajan, rising through patches of fog. "Two thousand eighty-five meters high," he told me, and began giving me equally precise geographic data about the island it dominated. Palawan is one of the larger of the seven thousand or so islands that form the Philippines, and the skinniest—275 miles long and maybe 35 miles wide. It angles southwest from Luzon almost to Borneo with about three hundred miles of dark blue Sulu Sea separating it from the bulk of the country.

As I previously noted, the famously low pay of newspaper reporters causes those who survive to develop a habit of recycling the stuff they write. In my newsroom days, for example, I was selling by-product stories to journals ranging from *Film Daily* and *IBM World News* to *Capper's Farmer* and the *Portland Cement Assn. Journal*. (A friend won the admiration of us all by selling a little feature he'd done on the difficulties of making a dry climate compost pile actually produce compost to eleven different magazines and papers, with slight modifications to fit each editor's needs.) So here I am, collecting stuff for a book that nobody wants to publish, and taking my habitual notes for the magazine piece I think I can sell. To demonstrate how it works, I will recycle here part of the article I sold to *Islands*.

My exporter friend and I are about to land at Puerto Princesa.

"Just below was a jumble of buildings roofed with sheet metal, palm fronds and tile; and the docks of the seaport, mostly occupied by barges and a gaggle of small craft. The biggest ship was a rusty minesweeper, probably abandoned by the US Navy in 1945. But what caught my eye was a two masted sailing ship with fresh paint as white as snow—a pearl set in a field of barnacles. Even before our plane touched the weedy landing strip, I had collected two characters—my seatmate and this dazzling ship."

The airport existed, my seatmate explained, "because Imelda wished it." Imelda owned the island's only lodging (adjoining the airport) and an uncle was developing a resort twenty miles away on the South China Sea. A road was to be paved to that resort—thereby more than doubling the island's present eight miles of pavement, but he suspected that Cory Aquino would now pave a road for one of her family instead.

The route to Palawan's maximum-security prison was not among those paved. The Jeepney taxi (Puerto Princesa had six of these) followed a narrow dirt road crowded by rice paddies stretching away on both sides to jungle-covered mountains. The cabbie, having explained the biographies of the gallery of saints welded to the Jeep's hood, spoke disapprovingly of the way the men cultivating the paddies were handling their water buffalo.

"All city people," he explained. "Nobody taught them how to plow."

I wondered why these urbanites were plowing so far from a city.

"They're convicts," he said.

Indeed they were.

The gate to Palawan Prison was a palm log laid across the road. The cabbie blew his musical horn. A plump middle-aged man emerged from a bamboo shed, chatted, pulled aside the log, and waved us through. A mile or so onward we reached a compound of concrete buildings put up by the U.S. Army during the Philippine Insurrection. The warden had his office in the largest of these with a chart on his wall showing the number and nature of his charges. The population was 3,318, a much smaller number was under a category that I would call "sharecropper," and an even smaller group were finishing their terms and preparing for release. Smallest of all (a total of three) were noted as "absent."

Did that mean they had escaped?

No. That category was for those who had missed two consecutive daily roll calls. They go out in the jungle but there's nothing to eat, snakes, stinging insects, spiders, etc., so they come back.

They don't leave the island?

There's no way to get off, said the warden, and the official statistics backed him up. No escapes listed, ever.

Did they launch manhunts for those listed as absent?

Why do I ask this? They get hungry. They come back.

I ask this, of course, because my plot require an escape from this place. I need to know the details.

Having covered prisons in two states I was impressed. There were no walls; if the guards were armed I saw no sign of it. The sharecropper convicts cut bamboo to make their own houses, brought in their wives and children after six months of good behavior (a bus took their kids into town for their education), and they shared in the profits of their rice crops after deductions for water buffalo rental. In the dirt-floored prison workshop, convicts were making hardwood canes and other salable items, shooing away the pigs (convict-owned) that shared the place.

Before leaving Puerto Princesa I visited the port for a close look at the two-master. Painted in precise gilt on its bow was its name: *The Glory of the Sea*. It will carry my hero, whom I have now named Mathias in memory of the late Sergeant Carl Mathias, a very brave man, across eight hundred miles of South China Sea to the muddy mouth of the Mekong River, from whence I'll get him to Cambodia. At the market I buy an efficient-looking bamboo blowgun with a quiver of bamboo arrows and head back for Manila.

There I hire a cab with a driver old enough to remember what the city was like in 1975 and we find a low-rent office for the questionable lawyer I'll need to create a sleazy bar for a meeting. Another long cab ride takes me to the Luzon village I'll have to describe, and to a cockfight where I pass the wager money around the arena but do not partake of the fresh-cooked rooster (a loser) sold at the ticket booth.

The evening before flying home I take a long walk along the waterfront, collecting sounds, smells, and images, including that of a cockroach migration that flows down the sidewalk toward my feet like a flood of black water. I spend an hour in a casino, with soldiers armed with automatic rifles guarding the door and an all-male mix of Japanese and locals, silent and grim, playing blackjack and roulette. Then more of my good luck. Rain drives me into the empty cathedral, and while I wait in the darkness for the squall to pass, the candles, the smell of incense, lead me to imagine the scene that was the key to making *Finding Moon* work. Moon becomes a lapsed Catholic. I have him waiting out the rain in the cathedral, ducking into an empty confessional booth where he hasn't been since boyhood, remembering the prescribed introductory prayer for forgiveness. Reciting it, he finds a young priest has been sitting behind the screen, quietly waiting for penitents. It's been about fifteen years since I wrote that chapter, and I still remember it as one of those rare and joyful moments when you know you're writing well.

Nothing to be done in Manila now except get through customs with my new passport. Things are calmer now and the official has time to inspect the entry page and find it lacks any official evidence of my arrival. He asks me the date. I tell him. He looks at the page again. It is still blank, but the official's expression is now skeptical. Am I sure of the arrival date? he asks, and before I can answer motions to a policeman. A lady in the next line waves at me—one of the travel writers I'd met on the flight in. I ask her the date we arrived. She shouts back the answer.

"Is that your lady?" asked customs.

I nod, ask her if we can look at her passport. She brings it over. Customs checks the date, writes it into the back of my passport. The problem is solved. I'm even allowed to tote my blowgun and arrows aboard.

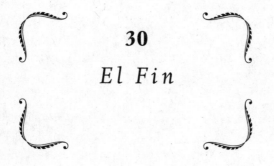

30

El Fin

When I interrupted my next Navajo police book to begin this memoir the lawn outside my window was ablaze with April dandelions and Lieutenant Leaphorn (retired) was sipping his inevitable coffee in the Navajo Inn awaiting a friend to learn more about a motiveless murder. Today the yellow on our lawn is autumn's crop—leaves shed by our cottonwoods—and Leaphorn still waits to do his thing. Bits and pieces of Next Book have built in my mind for months. It has that familiar feeling books cause in their formative state of finally being the really good one. I want to get on with it. Aside from that, wringing useful memories from one's subconscious produces unpleasant self-absorption. It puts you in contact with long-dead friends, good buddies, people you have loved, who have been kind to you, whose death left a vacuum, playmates, men of Charlie Company whom I hadn't thought of in years. There's sadness in that.

But when I try to sum up my seventy-five years I must admit the happy times were the overwhelming majority. And how does one quit writing an autobiography when he still has hundreds of happy memories left unreported?

I asked the fellows with whom I've been playing poker for almost forty years how one can end the account of one's life.

How about suicide? says one. That would end it.

Wouldn't work, says another, you'd have to do it with a suicide note.

It seems to me that Stendhal had a better idea when he tired of writing his very autobiographical *Promenades dans Rome.* The scholars tell us he was considering suicide. And they tell us that while writing this highly personal journal, he got the idea for *The Red and the Black* and wanted to get going on it. And so he finished *Promenades* by writing:

"Tomorrow we leave Rome, to our great regret. [The "we" being the fictional companions Stendhal used to beef out his tale.] We are going to Venice; we shall spend two weeks at the baths of Lucca this summer and a month at the delightful baths of la Battaglia."

That said, Stendhal wrote *The Red and the Black*, his classic. If the Frenchman can get away with it, why can't I?

Therefore, the next time I turn on this computer I will be with Lieutenant Joe Leaphorn (retired) awaiting a luncheon guest at the Navajo Inn. He will be casually eavesdropping on two elderly teachers recalling an odd Halloween incident of fifteen years ago. Truant students cutting across the long abandoned grounds of old Fort Wingate had been terrified by a prankster—someone imitating the screams of a woman pleading for help. And that reminding Leaphorn of an odd Halloween homicide, also fifteen years ago, and suddenly wondering if . . . But that's for tomorrow. First a final summary look at my seventy-five years is required.

They've been far better than anyone deserves, two thirds of them brightened with Marie, who rarely saw a disaster in which she couldn't find something funny, and a lot of them made tense, nerve-racking, interesting, and joyful by the bringing up of six children. My three fourths of a century has been notable for fortunate outcomes and rare disappointments.

There are two primary reason for this. First, Mama and Papa sent us out into life knowing it was just a short run toward that Last Great Adventure, and understanding that the Gospels Jesus used to teach us were the road map to make getting there a happy trip. That covers the first years. The last fifty-two years have been filled with love, joy, and laughter by a wonderful wife, partner, and helpmate named Marie.

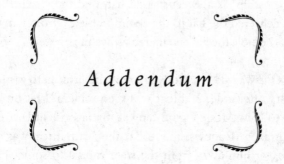

Addendum

In various ways the foregoing has explained the genesis of six of my books from the first *(The Blessing Way)* to the most recent *(Hunting Badger)*. Each of the others presented its peculiar problem and had a lesson about plotting to teach.

Examples, in chronological order:

The Blessing Way (1970). It was easy enough to make the Enemy Way ceremonial germane to the plot. It is used to cure illness caused by exposure to witchcraft and my villain was trying to keep the Navajo away from his territory by spreading witchcraft fears. The problem was devising a way for Joe Leaphorn to connect the ceremony and the killer. The solution came to me when I noticed the peculiar pattern of sweat stains on a felt hat caused by a silver concho hatband. With that in mind, I skiped back to an early chapter, write in Leaphorn at a trading post seeing the villain buying a hat to replace one stolen and wondering why someone would steal an old hat and not the expensive silver. That done, I then skiped forward to the "scalp shooting" phase of the ceremony, have Leaphorn notice the "scalp" is a sweat-stained hat, find the "scalp shooter" who has delivered the hat to the ceremony, learn from him where (and why) he stole the hat and thereby solve the mystery.

The Fly on the Wall (1971). Motivating my unheroic hero to pursue a news story after a death threat was the problem. I hit on having him flee to New Mexico, go fishing at my favorite little stream in isolated Brazos Meadows, and realize the death threat was merely a ruse to get him away from the state capital to somewhere he could be murdered quietly. Thus he knows his only hope is to solve the crime.

The Boy Who Made Dragonfly (1972). While doing the research on the complex Zuni religion to write *Dance Hall of the Dead* I ran into versions of the Dragonfly story told to children to teach ethics, morals, hospitality, and the evils of selfishness. It's a beautiful story of the power of love and the only problem was simplifying it for non-Zuni readers.

The Dance Hall of the Dead (1973). The problem here was how to have Leaphorn understand what was motivating the behavior of George Bowlegs, a fugitive Navajo boy. To do this I had Joe gradually understand Zuni theology as a Navajo (or a white mystery writer) would, and realize the boy was trying to make contact with the Zuni Council of the Gods. Thus the boy (and Leaphorn) would come to the Shalako ceremony, at which these spirits make their annual return to the pueblo, and thus I would have my excuse to describe this incredibly beautiful ceremony.

The Great Taos Bank Robbery (1973). Most of the essays in this book were written to meet requirements for a master's degree in English. As required, they displayed whatever command I had of dealing with a variety of subjects—ranging from the zaniness of Taos, to the nature of an ultramilitant Chicano leader, to the detective work done to locate the source of bubonic plague.

New Mexico (1974), *Rio Grande* (1975), and *Indian Country* (1977) were the texts of books done in collaboration with photographers.

Listening Woman (1978). This book taught me that inability to outline a plot has advantages. The plan was to use Monster Slayer and Born for Water, the hero twins of the Navajo Genesis story, in a mystery involving orphaned brothers (a "spoiled priest" and a militant radical) who collide in their campaigns to help their people. I would use a shaman, the last person to talk to my murder victim before he is killed, as a source for religious information meaningless to the FBI but revealing to Leaphorn. After a series of first chapters that led nowhere, I wrote a second chapter in which Leaphorn stops the villain for speeding and, more or less out of whimsy, I have him see a big ugly dog in the backseat of the car, intending to use the delete key on my new (and first) computer to delete said dog later. That unoutlined dog became crucial to the plot. No more trying to outline.

People of Darkness (1980). Older, wiser, urbane Leaphorn refused to fit into my plan to set a plot on the Checkerboard Reservation, in which the goverment gave alternate square miles of land to the railroads and in which Navajo was intermixed with a plethora of whites, Zunis, Jemez, Lagunas, etc., and a dozen or so missionary outposts of different religions. Since Joe wouldn't be surprised by any of this I created younger, less culturally assimilated, Jim Chee.

The Dark Wind (1982). One of the many facets of Navajo culture that appeals to me is the lack of value attached to vengeance. This "eye for an eye" notion pervading white culture is looked upon by the Dineh as a mental illness. I planned to illuminate this with a vengeance-motivated crime—the problem being how to have Joe, who doesn't believe in vengeance, catch on. The answer came to me in the memory of a long interview I once did with a private detective about his profession. I never used any of that, but a card trick he showed me proved to be just what I needed. My villain, a trading post operator, showed the same trick to Leaphorn, and when he solved it he knew how the crime was done.

The Ghostway (1984). The trigger for this book was a roofless stone hogan with adjoining shed in a little spring-fed pocket on Mesa Gigante, which dominates the Canoncito Navajo Reservation. I happened across it one autumn afternoon, noticed a hole had been knocked in its north wall, the traditional exit route for the body when death has infected the hogan. But why had the dying person not been moved outside before he died, so the *chindi* could escape?

From this the story grew. The dead person becomes a wounded fugitive from the mafia who had come to the home of his Granddad to die. But Chee notices this poor fellow had been given only part of the burial ritual and denied other parts, and that the old man who abandoned the hogan left behind his Four Mountains Bundle, the sacred objects that traditional Navajo collect from the reservation's Four Holy Mountains. Of course the FBI neither knows these oddities are crucial nor how to explain them. Chee does, and thus I have my chance to lead readers through some of the margins of Navajo culture.

Skinwalkers (1986). How do I awaken Jim Chee, sleeping in his cot beside the paper-thin aluminum wall of his trailer home, so he will not be killed when the assassin fires her shotgun through said wall? Everything I try sounds like pure psychic coincides—which I detest in mysteries. Nothing works until I remember the "clack, clack" sound made when a friend's cat goes through the "cat door" on his porch. I write in a spooky stray cat, for whom Chee makes this cat door (thereby establishing him as a nice guy and giving me a chance to explain Navajo "equal citizenship" relationships with animals). The cat, spooked by the assassin's approach, darts from its bed under a piñon into the trailer and awakens Chee. At book's end, when I need to terminate a budding romance, the cat serves a wonderfully symbolic role. This was the first book in which I used both Leaphorn and Chee. It made a great leap forward in sales and hit a bunch of best-seller lists, but not the crucial one in the *New York Times*.

A Thief of Time (1988). My "breakout book" was described earlier in considerable detail. It was a "breakout" in more than sales and eventually led to the Public Service Award of the U.S. Department of Interior, an honorary membership for life in the Western Literature Association, the American Anthopolgy Association's Media Award and the Center for the American Indian's Ambassador Award, a beautiful bronze of a Comanche warrior holding his coup stick.

Talking God (1989). A book modified by coincidences. While writing Chapter 3 I stop because it's time for Sunday Mass. But the problem stays with me during the ceremony—how to describe a corpse found beside the railroad outside Gallup. I notice an elderly Hispano usher with an aristocratic face dressed in an expensive but well-worn suit. He becomes the victim. But such a man refuses to fit my gang murder plot and turns the book into a Central American political conspiracy assassination. Next, old writing friend Bill Buchanan (*Shining Season, Execution Eve*, etc.) mentions a man responding to Bill's refrigerator sale want-ad was not a potential buyer but a lonely fellow needing to exchange words with a fellow human. That, too, sticks in my mind. I use it. It turns my assassin into a terribly lonely man and provides a much better ending. The first chapter was no problem at all. I have an urban wannabe Navajo send a Smithsonian official a box of her ancestor's bones, dug from an ancient Episcopal graveyard, for her to display along with the bones of his ancestors. I received "good-for-you" applause from about twenty tribesmen for that one.

Coyote Waits (1990). When Barney and I were prowling the Four Corners with me writing and him photographing stuff for our *Hillerman Country* he taught me a lesson in optical perspective that solved Leaphorn's problem in finding the needed witness. Barney anthromorphized cliffs, canyons, trees, etc., turning their reflected lights and shadows into presidential profiles, bears, and so forth. (Something I do with cloud formations, seeing in them not only God's glory but dragons, Popeye, and aircraft.)

"Stop," Barney would say, and point at a rock formation. "See the zebra with the pipe in his mouth?"

I'd say no. He'd say back up a little. We'd stop where all the necessary elements would line up properly and I would either see suggestions of a zebra or, often, simply say I did and drive on with Barney explaining how viewer position and the optics of telescopic lenses affect what you see. It was the sort of data I usually find easy to forget, but I remembered it when stuck for a logical way to have a witness out in empty country witnessing a murder. He became a lonely high school kid whose hobby was landscape photography and who found a way to declare his love for a girl by careful placement of white paint on basalt rocks so the message could be read only from the perspective of her hogan.

I spent weeks trying to have Leaphorn figure that out, wishing I'd never heard of optical perspective.

Hillerman Country (1991). The first time Barney and I had a chance to work together since digging postholes in 1942 produced this book, and it was a labor of love. I sent Barney a lengthy listing of places he needed to photograph to go with my text. He'd send me great sheets of contact prints of totally different landscape—proving that I was still Little Brother and that photographers march to their own drummers. So I bent a bit, and so did he, and we were both delighted with the finished product. Barney, who always felt hospitals were entered only to visit sick friends, died while out shooting another book assignment just a few weeks after our joint venture was published.

Sacred Clowns (1993). This book grew from something left over from an earlier one. *The Dark Wind* had required me to learn about the Hopi. I had slept in my pickup at the edge of Walpi, awaiting morning to interview a fellow for a magazine article. I awoke at sunrise (easy when you've been cramped in a Toyota truck) and saw a man emerge from a house. He held the bundle he was carrying up toward the rising sun, stood like that for a long moment, apparently chanting, and then disappeared again into his house. I learned he had been presenting his eight-day-old child to God, symbolized by the rising sun, in a ceremony in some ways like a Christian baptism and in some ways more than that. The elder I interviewed explained that the chant he had sung presented the infant as a child of God, and recognized the human father and mother as foster parents—promising to nurture God's child by the Creator's rules and asking God's blessings on this task.

Sacred status given children in the religious philosophy of many of the pueblos cast light for me on the role of the Koshare, Mudhead, and other "sacred clown" societies and helps explain why one rarely sees a pueblo child thumped on the ear or otherwise physically punished. I share this belief that each human has this special relationship with God who ("Judgment is mine, sayeth the Lord") will take care of meting rewards and punishment. Therefore, I spent untold months trying to come up with a way to use it in a plot in a book we named *Mudhead Kiva*.

During this process I discovered I have cancer, spend some time in the hospital—wonderful periods away from the telephone for thinking. By the time I got back to serious writing, *Mudhead Kiva* has died and *Sacred Clowns* has emerged, leaving HarperCollins to explain an imaginary book they had been advertising. However, the story improved as much as the title.

Finding Moon (1995). Closest to my heart, but not to those of editor, publisher, and many of my readers. Peter Thorpe, the talented jacket designer of my Navajo police books, did a beauty for this one—painting a moon rising over Cambodian mountains with the figure of man outlined against its face. I got an early look and endorsed it, whereupon it was redesigned to fit more into the pattern of my previous books—the sort of development that reminds writers of their place in the publishing world.

The Fallen Man (1996). Several notions in my collection of potential story ideas collided for this one. Idea one was to leave a mountain climber trapped atop Shiprock, as was Monster Slayer in the Navajo origin story. Two was having a custom-made competition rifle firing custom-made ammo used by a sniper on the rim of Canon de Chelly to assassinate a witness far below. Three was to involve cattle rustling and the antirustler tactics of working with "watchers." Some of these worked but a half dozen others misfired, forcing me to learn a lot more about serious mountain climbing than I wished.

The First Eagle (1998). This book was trigged by a new death penalty law for certain felonies on federal reservations. Since about 95 percent of federal reservation acreage is also Indian Reservation acreage this looked like a special "Death Penalty for Indians Law." Making the book work required a plot even more convoluted than those I usually impose upon readers. Luckily Marie was a bacteriology major, a big help in working bubonic plague into the plot—as were the vector controllers who hunt down the sources of the disease and the bacteriology professors upon whom I imposed.

I gave myself a problem by picking Gold Tooth, Arizona, as a crucial location because my map showed it in the very empty country where Hopi and Navajo territory abut. Wonderful name, Gold Tooth, and a ghost town, too, but I couldn't find the unimproved dirt road that was supposed to lead to it to get a visual fix. That bothered me. So Marie and I made another "find Gold Tooth" journey along the road between Moenkopi and the Hopi Mesa, looking for some sort of junction. We failed again, but at the Tuba City Trading Post found a Navajo woman who knew the way.

"Past the top of the hill out of Moenkopi Wash, drive slow and keep a close watch beside the road to your right. In about a mile you see a place where people have turned off the pavement. Follow the track maybe fifteen miles or twenty miles or so."

We found the tire tracks, drove the fifteen or so miles, past one distant windmill, past three cows, and came finally to a roofless, windowless stone building to our right and an old-fashioned round hogan to the left. It didn't look much like what I'd described, but Marie consoled me with the reminder that not many of my readers would be seeing it.

Hunting Badger (1999). An actual crime—odd enough to fill the need of any mystery writer—was the seed from which *Hunting Badger* grew. I planned to use the sour memories of the event: theft of a water tank truck by three heavily armed men, murder of the policeman who stopped them, an FBI-orchestrated, incredibly bungled, Keystone Cops manhunt, evacuation of Bluff, Utah, quarter-million-buck federal reward offer, which attracted a horde of bounty hunters, vast waste of tax money, etc., as the background for my plot. I thought it would make an easy book to write. It didn't. I was left with the problem of how to have my own *bandidos* escape. Help came from some elderly aviators who filled me in on the sort of vintage aircraft I needed to delude my FBI characters, and from Patti Collins and her Environmental Protection Administration helicopter crew, who provided data on abandoned coal/uranium mines where I needed them.

The three anthologies that bear my name, *Spell of New Mexico*, *The Best of the West*, and *The American Detective Story* all sprang from the ideas of others. *Spell* was the result of lunches at Campus Drug with Jack Rittenhouse, history editor of the University of New Mexico Press and lifelong book collector. At these, we fell into the habit of remembering what famous folks, from D. H. Lawrence to Karl Jung, had written about New Mexico. Jack suggested we collect a bunch of these into an anthology. I liked the idea but not the work. Jack said he'd do the collecting, editing, etc. (95 percent of the work), if I'd write the introduction and the connective tissue. When the book was being published Jack said he couldn't put his name on it due to University Press rules.

Best was another product of those lunches and another of Jack's ideas, which was to go back to the beginnings of literacy in our part of the world and collect bits and pieces that reflected on the territory and the times. It would range from letters, diaries, documents, and even tombstone declarations and warnings inscribed into rocks, all the way to fiction. It sounded to me like a staggering job, but Rittenhouse had most of the books and other documents needed in his own collections and knew how to find what he didn't have. I would simply help with the sorting and write the explanatory notes. Jack was ill now, had retired from his post at the University Press and therefore the rule that kept his name off our first venture wouldn't apply. Now I learn that the rule existed only in Jack's imagination. He loved books more than anyone I've ever known. But he didn't want to have his name on one. While we were still debating that, Jack came by my house and said we'd have to rush the job. His doctor had told him his cancer would give him about four more weeks of life. We finished just in time and while the Rittenhouse name isn't on the dust jacket, I bent my promise a little by telling the story in the Foreword.

The American Detective Story was the idea of Rosemary Herbert, now book editor of the *Boston Herald*, who wanted to illustrate the evolution of the American version of this genre—from the cozy British "tale of ratiocination" to the "mean streets" of the United States. I had written some about that and liked the idea. But Rosemary knew much more about the form and, as usual, she did most of the work. She even posed for the dust jacket photo.

Bibliography
Books by
and about
Tony Hillerman

Books by Tony Hillerman

The Blessing Way. New York: Harper & Row, 1970.
Lt. Joe Leaphorn must stalk a supernatural killer known as the "Wolf-Witch" along a chilling trail of mysticism and murder.

The Fly on the Wall. New York: Harper & Row, 1971.
A dead reporter's secret notebook implicates a senatorial candidate and political figures in a million-dollar murder scam.

The Boy Who Made Dragonfly: A Zuni Myth. New York: Harper & Row, 1972.
Retells a Zuni myth in which, through the intercession of a

dragonfly, a young boy and his sister gain the wisdom that makes them leaders of their people.

The Great Taos Bank Robbery and Other Indian Country Affairs. Albuquerque: University of New Mexico Press, 1973.
Hillerman, who knows the Southwest like no other contemporary writer, presents nine extraordinary, true tales that capture the history and rhythms of daily life in New Mexico.

Dance Hall of the Dead. New York: Harper & Row, 1974.
An archaeological dig, a steel hypodermic needle, and the strange laws of the Zuni complicate the disappearance of two young boys.

New Mexico, Rio Grande, and Other Essays. Portland, Ore. Graphic Arts Center Pub. Co., 1975.
Gives the reader a deeper appreciation of how Hillerman sees the land he loves, as well as the places from which he draws his inspiration and his intimate knowledge of the backgrounds upon which he casts the characters of his mysteries. The essays are complemented by the extraordinary photography of David Muench and Robert Reynolds.

Hillerman, Tony, and Robert Reynolds. *Rio Grande.* Portland: Charles H. Belding, 1975.
Hillerman's essay on this beautiful river accompanies Robert Reynolds's award-winning photography.

Listening Woman. New York: Harper & Row, 1978.
A baffling investigation of murder, ghosts, and witches can be solved only by Lt. Leaphorn, a man who understands both his own people and cold-blooded killers.

People of Darkness. New York: Harper & Row, 1980.
An assassin waits for Officer Chee in the desert to protect a vision

of death that for thirty years has been fed by greed and washed by blood.

The Dark Wind. New York: Harper & Row, 1982.
Sgt. Jim Chee becomes trapped in a deadly web of a cunningly spun plot driven by Navajo sorcery and white man's greed.

Hillerman, Tony, ed. *The Spell of New Mexico*. Albuquerque: University of New Mexico Press, 1984.
Hillerman has organized an impressive collection of writings about New Mexico: Oliver La Farge, D. H. Lawrence, Ernie Pyle, Conrad Richter, Mary Austin, and many others.

The Ghostway. New York: Harper & Row, 1984.
A photo sends officer Chee on an odyssey of murder and revenge that moves from an Indian hogan to a deadly healing ceremony.

Skinwalkers. New York: Harper & Row, 1986.
Three shotgun blasts in a trailer bring Officer Chee and Lt. Leaphorn together for the first time in an investigation of ritual, witchcraft, and blood.

Indian Country: America's Sacred Land. Flagstaff, Ariz.: Northland Press, 1987.
Exciting essays of the American Southwest and its people, accompanied by photographs by Bela Kalman.

A Thief of Time. New York: Harper & Row, 1988.
When two corpses appear amid stolen goods and bones at an ancient burial site, Leaphorn and Chee must plunge into the past to unearth the truth.

Hillerman, Tony, Florence Lister, and Peter Thorpe. *Tony Hillerman's Indian Country Map & Guide*. Mancos, Colo.: Time Traveler Maps, 1998

This hardcover "European style" companion map captures events, locations, and quotations from all Hillerman's bestselling Indian Country mysteries. Extensive illustrations by Peter Thorpe and a highly detailed map bring one of America's most intriguing and mysterious regions to reality.

Talking God. New York: Harper & Row, 1989.
A grave robber and a corpse reunite Leaphorn and Chee in a dangerous arena of superstition, ancient ceremony and living gods.

The Joe Leaphorn Mysteries: Three Classic Hillerman Mysteries Featuring Lt. Joe Leaphorn: The Blessing Way/Dance Hall of the Dead/Listening Woman. New York: HarperCollins, 1989.

Coyote Waits. New York: Harper & Row, 1990.
When a bullet kills Officer Jim Chee's good friend Del, a Navajo shaman is arrested for homicide, but the case is far from closed.

The Jim Chee Mysteries: Three Classic Hillerman Mysteries Featuring Officer Jim Chee: People of Darkness, The Dark Wind, The Ghostway. New York: HarperCollins, 1990.

Hillerman Country: A Journey through the Southwest with Tony Hillerman. New York: HarperCollins, 1991.
Take a tour of the American Southwest through this book, which also contains photographs by Hillerman's brother Barney.

Block, Lawrence, Sarah Caudwell, Tony Hillerman, Peter Lovesey, and Donald Westlake. *The Perfect Murder: Five Great Mystery Writers Create the Perfect Crime*. Edited by Jack Hill. New York: HarperCollins, 1991.

Hillerman, Tony, ed. *The Best of the West: An Anthology of Classic Writing from the American West*. New York: HarperCollins, 1991.

A sterling collection of classic and contemporary fiction and nonfiction, evoking the unique spirit of the West and its people.

Charyn, Jerome, ed,. *The New Mystery: New & Classic Stories by P. D. James, James Ellroy, Sue Grafton, Tony Hillerman;* New York: Dutton, 1993.

Sacred Clowns. New York: HarperCollins, 1993.
Officer Chee attempts to solve two modern murders by deciphering the sacred clown's ancient message to the people of the Tano pueblo.

Hillerman, Tony, ed. *Mysterious West.* New York: HarperCollins, 1995.
Edited by Tony Hillerman, this first-ever collection of mystery stories set in the West contains twenty original entries by such luminary mystery writers as Marcia Muller, Susan Dunlap, and Robert Campbell.

Finding Moon. New York: HarperCollins, 1995.
Moon Mathias discovers his dead brother's baby daughter is waiting for him in Southeast Asia—a child he didn't know existed. Finding her in the aftermath of the war brings out a side of Moon he had forgotten he possessed.

Indian Country: America's Sacred Land. Albuquerque: University of New Mexico Press, 1995.
Hillerman describes the intangible yet powerful aura of the Southwest, America's sacred land, while photographer Bela Kalman captures its beauty through his color photographs. The book is a tribute to a land where the land's spirits are as real as its inhabitants.

Fallen Man. New York: HarperCollins, 1996.
A man met his death on Ship Rock Mountain eleven years ago, and

with the discovery of his body by a group of climbers, Chee and Leaphorn must hunt down the cause of his lonely death.

Herbert, Rosemary, and Tony Hillerman, *The Oxford Book of American Detective Stories*. New York: Oxford University Press, 1996
For this collection, Hillerman and Herbert have selected thirty-four stories that demonstrate the vigor and diversity of the American Detective Story genre.

The Great Taos Bank Robbery and Other Indian Country Affairs. New York: HarperCollins, 1997.
Tony Hillerman, who knows the Southwest like no other contemporary writer; presents nine extraordinary, true tales that capture the history and rhythms of daily life in New Mexico.

First Eagle. New York: HarperCollins, 1998.
When Acting Lt. Jim Chee catches a Hopi poacher huddled over a butchered Navajo Tribal police officer, he has an open-and-shut case—until his former boss, Joe Leaphorn, blows it wide open.

Hunting Badger. New York: HarperCollins, 1998.
Hunting Badger finds Navajo tribal police officers Joe Leaphorn and Jim Chee working two angles of the same case—each trying to catch the right-wing militiamen who pulled off a violent heist at an Indian casino.

Randisi, Robert, ed. *First Cases: New and Classic Tales of Detection*, Vol. 3. New York: Signet, 1999.
The third volume in this indispensable series offers more fictional detectives' inaugural cases—and includes two never-before-published stories

Hillerman, Tony, and Otto Penzler, eds. *Best American Mystery Stories of the Century*. New York: Houghton Mifflin, 2000.

An anthology of fifty-five brief mystery stories ranging from O. Henry to Dennis Lehane.

Bibliographies:

Tony Hillerman: From The Blessing Way to Talking God, A Bibliography. By Louis A. Hieb. Tucson: Press of the Gigantic Hound, 1990.
Chronology, bibliography, including contributions to books and periodicals, and works about Hillerman.

Tony Hillerman Abroad. An Annotated Checklist Of Foreign Language Editions. By Louis A. Hieb. Santa Fe: Parker Books of the West, 1993.
An expanded version of the earlier publication with beautiful colored illustrations and listing books through *Sacred Clowns*.

Hillerman, Tony, and Louis A. Hieb: *Collecting Tony Hillerman: A Checklist of the First Editions of Tony Hillerman with Approximate Values and Commentary.* Santa Fe: Vinegar Tom Press, 1992.
This is a checklist that updates identification information for Hillerman's American first editions and that has been augmented by values and commentary.

Hillerman, Tony, Hieb, Louis A.: *Fifty Foreign Firsts: A Tony Hillerman Checklist.* Santa Fe: Parker Books of the West, 1991.

Tony Hillerman: A Reader's Checklist and Reference Guide. Middletown, Conn.: Checkerbee Checklist, 1999

Books about Tony Hillerman

Bulow, Ernie. *Words, Weather and Wolfmen. Conversations with Tony Hillerman.* Gallup, N. Mex.: The Southwestern Books, 1989.

Bulow, Ernie. *Talking Mysteries: A Conversation With Tony Hillerman*. Albuquerque: University of New Mexico Press, 1991.
Illustrated with photo-portraits of the contributors, gallery of black-and-white drawings by Ernest Franklin. Hillerman discusses the craft of mystery writing and contributes an autobiographical piece. Bulow adds an extensive interview. As an additoinal treat, a Jim Chee mini-mystery, originally published in 1981 and long unavailable, is included here.

Coale, Samuel. *The Mystery of Mysteries: Cultural Differences and Designs*. Bowling Green: Popular Press, 2000.
Four American mystery writers have contributed new dimensions to the mystery form. Tony Hillerman's Navajos and their customs, Amanda Cross's (Carolyn Heilbrun's) academics and their feminist credentials (or lack thereof), James Lee Burke's southern Louisiana Cajuns and his own fiercely moral "take" on Southern gothic fiction, and Walter Mosley's urban blacks and their close-knit culture have challenged the conventional mystery's focus.

Using feminist and black critical theory, mythic and historical patterns, and literary genre theory, Samuel Coale examines their works and investigates the compromises that each is forced to make when working within a recognizably popular literary form.

Erisman, Fred. *Tony Hillerman (Western Writers Series No. 37)*. Boise: Boise State University Press, 1989.
A brief biography of the author as part of a series from Boise State University.

Freese, Peter, *The Ethnic Detective: Chester Himes, Harry Kemelman, Tony Hillerman*.

Greenberg, Martin. *The Tony Hillerman Companion: A Comprehensive Guide to His Life and Work*. New York: HarperCollins, 1994.

The first authoritative guide to Hillerman's "world," which includes the geography of his novels, a personal interview, clans in Hillerman fiction, a concordance, and photographs.

Reilly, John M. *Tony Hillerman: A Critical Companion.* Westport: Greenwood Publishing Group, 1996.
Critical companions to popular writers series. This study examines each of his thirteen novels and includes a biographical chapter and a chapter on his innovations in the genre of detective fiction.

Sobol, John. *Tony Hillerman: A Public Life.* Toronto: ECW Press, 1994.
A brief biography of Tony Hillerman.

Englade, Ken. *Tony Hillerman's Frontier: People of the Plains.* New York: HarperCollins, 1996.
Tony Hillerman endorses this richly evocative new series that portrays the day-to-day lives of Native Americans in the West during a volatile time of betrayals great and small.

————.*Tony Hillerman's Frontier: The Emigrants.* New York: HarperCollins, 1996.

————.*Tony Hillerman's Frontier: The Tribes.* New York: HarperCollins, 1996.

————.*Tony Hillerman's Frontier: The Soldiers.* New York: HarperCollins, 1996.

————.*Tony Hillerman's Frontier: Battle Cry.* New York: HarperCollins, 1997.

————.*Tony Hillerman's Frontier: Brothers in Blood.* New York: HarperCollins, 1998.

Preston, Lewis. *Tony Hillerman's Frontier: Cold Justice*. New York: HarperCollins, 1998.

Camp, Will. *Tony Hillerman's Frontier: Comanche Trail*. New York: HarperCollins, 1999.

Forewords and Introductions by Tony Hillerman

Varney, Philip. *New Mexico's Best Ghost Towns: A Practical Guide.* *Albuquerque: University of New Mexico Press, 1987.*
Foreword by Tony Hillerman.

Bryan, Howard. *Robbers, Rogues, and Ruffians: True Tales of the Wild West in New Mexico.* Santa Fe: Clear Light Publishers, 1991.
Foreword by Tony Hillerman.

Campbell, John Martin. *Few and Far Between: Moments in the North American Desert.* Santa Fe: Museum of New Mexico Press, 1997.
Foreword by Tony Hillerman.

Rutland, Robert Allen. *A Boyhood in the Dustbowl 1926–1934.* Boulder: University of Colorado Press, 1995.
Introduction by Tony Hillerman.

■ **Perennial**   ■ **HarperCollins**_Publishers_

Hardcover and Paperback Books by Tony Hillerman:

WAILING WIND
ISBN 0-06-019444-8 (hardcover)
A new novel featuring Hillerman's investigative heroes: Joe Leaphorn and Jim Chee.

The Golden Calf mine's location had been forgotten for decades, but rumors of the wealth it holds had not—wealth that led to murder and a strange unsolved disappearance two years ago, and that now seems to be connected to a body found in a pickup truck at the bottom of Coyote Canyon.

"Hillerman is never better than when he is circling a puzzle from various angles, playing with the perceptions of his detectives as well as the reader's."—_New York Times Book Review_

THE JIM CHEE MYSTERIES
Three Classic Hillerman Mysteries Featuring Officer Jim Chee:
People of the Darkness, The Dark Wind, The Ghostway
ISBN 0-06-016478-6 (hardcover)

SELDOM DISAPPOINTED
ISBN 0-06-050586-9 (paperback)

Tony Hillerman looks back at the 76 years he spent rising from hard-times farm boy to bestselling author. In this wry and whimsical memoir Hillerman offers frequent backward glances at where he found ideas for plots of books and the characters that inhabit them.

"An amazing reporter's eye at work." —_Fort Worth Star-Telegram_

THE BEST OF THE WEST
An Anthology of Classic Writing from the American West
ISBN 0-06-092352-0 (paperback edited by Tony Hillerman)

In this extraordinary treasury, Tony Hillerman has gathered over 140 remarkable texts— from diaries, news dispatches, travelogues, letters, short stories, stone inscriptions, and well-known documents—from and about the West.

"Anyone who enjoys a slumgullion stew can find something tasty in this campfire collection." —_Entertainment Weekly_

THE GREAT TAOS BANK ROBBERY
And Other True Stories of the Southwest
ISBN 0-06-093712-2 (paperback)

The present and timeless past of one of America's most beautiful and haunting regions is re- vealed in this fascinating collection of true stories about the Southwest, compiled and told with inimitable wit and wisdom by Tony Hillerman.

"Hillerman has become a national literary and cultural sensation." —_Los Angeles Times_

(((LISTEN TO))) A TONY HILLERMAN AUDIO!